BORDERLINE
A Poetic Memoir

While based on real events, certain details and names have been altered for narrative purposes.

Copyright © 2024 by Diana Kouprina

All rights reserved.
Published in the United States by
Wild Press.

www.wild-press.com

ISBN: 979-8-9917903-1-4
Library of Congress Control Number: 2024926225

Cover design by Ashton Loren Ryan

For Margie

Contents

Prologue	17
Book I	15
Book II	81
Book III	135
Book IV	315
Epilogue	377

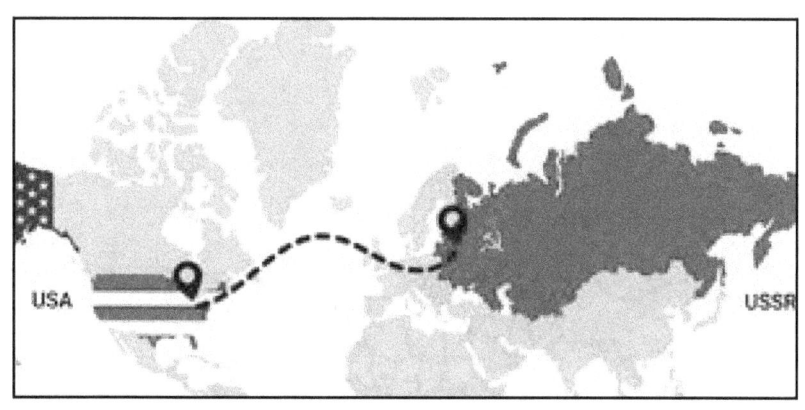

Forest Edge

Have you ever found yourself lost at the edge of the woods with no point of return?
Have you ever been stuck in the crippling darkness where the tree shadows grow?
Have you ever felt the chill of the night creep in,
And the whispers of the wind curl around your thoughts?
Have you ever watched the flicker of moonlight slip away,
Each moment a reminder of paths not taken?

Beneath the tangled branches, fears weave like ivy,
Wrapping tightly, squeezing out the light.
Where you try to reach for something solid, something true,
Yet the ground shifts beneath the feet,
A maze of doubts at every turn of the woodland forest.
And in that stillness, a question lingers—
Is it the woods that confine me, or the shadows within?
Each step deeper feels like a surrender,
Yet within the darkness, a spark remains,
A whisper of hope whispers through the branches,
It's heard through the wind-blown yellow crispy leaves,
Covering the path
With red,
Brown, orange, magenta
Burgundy, pink, green.
Guiding me gently into a moonlit night,
Into the field where fresh gulps of air are consumed in hunger.
The first breath of life is finally there.

Have you ever gotten lost within the road less taken?
Or is it just me who has wandered off the edge with Frost?

Diana Kouprina © 2024 all rights reserved

Human beings do not stand in one world only but between two worlds and must distinguish themselves from their functions in both worlds.

That is individuation.

– Carl Jung

Introduction

I lay in bed, staring into the shadows that curled across the ceiling, restless and raw. Sleep wouldn't come. My veins felt alive, coursing with a searing heat, anger boiling like   poison I couldn't purge. The same thoughts circled endlessly, tightening their grip.

I had really done it this time.

I didn't meant to ruin my sisters "wedding"(it wasn't even a wedding it was just the two of them and my mom and brother all going to city hall in Cambridge), how was I to know that five hundred I stole was the only cash they had with them and since she didn't know it was missing she didn't stop at the bank, so ultimately she couldn't pay for her marriage license and would need to reschedule the whole thing, and they couldn't reschedule because their flight was leaving the next day.

My mom as always got mad at me, and yelled,

I finally snapped.

I fought back.

I punched her in the face.

But she deserved it. Didn't she? She always knew how to draw blood, to press the tender parts of me until I snapped. Behind closed doors, her voice would rise—a blade cutting through my silence. Her words, sharp and cruel, twisted themselves around me, their venom sinking deep. Her brown eyes burned darker in these moments, alive with some animal need to release her rage, to unburden herself onto me.

Always me.

And then, as if by some cruel magic, she'd step back into the world, radiant and kind, pouring love and warmth into my brother and sister. The contrast was unbearable. She was a saint to them.

To me, she was the villain, the wicked stepmother from Cinderella. She used to be my best friend. My ally. My mother. Once, it was the two of us against the world. But now, it feels as though her love has drained away, drop by drop, until there was nothing left for me. I hadn't meant to lash out at my sister. But I did. And now I couldn't take it back.

The damage was done.

Still, I didn't care.

I felt no guilt, only fury.

Fuck them. Fuck them all.

They couldn't possibly understand the labyrinth of my mind, the hell that twisted inside me. I couldn't tell them what I'd been through.

How could they ever comprehend?

I was exhausted.

I was the one who deserved their love, not their hate,

More than they could ever understand.

I felt so tired, but sleep was elusive.

I felt exhaustion and pain upon my shoulder, as though there were heavy bricks pressing down on my shoulders, the pain was unbearable. I tossed and turned.

My legs felt restless. I told myself I would save it.

I wouldn't do it.

But the hate, the pain, the anguish and the turmoil I felt left me with no choice.

It grew inside me like a monstrous vine, curling tighter and tighter around my ribs. Every thought birthed more hate, sharper, more pointed, until it turned outward.

I hated my mother.

I hated my father.

I hated my brother.

And most of all, I hated my sister.

She never faltered, never defied.

She was their masterpiece, the golden child who knew exactly how to be everything I wasn't.

She even managed to find a husband with a PhD from Yerevan. They flew to the U.S. for their wedding, a celebration masked as a strategy to secure his visa. He would become a U.S. citizen before me.

Before me!

This one thought stung more than the rest of them.

I belonged in the U.S., I grew up here, never leaving the country. And, he! He only just now stepped foot on U.S. soil, and he would be a U.S. citizen in five years maximum.

No one cared to help me. No one ever has.

And then they wonder why I do what I do.

I felt the anger rise up to my throat, combining with bile.

I am nothing.

I am no one.
I am broken, shattered into a million pieces.

For me to feel anything, I need to be high. Drugs are expensive now—so expensive. And I'm not even good at this anymore. I'm a terrible escort, too old for it, still sneaking around my parents like I'm sixteen again, fumbling through a life that feels frozen in time.

I'm stuck. A controlling mother presses her weight against my chest, suffocating me. Everything I do is wrong in her eyes. I needed money. I needed to get high.

I didn't mean to take all their cash. But I did. And they'll survive—they could've stopped at the bank and withdrawn more money. What's the big deal? My sister's always dripping in Chanel, gliding around in her Louboutins like life is effortless. Her engagement ring is a five-carat diamond, glittering in the center of everything she does. And she has the nerve to yell at me for stealing their cash and "ruining" her perfect little wedding plans?

Honestly, what the fuck? I needed it more than they did.

I tossed and turned that night, my thoughts heavy, my body restless.

I didn't want to shoot up. I told myself I wouldn't.

But I did.

Needle to vein has a fast release—sharp, sudden, a clean escape. Unlike snorting. The world blurs quickly, the body letting go before the mind can catch up.

I ran to the bathroom and threw up.

And only then did peace embrace my mind and begin to lull me into another dimension.

The dream was like no other. I was lying next to my ten-year-old daughter. I knew it wasn't real because I don't have children. I can't have children. PCOS sealed that truth long ago. It's an emptiness I've come to live with. But in this dream, I did have a child—a daughter. And she was beautiful.

We were somewhere tropical. The hum of the AC filled the room, and I woke to see a white kitten climbing up and down the long navy-black velvet curtains. My breath caught; I feared the kitten might fall and scratch my daughter's angelic sleeping face. She looked so peaceful, her innocence untouched.

I got up carefully, pulling the covers snug over her small body. I reached for the kitten, plucking it from the curtain as though saving it from falling out of the sky.

And then I woke up.

I wanted to sink back into that dream, to slip into the tropical air, to stay in that realm of existence.

It felt safe, warm, **alive.**

But reality had other plans.

I was startled awake not by the silky white kitten climbing up the dark navy curtains, but by my sister, throwing my clothes into trash bags.

She stood over me, her eyes sharp with anger. In her hand was a phone, her lifeline to our father—her ally, her best friend. She thrived in his favor, always the golden child. Anything she wanted, he gave without question.

She thrust the phone toward me. *"He wants you out of the house."*

I didn't want to take it, but I had no choice. The weight of his voice on the other end pressed against my skull, thunderous and unrelenting.

"You better be gone by the time my flight lands in Boston," he said, his tone slicing through me.

I couldn't stop myself. *"But I can't be stateless and homeless."*

His response was cold, final.

"I know everything, I have warned you before. Your mom always intervened, but now, no more warnings, you are not a part of this family anymore. Get your belongings and get out."

It was official. I was out of the house.

Out of the family.

I jumped myself awake in bed.

I checked my arms, a voice in my head said,

That was just a dream, you have never shot up heroine. You never did. You are safe.

I began to slowly realize I had a nightmare, that led to a dream of this current reality, only to be awakened by my fear into my truth. As though I was pulled out of a different   dimension, parallel universe. My father's words were still replaying in my head. My heart was pounding, I felt disoriented.

But this time, it wasn't the dream.

I was awake in my reality.

The dream within my nightmare was my reality and I was so happy to wake up into it.

The white kitten had in fact been climbing the curtains, her small body defying gravity. I reached for her, pulling her close. And when I turned back to the bed, there she was—my daughter, fast asleep beside me.

We were in Miami, my sister had recently gotten married to a wonderful woman from Yerevan, Armenia and to add to further joy they brought a white kitten they had rescued. The kitten was a birthday present for my daughter who had just turned ten years old.

This was my reality.

As I tucked the kitten under my chin, snuggling her warmth, I thought of the nightmare, the dream within the nightmare, and waking up to my current reality. How vivid it had been, how it had lingered even after I opened my eyes.

It wasn't just a nightmare; it was a glimpse into a parallel world, one where the choices I made had led me somewhere darker, emptier.

The truth is, that world could have easily been my reality. I've always found myself

straddling the borderlines—between life and death, light and dark, hope and despair.

Book I

Prologue:
I Need Love

I can remember being thirteen, thinking, if I just find the boyfriend—someone to love me forever—I'll be okay. It was a belief I held close, like a secret key to a door I couldn't find. The idea of love was my salvation, my promise that life would make sense if I could just be somebody's someone.

I knew then, in a way that most girls my age didn't seem to, that I couldn't love myself. It wasn't that I didn't want to—I just didn't know how. Loving myself seemed foreign, an impossible task. So I thought I could outsource it, hand the job to someone else, let them show me how. I imagined that if I could find him—the one who would hold me, see me, want me—the emptiness would dissolve. At thirteen, I was certain love was the answer. What I didn't understand was the question I was asking.

So when it all fell apart—as it did, as it always seemed to—I was left clutching at pieces, shattered and confused. And all I knew to do, all I'd been trained by my own heart to do, was repeat the pattern. Find another man. Patch over the cracks left by the last one.

Replace the man who broke me with someone new, like a rotating cast of characters in a play I didn't know how to stop performing. Each time, I hoped it would be different. Maybe this one will fix it, I'd think. But no one ever did. They couldn't, because the thing I was asking for wasn't theirs to give.

Then it got to the point where it wasn't just me and my fragile sense of love holding onto this belief. Even attorneys, my parents, and what felt like the entire U.S. government had enforced the pattern. My path to being okay, to being a U.S. citizen, to restoring my life, all seemed to hinge on one thing: Just get married again.

The divorce had been simple. No children, an ironclad prenup—clean, easy, clinical. All I had to do, they said, was move fast. Get married as soon as you can. As if that, once again, would be the fix. Another man, another ring, and I'd be whole again, on paper if not in spirit.

And looking good on paper had become vital to my survival. It was my only hold on U.S. citizenship, my way to keep everything from unraveling. My existence, my future, my very identity—reduced to the neatness of a signature and the promise of love from yet another man.

But I can't say I didn't meet the one. My twin flame came after John—the one who would teach me independence, the one who didn't want to get married. Even if, by some random chance, he did, it would only be another paper arrangement. He didn't meet the financial requirements to be a "good husband candidate" in the eyes of the USCIS.

The government wouldn't have approved of him, no matter how right he might have been for me. So even the idea of love felt out of reach unless it ticked the right bureaucratic boxes.

Even after I had my miracle baby, and even with my twin flame, I was still in search of a husband. There was no other way I could see my bleak immigration situation unfolding, from being documented to turning undocumented.

I needed citizenship—my U.S. citizenship—in the only country I had ever known.

About, Letting Go

I have hang ups, I hold on too tight,

A broken record playing on the loop,

I seek to find my flaw, my fault, my failure.

I play it all on repeat mode inside my brain.

Always too terrified to seek the truth

Thinking it's me, the problem, the flaw, the failure

Believing that I am the monster in the mirror,

Too scared to look and see, of what I would find staring back at me,

All the while needing, craving love, like air.

©**Diana Kouprina**

I can clearly remember, as if it happened yesterday, the time I messaged Mrs. B.

I wrote to her on Facebook Messenger: I'm so sorry for everything, for how it all ended. I just want you to know you have always been my family. I will always love John, and I hope he's doing well.

That simple message unlocked a new door—a way back to John, to returning to a place I had forgotten I'd left, with that final phone call where I said, I need to come home.

Mrs. B invited me to a baby shower at their house, for John's middle sister. So I packed up my two-year-old daughter, Polina, into her bright pink and black Bugaboo stroller, and we went.

I told my mom I was going. We had a fight—she couldn't seem to grasp why I had to go back there with Polina. But I had to go. I believed that by going, everything would be solved. This was meant to be.

John and I.

It was almost a two-hour journey to get from Belmont to the "Big" estate house. I didn't—I don't—drive, so it made it more difficult. We took a bus, then a train, then another train, and from the train station, I took a cab. I did it all with my two-year-old in tow. All I had to do was get to John's.

We made it to the party. John wasn't even there for most of it, but the house—it felt like it was calling me home. Our wedding pictures were still up on the side tables, the picture collage from 2005 that his sister had made of all the family pictures was still there. I was everywhere in that house, like a ghost of the life I thought I'd left behind.

Borderline

Always, I find myself stranded between black and white,
Good and bad, the razor-sharp line that slices the air.
The border no one seeks, yet I walk it, barefoot,
Finding balance in the grey—an impossible dance.
A tightrope strung between right and wrong,
Words hushed, for fear of falling into the silence of grey,
Where shadows move like ghosts—
The sea of black and white crashes on either side,
Waves gnashing like teeth against the tightrope borderline.
I have tumbled from this border before,
Flung back and forth, a tennis ball in the cruelest match.

When I fell— Into the black abyss, I drowned in its triangle of evil,
Sucking in water like air,
Grasping for the border to hold my soul above the flood.
I've wandered, too, into the whitewashed brightness,
Where the good was no more than an empty glare.
No contrast to be found within its blinding whiteness.
The good did not breathe joy into me,
Did not drive away the fear— No, it spun me back into the dark,
Until I found the balance between it all.
I do not mind this life on the border,
Between black and white, good and bad.
In the shifting light of grey,
My soul has learned to harden and soften in equal measure—
A flicker of light above the staircase I climb,
barefoot still.

©Diana Kouprina

*Then – in my childhood – in the dawn
Of a most stormy life – was drawn
From ev'ry of good and ill
The mystery which binds me still*
– Edgar Allen Poe

The day I died is the day I began to survive…

Chapter 1
I Love Alone

I was an extremely empathetic, sensitive child and am convinced I had the misfortune of being born 10 years too early, but be as it may. I was born in the mid 80s in the Soviet Union and in 1993 my mother and I arrived in the US under my father's student visa which was granted to him by Yale University. When we arrived he had one more year left in his studies. After he graduated he began working for Harvard University, my father's H1B visa cemented that he was an extraordinary human being and vital to the US, as the *"H1B visa is only granted to individuals who have skills that are unique and
extraordinary and vital for the US economy" (USCIS.gov).* This is the story that helped me gain a bit of status later in private school. After all, I wasn't an *"illegal immigrant"* and my father went to Yale, an Ivy League University, therefore I belonged, *kind of, maybe.*

For the first seven years of my life I remember a happy childhood, filled with love of
affectionate babushkas, aunts, uncles, and two best friends. We lived in Tbilisi, Georgia in a one bedroom apartment with my mother, my grandmother, my grandfather and my great grandmother; the same apartment my mother and my uncle were born in. The apartment was a part of a large housing complex, almost like a community of neighbors where

everyone knew one another. The kids, on hot summer days, would run around in the streets as the men would sit around large tables playing checkers and chess. Babushkas would sit outside, selling fried sunflower seeds in newspaper cones, but the best was when the sweet, sugary scent would rise in the air. That's when, we as kids, knew the neighborhood babushka was making red rooster lollipops, and selling them for a few kopecks out of her apartment. I would run to her apartment complex down the little dirty hill road, across from the playground, clenching my kopecks in hand, mouth watering over the sheer thought of licking the red rooster lollipop.

I had two best friends, Melhouse and Bella, we were all around the same age. Mel, lived right
across from us, with his mother and grandmother, his father was a real life soldier. Bella lived
below us on the first floor. We played outside and had grand adventures. When the civil war
came to Georgia, and Mel's dad was a part of the war, I packed a white purse with a
drawing of red riding hood and the wolf on the front; I have no idea what I put in the purse. It
was little, didn't fit much, I remember that. I remember how Mel and I ran away when no one
was watching, to go to the bus that would bring us to his dad, where the war was happening. I
remember standing with him at the bus stop, ready for whatever journey that was laid out for us. We were eight. We never got on the bus. Our parents found us. But I loved Mel, he was my partner in crime. Until he wasn't.
I have so few of these cherished memories, memories of childhood joy, love and friendship. I remember loving to build snowmen in the winter. I would be the first one out in the snow,
followed by Mel and Bella. I would be the last one in, perfecting our snow masterpieces. I
remember when the electricity would go out and we would resort to the use of candles and oil
lamps. We would fry sunflower seeds on the stove and I would perform in front of my
grandparents. I loved to dance, perform, pretend, and play the piano. In those moments and
through their eyes, I believed in myself and my magical abilities of creation and performance.

As a child I believed myself to be an artist, a ballerina, an actress.

Butterfly Wings of Für Elise
On those silent Soviet nights, beneath a starry sky, heavy with stillness,
When the world outside was cold, familial bonds formed around me, the only child who played so well.
The blockade held its breath, and the flicker of kerosene lamps led us well into the night.
My favorite time, when I could entertain with grace.
Aroma of fried sunflower seeds filled the air.
The dim light danced across the walls,
The mix of —sharp, faint—scents perfumed the air,
Drawing me inward, deeper into the rhythm of melody,
Beethoven's voice guiding me into a lull.
My fingertips, then so pure,
So sure upon the ivory keys,
Danced in perfect harmony.
How I loved the piano—both of them, two of them,
I had, one in Yerevan, the other in Tbilisi— my silent companions,
Each a doorway to another world.
They were my iPhone, my iPad, my television,
My evening sonnet whispered in the glow of flickering flames.
My bestest friends.

Für Elise (playful, light)
Yet still, in the quiet, I hear my laughter— Faint, like the wind, a melody that circles me.
I close my eyes; there is traffic up ahead, the ride is long, the trees flicker past my window.
The suns bright rays glimmer in my eyes, I feel the breeze coming through the open windows, the warming of the day.
I hear the melody once more. I skip through time, playful, light,

My song an echo in the distance,
A whisper I try to grasp.
This is for me, my inner child.
For me,
The memories:

I remember when my great aunt, would come to visit my great grandmother. She was tall and
beautiful, she always brought bagels and sushki for me everytime she came over to visit. I loved her, she smelled like springtime flowers and Paris. In her apartment she had an
array of perfume bottles made of crystal, all arranged on her vanity, along with her makeup and jewelry. I would always arrange and re-arrange her make up, gently feeling the silky smooth like textures with my
fingertips. In her "gardirobe" (wardrobe), amongst her clothes, hidden and neatly tucked in the back I would always find, waiting for me, her wedding veil made out of French tulle. I loved running my fingers through the exquisite texture of braided silk.

Chapter 2
Vanilla Memories

We had a light green balcony, in spring, it matched the butterflies

Ivory wings, yellow-bellies, vanilla-scented

Dancing gently in the summer breeze.

Our hallway floor, thick in burgundy pain, cool cement beneath bare feet,

The memories linger alive in me still, stored deep within my treasure chest of dreams.

A past life, now foreign and strange, but woven into me,

Where love flowed freely, without change, and fear knew its place,

Where laughter echoed, and joy bounced off into outer space,

Until the day, it crumbled down like a house of cards,

blown away in a single breath, gone within a blink,

Never to be built,

The same,

Again.

Between 1991 and 1993, Georgia, a Soviet Union Republic faced its own civil war during the
collapse, "perestroika", of the Soviet Union.

 My mother's family due to lack of finances and lack of desire to move remained in Tbilisi, Georgia.. My deduk, (grandpa) had already passed away, and my uncle fled to follow the love of his life to Luithvenia. My father was at the time in America, working on his masters and my father's parents had purchased an apartment in Yerevan, Armenia. It was decided by the grown-ups that my mother and I would be safer living in
Yerevan, with my father's parents so my mother and I followed

them to Yerevan.
It was just my two babushkas left and this would be my first experience of feeling
abandonment, heart ache, and loss.
I attended first and second grade in Yerevan's Russian school, as my primary language

was Russian, and during winter and summer vacations, my mother and I would take the train to Tbilisi to stay with my babushkas. But even there, it was no longer the same. My friends had all moved, all escaping the war that was coming to the city of Tbilisi. Slowly everything I had known and loved truly and deeply was crumbling down around me. There was nothing I could do to stop it. All I could do was hide deep within the safety of my past memories.

My earliest memory of dissociation occurred when my mother and I lived in Yerevan, Armenia.
I was 7 years old. I remember it as though it was yesterday. My mother and I were
walking home from my piano lesson. I loved my piano lessons at the time. My piano teacher was a warm, loving, Russian speaking, Armenian woman, whose apartment was filled with cozy, plush trinkets. I felt love and joy every time my mother and I entered her apartment, where we would be greeted by a big, shaggy dog, as memory serves me he was almost the same height as I was at the time. The lesson itself went smoothly and I received all the necessary praise to keep going on my piano journey. Yet, on that walk home, I remember feeling dread. I was worried my grandparents, my father's parents, would be arguing when we got home. I hid inside my mind on that walk home and played around with different scenarios. I refer to them now as *"The what ifs"*.
I tried to focus on positive outcomes, visualizing so hard on imagery popping inside my mind that I no longer could feel the surroundings around me. I no longer felt myself in my body. I was somewhere else, watching a movie of what if's, playing inside my mind. The imagery was so vivid I recall it today as though I had just experienced it. Ironically I can't recall how long the walk was from the lesson to the apartment. I can't recall if it was fall or winter. I can't recall what I was wearing. Did mother and I speak during this walk? Or did we walk in silence.
All I can recall is the movie called "What if", playing in my mind.

The first scene was what if, I have it all wrong and when we get home everyone will be happy. What if my grandmother was happy and smiling when we entered the apartment? What if my grandpa decides to hug me? What if they are both really, really nice to my mom and she smiles? What if I smile and we all smile? What if I pray now and by magic, this imaginary reality comes true.
What if….?
When we finally got back to the apartment, my grandparents were mad. There was a fight. I hid myself in the depth of my mind and stayed there. I don't know what my body did. I don't know if it cried or hid. I don't know if I froze. But I do know I would learn to hide myself far in depth of my mind from then on when something bad happened.
I found safety in hiding on the little balcony which was joined to my mother's bedroom.

I would sit out in the evening on the little balcony outside my mother's bedroom and stare out at the other tall buildings that surrounded our tall apartment complex. I would stare into the windows that had lights on inside them, hoping to see glimpses of the people who lived there and make up stories of their lives. I always saw them as being these loving, happy people and wishing I could be one of them.
If I could just be someone else, anyone else, anyone but who I was and how I lived, I would be happy. The longer my mother and I remained in Yerevan, the more and more my inner self dissatisfaction began to fester. My father's parents weren't the most
loving grandparents. From what I can remember my grandfather lacked kindness and joy. I didn't quite fear him but I can't say I liked him at times although I had no fear of
speaking up with confidence and I loved him deeply. The whole time we were in Yerevan, I longed to be back in Tbilisi with my loving grandmother and great-grandmother, where I felt safe, where I wasn't judged or criticized, where love was honest and pure, where I could be my true self.
Oh how I hated Yerevan, in the first year, and how I longed to just live in Tbilisi; by the time I found my footing in Yerevan it was time for the biggest move of all to which

nothing truly compared in 1993; when all I had known would be completely forgotten and I would have to become something and someone else entirely.

One day, without a thought,

I caught a butterfly in my net. Excitement soared through me as I held her by her wings.

Perched on top of my tippy toes, in a ballerina pose, gripping unto the rail,

I marveled at my catch –

What wonder, what a feat!

I brought her up to my nose, I smelled her yellow pollen belly,

Inhaling the vanilla scent.

I rushed to the kitchen, where my mother stood,

Breathless, eager to share –

I inhaled for the last time her sweet vanilla scent,

Then set her free, watching her flutter in air.

My mother's scream, sharp and shrill,

Carved itself into memory,

Her terror born of vanilla wings, still echoes in laughter of today.

Standing on that balcony, catching butterflies in a world so distant now

A foreign land of dreams, until I catch a glimpse of a white butterfly fluttering about

On a summer's day, bringing whispers of lost lands, memories wrapped in vanilla wings.

Chapter 3
The Little Mermaid

A year prior to our departure, my father sent me a video tape of the Little Mermaid. As a child I loved fairy tales and to my dismay the fairy tales told by Hans Christian Anderson didn't always have a happy ending. I remember when I first read the tale of the Little Mermaid, how she sacrificed all for love to, in the end to not get the prince, but be redeemed by becoming one of the daughter's of the air. For years I would obsess over the story, and later I would wonder why was I so scared of embracing the potent lesson of the fairytale to never give up one's voice. I forgot that lesson and denounced it. Yet, the fact remains and lays in the haunting warning of what could happen if one gave up their voice for someone else:

"She saw that on the ship, life and merriment were still going on. She saw him and his beautiful bride who was thought to be his savior; she laughed and pressed her lips to his, while he played with her long, black hair.
Morning was breaking; the sun would soon rise. And with it she knew she must die and dissolve into foam on the sea.
But all at once, her sisters rose out of the water before her. Their faces were pale, and their long, beautiful hair no longer waved in the wind; it had been cut off.
'We have given our hair to the witch,' said they, 'so that she might bring help to you and save you from death this night. She has given us a knife. Here it is! Do you see how sharp it is? Before the sun rises, you must plunge it into the heart of the prince, and when his warm blood falls upon your feet, they will grow together into a fish's tail, and you will be a mermaid again, and can come back to us, and live your three hundred years before you turn into dead, salty sea foam. Hasten! He or you must die before the sun rises.'
Then they sighed deeply and mournfully, and vanished beneath the waves.
The little mermaid drew aside the crimson curtain of the tent, and saw the fair bride
resting her head on the prince's breast. She bent down and kissed his beautiful brow, looked at the sky where the dawn was spreading fast, looked at the sharp knife, and again fixed her eyes on the

prince. He dreamed in his dreams of her, and of the love she had brought him.

She raised the knife—then threw it far out into the waves. The water turned red where it fell, and the drops that spurted up looked like blood. She cast one more lingering, half-fainting glance at the prince, then flung herself from the ship into the sea, and felt her body dissolving into foam.

And she flung herself from the ship into the sea, and felt her body dissolving into foam.

But as the sun rose, she felt warm rays fall upon her, and the little mermaid was lifted up out of the sea.

She saw above her a host of lovely transparent beings, and through them she could see the white sails of the ship and the red sky of the morning.

Their voices were melodious, but so ethereal that no human ear could hear them, just as no earthly eye could see them; the little mermaid perceived that she had a body like theirs, and that she was gradually rising higher and higher out of the foam.

'Where am I?' asked she; and her voice sounded like that of other beings, so spiritual, that no earthly music could imitate it.

'Among the daughters of the air,' answered one of them. 'A mermaid has not an immortal soul, nor can she obtain one unless she wins the love of a human being. Her eternal existence depends upon the power of another; but the daughters of the air, although they do not possess an immortal soul, can, by their good deeds, procure one for themselves. We fly to warm countries, and cool the sultry air that destroys mankind with the pestilence. We carry the perfume of the flowers to spread health and restoration.

After we have striven for three hundred years to do all the good in our power, we receive an immortal soul and take part in the happiness of mankind. You, poor little mermaid, have tried with your whole heart to do as we are doing; you have suffered and endured, and raised yourself to the spirit-world by your good deeds. And now, by striving for three hundred years in the same way, you may obtain an immortal soul.'"

– The Little Mermaid, Hans Christian Anderson

In hindsight, today I can say, bravo Hans Christian Anderson for teaching young girls about the power of their voice, through a haunting tale of what happens to a woman when she sacrifices her voice for a man, and what true redemption looks like. I apologize here dear, reader if I sound too repetitive, but I can't help but stress the urgent warning that Hans Christian Anderson embedded into the tale of the Little Mermaid, the warning I myself did not heed, as the ending that Disney created was so much more romantic. Yet, today especially for girls, the ending that Hans Christian Anderson wrote originally should be read, taught, discussed, turned into a movie because the truth of life lies within the original ending of the story.

 Unfortunately, that is not how I felt when I initially read the fairy tale. I loved the tale, I identified with the little mermaid, but I hated the ending, I despised it. It tormented me. I didn't even care about the part where ultimately Ariel is rescued from becoming sea foam, and becomes one of the daughter's of the air. For me it ended when Eric chose the other woman, the one who had a voice, instead of the voiceless mermaid who had sacrificed herself, her voice, for him and he, the Prince couldn't see it.

It stood against everything I believed about love. After all I was being raised in a culture where young girls fantasize about their wedding day. That marriage was a way out of women's suffrage. My torment against the ending of the Little Mermaid came to an end a year later in 1992, when I got my hands on the Disney version of the Little Mermaid.

It proved to me that happy endings did exist, that after making a grand sacrifice, the prince in return would see me and rescue me right back. I watched that tape over and over again, driving my mother insane and relating to the parts where Ariel just wants more and viewing the sea king as a tyrant, relating his attributes to those of my own father. I saw a lot of myself in Ariel. I was Ariel, misunderstood, tormented and in desperate need of something different, something all together new to make me happy. I held on to the thought that once I arrived in the US, I would be HAPPY!
I was the little Mermaid after all, but the **Disney version**.

All I knew as a child was the Soviet Union—a vast, sprawling certainty that I thought would always be mine. I didn't realize then, in my smallness, that I would never know it again, never see it, never feel its rhythms beneath my feet.

Sometimes I wonder if my path wasn't carved out long before that day. Before I was even born. I was small, five or six, when my Babushka brought me to that Soviet apartment—a little flat indistinguishable from the others, yet full of warmth, of familiarity. It felt like home. Her friend was the palm reader, and her fingers traced my future on the surface of my hand, speaking words I could not fully grasp.

I wonder now if my Babushka Ira (*my mom's mom*) knew, that day she brought me to the palm reader, that she was letting me go forever. Letting me slip into a different world, into a future that none of us could quite fathom. Did they all know the magnitude of what was coming, while I remained blind to it? A child who didn't even realize she was living in a place and a time that would vanish, swallowed by history, never to return.

I wish I could ask her now—about the psychic, about that palm reader and her strange prediction that would cast its shadow across my life. Did my Babushka visit her to ease her own anxiety, to find solace in letting us go? By then, preparations were already underway. It was decided: one day, I would travel to America with my mother. It would be a journey that no one else would share with us. Not my Babushka. Not my Dedushka. Not the aunts or uncles or cousins who formed the fabric of my childhood. Just us: my mother, my father, and me.

The palm reader took my small hand in hers, examining its lines like an ancient map. "You have an interesting journey ahead of you," she said, her voice distant, as if speaking to something unseen. "You will suffer greatly in your first life, with your first husband, but you will survive it. After that, the rest will fall into place. Second love will come." At least, that's what my mind tells me now. The truth is, she wasn't speaking to me; she was speaking to my grandmother. The conversation flowed in Russian, words I barely understood then and have long since translated into English. I wonder: did my Babushka take me there on purpose, knowing somehow that my life would be shaped by this fleeting moment?

And yet, I see now how much I resisted it—my future, my fate. Even as I grew, I couldn't bring myself to face the demons crouched in my path. Instead, I wanted to run far away from them, to erase myself and start over. I wanted to rewrite everything: my morals, my values, my very identity. I became someone else entirely—a patchwork person, cobbled together from those around me, neatly packaged into a box that wasn't mine.
Even now, I'm not sure who she was, that persona I created; she was no one at all.

Prior to leaving for America from Moscow, my mom and I visited relatives in Saint
Petersburg, who would facilitate our final departure. The memories in my mind of those last two months are blurred but I remember a couple things clearly. I remember the white nights of Saint Petersburg, the water fountains made of cobblestones, the huge horse my mother placed me on to have my picture taken, and how the horse almost chopped of my mother's toe by nearly stepping on it. But most of all I remember McDonalds in Moscow.

My mother and I stood in a 2 hour long line in Pushkin Square to get into the first
McDonalds to ever open in Russia. After a two hour wait we were finally allowed
entrance into the magical world of McDonalds, where red and yellow colors dominated and seating resembled something out of a 1950s diner, with workers whose ensemble resembled that of candy canes. Waiters brought out plastic trays with colorful boxes of white, red and yellow to serve the awaiting patrons. I ordered a big mac, fries and a coke. To this day, I will remember it as the best meal I have ever had at McDonald's, by far better than the McDonald's I would taste a month later in NYC. That summer, I had a lot of hopes for America.
It's almost as though I could scrub off all the bad off myself, and step into a magical
princess world. After all, the country that created the Little Mermaid would love me and I would meet my prince charming.

I wanted to be a princess and I was going to a world filled with magic or so I thought.
We obtained our visas and said our goodbyes, being a minor at the time, I was
stamped inside my mother's Soviet Union passport. The irony of me not having my own passport would haunt me for the rest of my life. Of course, I didn't know that then. In those days, I was filled with hope, wonder, excitement and fear. Although I had all my hopes of magic placed in the dream of America, I feared what life would be like with my father. Even then I knew I was saying goodbye to all the loving nurturing that I had
received from my grandmothers. In my heart of hearts, I knew my parents had to love me, but they had the most critical way of showing it.
As a child I thrived on positive attention. I loved performing for

my great grandmother, singing songs, and dressing up. I knew anything that I came up with would be praised with words like brilliant, smart, beautiful. The more praise I received, the more I wanted to shine. It was though the positive words would continuously play on repeat in my mind making me want to be better and do better. The criticism on the other hand, those words, would sting and I would believe them as they would absorb themselves in my mind,
continuously playing on repeat. Later I would be very talented at being and believing that I was a "stupid chicken". It would become the best performance of my life.

But at the age of 8 going on nine, I buried the fear and the terrified emotions deep inside of me and clung onto the hope that America would make all my dreams come true. I would be a star, an actress, a writer. I would be someone. I would be an Artist.
I would win an Oscar.
I would become someone,
Someone Free.

Filled with magic, hope and wonder I boarded the plane on July 30th, 1993. It was my birthday. I was finally NINE years old. I was a big girl, stepping into a big world.
My dreams on the last nights in the USSR were of old ladies at night walking around and
sweeping the streets clean from all the hustle and bustle of everyday life, when all else was quiet and still. I pictured NYC to be the cleanest city on earth. Oh how little did I know, then. At the age of eight I had a very limited perception of what it truly meant to be moving to America. Everything I understood about this enormous country was what I had learned from Disney and I loved it.

For years later I would wonder, and dream of who I could have been. But in those early years I was filled with dreamers.

I have always wondered,

With years on end, and tears at hand,

Filled with regrets, of all I could have been.

A girl of visions, and of dreams,

Desire for stardom was rooted from within, on those nights

When blockades were real, roasted sunflower seeds perfumed the air,

Kerosene lamps lit up the way, as my fingers glided over black and ivory keys,

Creating a melody by memory of Fur Elise

High hopes, high dreams, always fueled the air

To be! Alas, it wasn't meant to be....

I think back, what if I could have been....

A ballerina filled with grace holding up my head up high, en pointe

Tendu and a plie 1, 2, 3, 4, to arabesque leading into a pirouette,

Or maybe, I could have been

A child Olympian for the USSR,

The shot was there, I just had to try,

If I just let go, but fear wouldn't let me budge or make a nudge,

My body frozen upon the sight, of high leaps and balance beams.

Or maybe,

I could have been...

The next Celine Dion,

With my spirit voice being my guiding star.

The desire burned deeply from within,

In this childhood realm upon which,

Dreamers dream.

Chapter 4
Hello, New York City!

The plane ride was long and it would be the only plane I would ever take that brought me across country borders. Little did I know then that I would never again have the
opportunity to step off US soil. After all, I was a big girl filled with big dreams arriving in New York City. What I knew about NYC then was what I have learned from movies, and my own imagination. For some reason in my mind I pictured the city to be sparkling clean, shining and shimmering. That was my first disappointment, when I learned that the city didn't sparkle like the green emerald city of OZ. It wasn't magical but extremely rushed, crowded and dirty. I felt little, lost and scared. I wanted to go back. I dreaded meeting my father, the dread and fear would remain within me for a long time.

My father met us at the JFK airport with his friend where we loaded up in the car and embarked on the journey from New York City to New Haven, Connecticut. As it was still my birthday, and my only birthday wish was to eat McDonald's in America we made a stop at the fast food joint, and that was when I experienced my second disappointment. The Mcdonalds in America was nothing like the magic I had experienced less than a month prior in Moscow. There were no happy, candy cane workers sweeping and wiping the tables or swiftly serving food. McDonalds, like New York City, appeared to be gloomy and it was then that the paralyzing fear of what life would be like in America set in, like a black mass setting in at the bottom of my stomach.

I am not sure exactly at what moment in time my father explained to me that Americans would not be able to pronounce Deanna. He explained that in accurate translation,
Deanna translated to Diana in English. I knew just a little bit of English at the time. I knew how to say that "my name is Diana"but what I didn't know was how to ask to be excused to the bathroom. My memories are hazy of the time period when I first stepped into a Catholic school in New Haven, Connecticut. I remember when my mom special ordered my uniform and I loved it, the plaid, deep red and blue skirt, white shirt, navy blue tights, black ballet flats. It was prettier then my 2nd grade uniform by far, and it made me

feel like a part of home was there with me on that first day of 3rd grade. I understood nothing and said nothing, except for that fateful moment when I realized I needed to pee and well, there was no way I was going to hold it in until the end of the day. I raised my trembling hand, and when the teacher called on me, I stood up because that is what I was taught to do when a teacher calls on you, you need to stand up and express your needs while the whole class stares at you. So, I stood up and in Russian asked if I could go to the bathroom. The nun did not understand me. So again, in Russian and louder, I said it.

And, again there was silence.
I was thinking to myself, on the first day of school in America, I am going to pee myself in front of everyone . I wished I was invisible.
The Nun left me standing as she left the classroom. I didn't dare sit down. It felt like
forever as I stood there waiting for her to return. All I could think about was "Please don't pee, Please don't pee, Please don't pee, Please don't pee".
When she finally returned, she came in with Luida, my only friend, and that's only because our families were friends and it was her parents who suggested that I attend the Catholic school with Luida, as New Haven didn't have any good public schools. Luida was in 4th grade and her classroom was next door to us.
Luida, in Russian asked me "Shto tebje nada?" (what do you need)

I responding "Hochu v toilete", Luida nodded at me, looked at the teacher and said, "she just wants to go to the bathroom" with a shrug.
I, in turn felt humiliated for causing such a commotion and not being able to say
something as simple as "I need to go to the bathroom" in English. Luckily through the whole commotion I didn't pee my pants and really held it in!

Chapter 5
Why, so serious?

I met Luida the second night after our arrival in New Haven. My mother and I didn't bring many things with us. We had two medium sized, brown, soviet suitcases that we packed all our livelihood into. So on that first night out, and since we were going to be guests in someone's house. I dressed up. My babushka prior to my departure had sewn me a baby pink sweater dress that had a large flower embroidery on the front of it. I loved it and I felt like a princess in it. I put it on for that eventful night, pairing it with white tights and simple black ballet flats. My hair was long, dark brown and frizzy, as curly hair tends to get when brushed. I hated my hair. I wanted straight, light colored hair.

When we arrived at the apartment Luida answered the door and I was mesmerized. She was in tights and a tee shirt, her hair straight in a neat bob, her nose fascinated me as it was a small button nose as opposed to my prominent, big nose. She had thin eyebrows and I was by the age of nine already struggling with a unibrow. As we entered the

apartment, my parents left me to make a friend, in the living room, while they themselves moved into the kitchen where my father's friends were gathering around the table to eat and drink.

In the living room, Michael Jackson was dancing around on the small, brown TV, and

Luida informed me in Russian she was trying to learn the moonwalk. I was fascinated and entranced.. We danced to Michael Jackson and Ace of Base and after a while of me watching and Luida showing off her dance moves, she tugged on my hand and said, "Let's go play in my room, I have dolls," and then she showed me her Barbie collection. She had dressed barbies and naked barbies, barbies whom she attempted to give haircuts to, she had the Barbie dreamhouse, she had Ken, she had the whole Barbie world, with an array of Barbie shoes and clothes. Some of her barbies could move their whole arm around and others could move their hips. I loved the Barbie shoes the most. I had only one Barbie, which I wasn't even allowed to have but she was a present from my babushka and she traveled across the country with me.

I was living in Yerevan when I first laid my eyes on Barbie. It was the time of Perestroika, and American brands and products were appearing everywhere. My babushka would visit us as much as she could, traveling by train from Tbilisi to Yerevan. The route I myself would come to love as a child. There was always something mystical and soothing when the train pulled out on its tracks, making a chugging sound. It was a three day journey of living with strangers in very close quarters, and sleeping on pull out bunk-beds, sharing meals that we had packed for the long journey. Everytime that she visited, I would bring her to a specialty store,

where I would show her Barbie. Always repeating to her the same phrase: "We are going to just look, not to buy."
Buy we couldn't; Barbie cost a ruble fortune at the time, the price was equivalent to two months rent; 1,300 rubles to be exact.
Until one day, after a lot of looking at Barbie, I walked into the store and I walked out with Barbie. That was the happiest I had ever been. To this day, I can still feel and taste the joy I felt when I held the coveted pink Barbie box in my hands.
I loved Barbie and all she stood for.
My father hated everything Barbie ever stood for so I wasn't allowed to have them. But the forbidden fruit tastes so much better. All I wanted was Barbies to play with, the ones my father forbid. Luida on the other hand had it all, all the Barbies, and dream houses, and she even got to keep her real name. She was Luida in Russian and in English. Her full name was
Luidmila, and she could have gone by Mila so Americans would have an easier way to pronounce her name, but she chose not to. She was Luida. I would wonder often as to why I had to become Diana, although I never voiced my questions to anyone, I just accepted that I did.

I fell in-love with Luida right then and there, wearing my baby pink sweater dress, with my long dark, brown frizzy hair pulled back by a bright-deep pink squishy headband. I knew as soon as I laid my eyes on her, I wanted to be just like her. I wanted to look like

her, but most of all, I craved to be as carefree and independent as she had seemed to be in that first instant that I met her. Luida soon became my best and only friend during those years in New Haven. She is the only one who I could relate to and who called me by my real name. I could talk to her in Russian and she taught me English, and how to be cool.
I worshipped her.

Chapter 6
Skipping Grades Can be confusing

By the time we made it to Cambridge I was in 5th grade, and had skipped 4 th grade. I don't remember much of 5th grade other then I was a new student once again and I didn't have many friends. OJ

Simpson was on trial, and I remember watching bits and pieces of the trial on TV at school. It was a historical moment, I don't think I understood. I felt lonely. I hid in my mind. By 6th grade I lived in the world of my own imagination and books. I studied and read obsessively.

It was also the time when the idea of private school was first presented to me. I jumped at it because I was in awe with the idea of being the best, that I could be among the best of the best.

Secretly I hoped to be just like my father, I wanted to be the genius in the family just like him, secretly I dreamt of Harvard University, of being one day accepted there, as that acceptance would solidify my greatness, as Ivy League education solidified my father's greatness. He had achieved what only a few Soviet Armenian immigrants could only dream about; he did it all swiftly, precisely, and with ease. I grew up hearing of my

father's greatness, his intellect from my babushkas. I never voiced those dreams, those visions, they were my secret fantasies; fantasies which I was too scared to voice aloud in fear of being laughed at, because even then I told myself I wasn't good enough, even then there was a voice in my head growing larger and larger telling me I wasn't good enough, mocking my dreams and laughing at me. It wasn't a loud voice than, rather a whisper, a slight uncomfortable feeling I couldn't quite place.

I met Araxie through my father's mentors, a prominent Armenian family whose prestige shimmered like a distant constellation. They were bound to Ivy League institutions, their lives threaded with the elegance of academia and the quiet wealth of tradition. This connection came through my father's affluent employment, part of an expatriate program that brought us into their orbit.

I adored the family—their cross-cultural warmth, their unselfconscious embrace of us. They offered love as naturally as sunlight through an open window, filling every corner of their home. They invited us to their sprawling Sunday dinners, where relatives and friends gathered in multitudes. Their dining room was alive with the rhythm of clinking glasses, overlapping conversations, and laughter that seemed to rise with the steam of lavash and lamb stew. I was drawn to those Sundays, to the children weaving between adults like errant threads in a tapestry. Most were boys my age, and we found

camaraderie over chess and our shared obsession with the film, *Searching for Bobby Fischer*; and well, Bobby Fischer in general. In those times I secretly dreamt of being the next Bobby Fischer, I dreamt of being someone, anyone great, and I would think to myself, why not maybe I could be the next Bobby Fischer, I would reason with myself that I did in fact play chess well, and I always beat the boys, and my computer, in
addition the Armenian family always praised me for my intuitive chess skills.
The whisper of a voice that told me I couldn't do it, had began to diminish. It was almost non existent, when I met Araxie.

The eldest daughter: the sun in their small solar system. She was twenty-five, her dark, bobbed curls refusing the discipline of perfection. She moved as though her body knew secrets the rest of us could only guess at, and she smelled of something more than perfume—confidence, perhaps, or simply the promise of a life fully inhabited. I wanted to be her, though I wouldn't have known how to put it into words.

Her appearances at the Sunday dinners were rare, fleeting as she was busy, writing her psychology PhD, disappearing into the labyrinth of her intellect. But in the few moments she offered me, she became something larger than a mentor—she became a mirror in which I saw my own potential reflected.

Araxie treated me as her equal, though I was only eleven. She spoke to me with the
gravity one reserves for peers, never once condescending. She told me about Dana Hall, its storied history and the pride she carried as an alumna. Her voice lingered on those memories, and I imagined myself following in her footsteps, stepping into a world she had already claimed as her own.

She helped me craft my admissions essay, a dissertation against the death penalty. We debated morality and justice, psychology and the weight of human choice. Araxie's words were like hands shaping clay, molding ideas I didn't yet know I had. On Friday evenings, she invited me into her world—her friends, all in their mid-twenties, gathered to watch The X-Files. I, a child among adults, was inexplicably welcomed. I reveled in their
debates about aliens, conspiracies, and the unsettling notion that truth could lie hidden

in the folds of everyday life. For the first time, I felt not just included but essential to a conversation.

Araxie was the first person to take me to the movies. I can still see the theater's dim glow, feel the sticky press of the floor beneath my shoes. Jumanji played on the screen, its chaos pulling me into another world. I clung to Robin Williams' character, his fear and wonder a mirror of my own. In that theater, the bigness of the screen made my own worries feel small, insignificant—a gift only stories can give. For a brief, magical window of time, my fears melted like shadows under a rising sun.

But as swiftly as Araxie appeared in my life, she disappeared. Her absence was not marked by any grand event, no falling-out or goodbye. She simply faded, like the last note of a song, leaving the room filled with a silence I didn't know how to fill. Looking back now, I wish I had her by my side to guide me after I was accepted to Dana Hall. Without her, the path felt lonelier, less certain.

It's almost as though her work was done after my acceptance, as if she had only ever been meant to lift me to that first, precarious step. I am left with the memory of her, a fleeting glimpse of what it means to see someone not as they are, but as they might one day become.

Chapter 7
I don't want to party
Christmas Party – 1995

It was around Christmas time of 1995, my mother and I were getting ready for the annual
Christmas party which was to be held at Roger Fishers home. My mother was in the shower and I was rummaging around. I remember the landline ringing. And as it was ringing, I began to feel like this is going to be a bad call. I answered the phone. On the other end was the voice of my babushka Ira. Her voice seemed shaky, although she tried to sound cheery and asked to speak to my mom and that it was important. The phone we had was portable and brought into the bathroom. My mom initially was irriated by my

intrusion, but took the phone. I left the bathroom before she said "private", but I didn't go to far. Something in me in that moment froze. I needed desperately to know what was
happening, I knew it was bad. I prayed no one died, but I knew someone died. I heard my mom sobbing in the bathroom. Each sob would pierce throw me, until I no longer could contain the tears from flowing down my cheeks. I wanted to burst and sob. I
just felt it. My beloved babushka Poli had passed away. I prayed it was a lie. I prayed something else happened to someone else. I bargained with God, I promised to be sad for

whoever it was that got hurt, as long as it wasn't her. But it was her.
My mother confirmed it when she had collected herself in the bathroom. She said in a cool, almost nonchalant voice. I knew she was restraining all her emotions. I felt a welt inside of me ready to explode. But I contained it. I had to. I had to contain all of it, to be strong for my mom.
Just tears streamed down my cheeks, I couldn't contain those, yet. And when I made it into my room for get dressed into some sort of Christmas outfit, I presume, I have no recollection of it.

It wouldn't be until I was alone, in the private safety of my room, I let out the heart wrenching sob that I could no longer contain. My mind and body disconnected.

To this day I wish I could recall the exact feelings I felt, the detailed conversations that flowed, the feel of the house that hosted the Christmas party. All I have though is a
memory of a "fancy" Cambridge house, like those ones that are located on
Brattle St, nestled between Harvard Sq, and Belmont MA, hidden by Mount Auburn St. Those are the houses that like it or not, just by looking at them you are transported back in time to the wealth and beauty of the Gilded age.
As for the interior of the house, I again fail to recall much of the exact details. I fear my
recollection is muddied with my childhood imagination. As for me I remember thinking this is from a scene of the Nutcracker, a large roaring firplace in the middle of the room that resembled a ball room, to the side a Christmas tree larger than any I had ever seen before, maybe in movies, not in real life. Presents, load of

presents under the Christmas tree, girls dressed in velvety dresses, with their flawless hair held back by burgundy, black headbands. I remember thinking to myself, that I wish I had worn something prettier. I wish I had owned a dress as pretty as theirs. I don't remember what I was wearing. But I do remember the harsh criticism of the self that went on in my mind.

I remember thinking to myself, I am not in my body, but rather, my body is a robot and someone, a little person inside my head is operating my robot body.

Smile, nod, shake someone's hand, do it right, not too firm, hold hand elegantly. Be like a

ballerina, like a princess would be. Repeat, smile, nod, shake hand, don't show emotion, stay by my mothers side, best not to take anything off the little trays being brought around by men dressed in tuxedos, I might make a mess eating, eating too much will make them think I am not fed at home, stay quiet.

Chapter 8
'Deti' Kids

I remember thinking to myself when my mother was pregnant with the twins, that   maybe in some way they would be little miracles, maybe one day they would grow to be my friends, and companions. I was a lonely child and I lacked my father's love. In   preteen years I would find myself continuously trying to find love. Not within myself, but within others.

My brother and sister were born May 14, 1996. Their birthday marked the day I stopped being a child, or rather treated as a child. I now was expected to help my mom around the house with chores and babysit, but I didn't mind more responsibility, I could prove and show I was good by taking on more responsibility, plus babies brought a new type of love into the house. What stung me deeply, was losing a lot of my mom's attention, it stopped being her and me against the world, and I developed jealousy towards my brother and

sister with a twinge of resentment. I felt left out, unloved, especially when I would

observe how my father interacted with the twins as opposed to me.

I secretly craved that attention my brother and sister were getting as

babies. But I couldn't ask for that affection, or attention, I was old now; a BIG GIRL. After all I was going on 12.

I missed my mother's attention, but she was always to busy with the babies. Only way I received attention was by helping out, and helping out I did. It was my mother and I, changing diapers, pushing the stroller with bundled up babies to Bread and Circus. It was me watching my brother and sister when it was too much for my mom to run errands with a stroller. It was us, a little family, but in the evening it would all change with the arrival of my father. He was an extra addition, to someone who my mother had to cater to. My father expected dinner served to him when he got home from work, and as he would
continue to work on his computer at home, my mom would become his servant. On weekends, my mother belonged to my father, giving all her love to my brother and sister.
I felt alone.

I listened to a lot of classical music those years, it would soothe me and bring back
memories of me dancing for my babushka's. I would close the door of my bedroom tune into the local classical radio station, and dance, I danced for me and I danced for my past, I danced for my babushkas. I could picture them smiling as I attempted to pirouette in my little bedroom. They were always with me, loving me. I missed their physical hugs, but in my dreams I felt them, right there with me.

This was also the time where I dreamt in ballet, idolizing Mikhael Baryshnikov. I felt a deep connection to his story – his daring escape from the Soviet Union to the United States, mirrored my own journey in ways I couldn't grasp or articulate, it was a c onnection I felt that gave me hope.

Chapter 9
Babushka Hasmik Comes to Visit

Babushka Hasmik, my father's mother, arrived in the United States as soon as she could after my brother and sister were born. She had crossed oceans, continents, and years of separation to be here, summoned by my mother's silent plea for help. The twins—two wriggling, demanding bundles of life—needed more care than I, at the fragile age of twelve, could provide. My mother needed her, and so she came.

It would be the first and last time I saw her after we left Yerevan.

At twelve, I didn't yet understand the weight of such moments—the finality wrapped in the ordinary. I didn't know that her visit was not just a fleeting encounter, but an ending. If I could go back, I would hold onto every fragment of her presence: her voice, her scent, the steady rhythm of her hands in the kitchen. But time moves with the stubbornness of the young. I let her come and go, barely noticing, barely reaching for her.

I couldn't then.

Three years had passed since we'd landed in America, and the child who left Yerevan was no longer there. In her place stood someone diminished—someone fearful where she had been confident, silent where she had once brimmed with emotion. Words that had once flowed easily in Armenian, in Russian, now felt foreign, ungraspable. I had shed my languages as if they were burdens, trading them for English, though I never truly carried it with grace.

I remember watching her from a distance, the way her movements seemed so certain, so her own. Her thick hands slicing apples, her voice—layered with the deep timbre of familiarity—singing lullabies to the twins. She spoke to me, but I could barely respond. I would nod or mumble in English, which she didn't understand. Our shared language had crumbled between us, a silent wall.

I was afraid to let her in.

Afraid of what attachment would mean, afraid of the sharp, clean ache that losing her

would bring. I shied away from her warmth, recoiling from what I couldn't name but felt deeply: the fear of love slipping through my fingers again. So I stayed on the edges, avoiding her eyes, retreating into the safety of my own quiet.

Now, I look back and regret what I couldn't give her, or myself. I didn't hold her hand, didn't let her hold me close. If only I had known that this was all we would have—a brief crossing of our lives, her visit as fleeting as a bird landing on a branch.

But I was twelve, and grief doesn't teach you until it's too late.

I still remember her as she was during that visit. When I close my eyes, I see her short gray hair, the sharpness of her Sophia Loren eyes, and the golden dress with eggplant-colored lines running through it. I can still feel the warmth in her hugs, the faint smell of her skin, and even her own quiet reservations, which mirrored my own.

In my mind and in my dreams, I hug her over and over now, wishing I could undo the distance I placed between us.

I know she was there the night I died—her and Babushka Polina. I remember it all so clearly now, as if that moment is etched into my very marrow. It's something that is never forgotten: dying. Only a few of us truly know what it is to die and come back to life.

It took me years to understand it, to make sense of the veil between life and death lifting, however briefly. When I go back to that night in my memory, I see it unfold as if it were happening in present time, a movie unfolding and I am just observing, I can do nothing else but watching, as though I am watching it happen to someone else: my babushkas, their souls there, holding vigil, holding my hands, as my body gives out. They were with me in a way I could never explain, guiding me back to life, when all I wanted to do was stay with them, their final hugs I felt, still feel, I received those hugs standing at the
tunnel between life and death, I wanted to go with them, but they said it wasn't time for me yet.

Even now, as I type this chapter I can sense them here with me, I can smell the fresh air of a spring day in the Caucasus, crisp clear air, mixed in with essence of fruit, herbs and sugar, as I type in present time. The fragrant scent surrounds me, on this cold fall day in Boston, where all my windows are shut and sealed tight, yet the scented cool air surrounds me.

Chapter 10
I don't know if I have friends?

During those first years in Cambridge I didn't have many friends. I had one best friend, Kyle. He immigrated with his family from

Asia, when he was two. We understood each other, and although our cultures seemed different they were also quite the same. Him and I bonded over our mutual love for movies, and books. He was obsessed with Drew
Barrymore, and I with Lucille Ball and Celine Dion, never quite understanding his
obsession with Drew Barrymore.
At, school I was not a popular kid, I was shy and awkward. I mostly kept to myself. I lacked confidence and would continuously obsess over how others perceived me.

To get out of my head I read, I wrote stories. I loved to write, to type, typing for me
replaced playing the piano. When I would type it would be as though a story that was playing in my mind was coming to life through smooth, clicking sounds and the
appearance of black letters on the white screen, bringing my imagination to life. That is also how I felt when I played the piano, and during the first initial year where I loved my piano teacher before it all was destroyed by the school of music in Yerevan and the strict authoritarian style of teaching. When I typed I created and felt at peace with myself.

That summer before entering Dana, I was floating in euphoria. I felt as though creativity was oozing from within me. I wrote my first book of fiction, a story about Witches, inspired by a story about Witches. Of course no one would ever read it and later when I would feel low I would delete the whole story with a click of a keyboard button, erasing it from the computer and from my inner being. But that summer, I wrote. I played chess and quite often beat the computer and I secretly practiced ballet in my room to classical music. There was no youtube at the time, my mentor was Mikhail Barishnikov, White Nights was my favorite movie in which Barishnikov plie's his way out of the Soviet Union, and into the safety of the US. He was my hero.

Chapter 11
I am REBEL!

I met Inna the summer before entering seventh grade, at the beginning of my rebellion phase against my parents—but mainly against my father. I wonder now if that was when I began craving his negative attention, and if, in fact, a part of me craved it more than anything else.

Inna was older, wiser—her presence shimmered with a kind of worldly allure I'd only ever imagined. She was well-traveled, she'd had boyfriends, and she carried herself as if life had already unfolded its secrets for her. She immediately won idol status in my mind. We bonded quickly, not just as friends but as kindred spirits, tethered by the weight of where we came from. Inna was from Tbilisi, Georgia, and fluent in Russian, Georgian, and English. Her mother had once worked for a high-ranking politician in Georgia. It seemed to me that everything about Inna was touched by a golden thread of
sophistication and experience.

We bonded over our culture—or more precisely, over our parents' culture and their heavy, suffocating ways. By then, I deeply felt the chasm between my parents and the parents of my American peers. Inna seemed to feel it too, and in her understanding, I found comfort. The best part of our budding friendship was that my father allowed me to go out with her.

We were allowed to venture to Harvard Square and even into Boston on our own, our movements unshackled, a rare indulgence. In retrospect, I wonder why we were
granted so much trust and freedom. Did my father trust me with her because he trusted her parents? Did he see in her the image of a good, hardworking girl—like all daughters of prominent Georgian families? She was that girl, but she also carried secrets, rebellion stitched into the seams of her life. She had it rough with her parents, though you wouldn't know it by the calm authority of her demeanor. This unspoken understanding made our bond even tighter.

She taught me ways to slip past the heavy bars of our parents' rules, to breathe in the quiet rebellion that lingered just out of their reach.

It was a beautiful summer day in Boston—not too hot, but warm enough to feel the sun's weight on our skin. The air was clear, the kind of sharp clarity that slices through the hazy edges of memory. Inna and I were allowed to explore the city alone, and this time, we went to Filene's Basement. Unlike me, Inna had spending money and could shop on her own. My family didn't shop at Filene's Basement; my mother loved Express.

Shopping with my mother always left a bitter taste, I always agreed with what my
mother recommended I wear, suggesting each outfit. I never felt as though I was picking the clothes myself, rather I was playing dress up for my mother.

I have this clear memory of once, during a migraine—one of the bad ones—I
hallucinated that she was dragging me around Express, forcing me to try on clothes, one outfit after the next in the dressing room. I remember crying, pleading with her to let me go home, but she only pulled me from rack to rack, her hands firm tugging me from one place to another. I remember vividly screaming out, "Please don't make me do this," in the hallucination. I could feel the carpeted dressing room floor under my knees, feel the sharp tug of her hands on my arms, pulling on my hair. I couldn't understand why I was on the floor being pulled around by my hair.

But when I came to, I wasn't at Express. I was at home, where I had been prior to the
hallucination, screaming, my mother kneeling beside me, her face tight with panic,
gripping my arms down, restraining me.

That's why Filene's Basement with Inna felt special, like a breakthrough through my
hallucination, through my nightmare of Express. Filene's Basement represented a space, untouched by the weight of obligation or parental control. But I still couldn't buy anything, and that left me restless, as I craved to shape a different identity for myself, to escape the horror of Express, even though I liked the brand and preppy fashion.

The next time we went, I told Inna how much I hated going shopping and even though I liked Filene's Basement, it wasn't fun for me because I couldn't afford anything. Her response was a revelation, a simple solution to a problem.

"Why don't you just take it?" she said, her voice calm, deliberate.
"Take it?" I asked, unsure I'd heard her correctly.
"Without paying," she said, as if it were the most natural thing in the world. She pulled a shirt off the rack and held it up like a trophy. "See? There's nothing attached to it—no sensors, no alarms. You just have to make sure the cameras don't see you." She looked up at the round eye of the camera above us, then back at me with a conspiratorial smile. "I'll buy something first. They'll give me a bag. Then you can put what you want inside it."

And just like that, I stepped across a line I didn't even know existed.

I picked a few shirts I liked and met her in the dressing room. There, we folded the stolen clothes into the shopping bag, mixing them with the items she had purchased and others

she had taken. My heart pounded as we walked toward the exit. My mind raced: They know. They've seen us. We're going to get caught.

But nothing happened.

The air outside was bright and clean, and I could finally breathe. My body hummed with adrenaline, the rush of it almost euphoric. After that, we returned to Filene's Basement again and again, growing bolder each time.

When we weren't stealing clothes, we searched for boys. At first, we stayed near Harvard Square, but the guys by the Pit were too punk, too metal, too far from what we were
looking for. So we moved on to Faneuil Hall, where teenagers roamed in clusters. Most of them were older—16, maybe 17. Inna was 14, and I wasn't even 12 yet, though I would be that summer.

"Don't ever tell them your real age," Inna said one afternoon as we skipped from one cobblestone to the next.
"Why not?" I asked.
"Because they won't like you if they know you're 12. If a boy is

16, you have to say you're 15. You look 15 anyway."

It wasn't a question; it was a command. And I obeyed. That summer, I wasn't 12
anymore. I was 15, a girl who stole clothes from Filene's Basement and skipped
cobblestones in search of boys, her lies carried lightly, like the wind through the narrow streets of Boston.

Chapter 12
I met the ONE- His name is Bryan, with a y!

The beginning of summer was filled with wonder, joy and breaking boundaries, I was able to do things, and was doing them, I felt free. It was yet another beautiful Cape Cod day in Boston, and Inna and I decided to go to Faneuil Hall to search for boys, and watch the street performers. I found it almost comforting being outside, and getting lost in the crowd. Inna saw a small group of boys by the Samuel Adams statue, and said:
"Let's go meet them," and meet them we did. Our search for boys finally was over. We found ones that liked us. Or rather, we found a boy that Inna thought was cute and he liked her and they hit it off. The boy's friend was stuck with me. And, even though I didn't really think he was cute, I tried to flirt with him, yet the whole time I was
obsessing over the fact that his feet appeared to be inverted, forcing him to have a bear

like walk. I had never seen anyone walk like that before.
That troubled me, what if we were to date and people thought he walked weird? On the other hand he looked like Joshua Jackson, from the Mighty Ducks; tall, cute, brown hair (just like Joshua's), brown eyes, similar built, only real difference was how they walked. Joshua Jackson had a confident walk and he was amazing on ice, from what I have seen of him in the movies.
But not like I had a chance with Joshua Jackson, but I did have a chance with this kid, by the name of Bryan with a y.

From what I can remember, Bryan was very nice, and proper, he was 16 years old and came to Boston from Hanover, MA. I told him I was 15, and my birthday was in July. We exchanged numbers and within a week, Bryan would become my boyfriend.
We would meet in Faneuil Hall, Inna, the boy she was seeing, me and Bryan. Bryan and I would hold hands and walk around Quincy

Market. I loved listening to him talk. I tried to appear more mature than I was. I would think to myself 'I am falling in love', 'I love Bryan, I hope he loves me. Can he love me? Am I really pretty enough for him?'

Truth be said, I don't remember much of Bryan's personality or what we talked about for hours on end, holding hands. I just remember desperately wishing for him to love me, and when he said "I love you" to me in July, I was flying high, I believed I would marry him. I let him kiss me. We saw each other often, I was still allowed to go out with Inna and no one was the wiser about the fact that Inna and I had 16 year old boyfriends, and we were secretly meeting them in Boston.

When the boys couldn't come in the city, and when Inna and I felt like we needed to
update our wardrobe, we would venture out to Downtown Crossing and "go shopping" at Filene's Basement.

We were getting very bold, confident and cocky. One thing I will say, about my stint as a
shoplifter is that when you get bold and cocky, and feel invincible, quit doing it or you will get caught. And caught we were. I would have been surprised if we hadn't been caught.

On this particular day, we were out of money. But we did have the Filenes Basement plastic shopping bags and receipts saved. The plan was to go into the store with the bags hidden inside our purses, and then fill them with clothes and walk out. We had 4
plastic bags and couple of receipts. We couldn't get into the dressing room and by then we thought we were invincible and we filled our bags right there in the open, in brazen view of the cameras which were recently installed, but would hide away from the sales associates as we did so previously and it worked. But on this fateful day, the greed and hunger I felt for getting a new fall wardrobe overpowered any clear thinking.

Hands shaking, I remember stuffing the clothes in the plastic bags. I remember feeling that something is off, stop don't do it. But I did it anyway.

With a pounding heart and a bag full of clothes, I made my way towards the exit door. I was at the door, I was about to pull it open when I felt the tap on my shoulder, my heart inside my body split in two, half of my heart dropped to the pit of my stomach, the other part made its way into my throat suffocating me.

"Excuse me, miss, can you come join me and your friend right over here, please?"

I turned, I saw a dark, security uniform, was that a gun?
I couldn't breathe. I don't know how my body turned to face him. I don't know how I made it into the little secret security room, clutching my bag of shitloads of stolen clothes. This was it.
This is the day I thought I died.. Goodbye world, it was good knowing you, I thought to myself.
Our four plastic bags, were filled with clothes worth over $500 combined. We had
officially committed a crime.
We could be sent to juvie, and then deported.
Parents were called.
We were handcuffed and brought to meet our parents at the police station.
They let us go, with a scheduled court date into the custody of our parents. I wished they had placed me in a solitary cell. I would have felt safer than in the custody of my parents.
My heart to this day pounds, as I think of my father, the terror I felt, hearing his vital threats of sending me back to Armenia. I wished I was dead. It would have been better if my heart had in fact imploded in my chest, immediately killing me, when the security guard gently touched my shoulder. Freedom, as I knew it was over. I would have been better off in juvie, there would have been more freedom of friendship allowed.

At home when the yelling calmed down, silence was bestowed upon everyone. I walked around feeling guilty, horrible and wretched for what I had done. I sought counsel, and friendship in Bryan, in our phone conversations. I told him I was grounded for the rest of the summer for something horrible that I didn't even do. I was able to blame it away all on Inna. After all, I didn't want him to think that I was a shoplifter. Plus he would never see her again.
Our families put a quick and abrupt end to our friendship. I wasn't allowed to go out or meet any other friends. Inna blamed it all on me to her parents, who in turn told my
parents that it was all my fault. I didn't argue it. There was no point. I was guilty too. But, I did feel some sort of relief being able to blame Inna for it all to someone who didn't know anything. I could lie smoothly, maybe it wasn't even lying, just telling a half truth.
I would soon need to be honest or half honest about my age. He thinks I am in high school and I hadn't even officially entered middle school.
Luckily end of summer was near, and all my hope for any type of

redemption lay in me entering Dana Hall.

Chapter 13
Welcome To Wellesley, Mass. EST. 1881

The Dana Hall campus is spread out in the vast suburban town that has an uncanny ability to transport you through time into history, through architecture and nature. The town itself was established during the Gilded age of 1881. The all girls school was established as a prep school for Wellesley College. From the stables, to the dorms, and around the pond, walking around the campus, especially in the fall, had a magical appeal to it. It was as though I would travel into a completely different world every morning and at the end of the day, return to the dark poverty of Central Square.
It wasn't all so simple for me to fit in amongst the wealthy elite of Boston. At the time my family didn't have a car and lived in a small two bedroom apartment in Cambridge . My route to get to school consisted of waking up at 5 o'clock in the morning, with a short walk from the apartment to the train station, with empty streets and the only people out would be the cast outs of society. My mom wouldn't allow for me to walk on my own to the train station. The early morning street around the T was filled with men and women sitting on the sidewalk, sharing a crack pipe or a needle. The entry way to the train station reeked of urine and alcohol from the night before.
So my mom, the hero, protector, would bundle up my brother and sister, put them in the double stroller and walk ten minutes with me to the red line, where the train would take me to south station. Although I would quite often wonder on these morning chilled walks:

What could my mom do to protect me if I were attacked in the center? By her going along isn't she putting herself and my brother and sister at risk? What is the worst a homeless person could do to me? Not like I had money, or whatever it was they were ingesting through needles and pipes.

At south station I would quickly learn how to maneuver around the hustle and bustle of
the morning and people arriving from the suburbs on the purple line. I was to take the purple line to Wellesley where another 10-15 minute walk awaited me until I finally would arrive on campus to start school. My day would conclude around 5pm, where I would

again board the purple line which would bring me back to south station, and the red line that would bring me back to central sq. I would arrive home around 7pm, with loads of homework and an LLBean backpack filled with books, binders, pens and pencils. My middle school schedule consisted of classes beginning at 8 AM and lasting till 230 PM, required classes included a language and Latin. Although I loved learning languages, I struggled with it. I found solace in my creative writing classes and English classes, hiding behind books and writing was my only escape from the inner hate and torment I

was experiencing.
Usually for an hour, I had a break between 230 and 315, during which time I would need to be ready for sport practice. For sports I played JV basketball and JV/V Lacrosse.
Lacrosse I loved, something about cradling a stick with a ball inside it and then trying to throw it into the net when a gaggle of girls is running after to you to steal the ball was thrilling for me. I wasn't a fan of basketball but I felt limited during off season of lacrosse in sports. So instead I took ballet classes. By the time I would make it home, I was spent after having a full day of classes and sports, but I still had hours and hours of homework, which I would be not be able to start until 8 or 9 pm. Never mind hours spent on thinking nothing I did was good enough and the best I could do was average, everytime I received a C I wanted to die. Yet, I kept right on receiving Cs.

Competition and jealousy of other girls was continuously palatable. Although I had friends I wanted to be at the top. I wanted to be like Emily W. or Alex B. who got the star roles in the Sound of Music Musical in which I was cast as a mere Baroness and a nun. I loved acting but my stage fright limited my true potential and it was something I could not work past. I was already continuously performing, wearing different masks to fit in, to do good, to excel, to cover up my truth, to forever hide my immigrant mark, and ultimately my true inner self. I was continuously acting. I feared the stage. I feared that everyone would see right through me and see me as a fraud, someone who didn't belong. Yet ironically, secretly I dreamt of the spotlight. I dreamt of one day winning an Oscar. The visual image of me receiving an Oscar; I could hear the Oscar speech I would say in my head. These dreams gave me drive, hope and courage.
7th grade, academically for me, ultimately proved to be the most

challenging. It was filled with extreme ups and downs. Almost as though, one term my mind worked its ass off and then it would just shut off for a little. Then it would spark back up again. I didn't have the support at home, nor did I know what support I needed. I lacked balance between two extremes.

I was unlike all the students at Dana, I was poor (although, I must admit here we were not poor by poverty line standards, we were lower middle class, but I felt poor, and ashamed around my peers in private school), an immigrant, a scholarship kid, which made me feel ashamed. I didn't want anyone to know the truth, and I rarely invited anyone over to our small apartment. I couldn't hide the fact that my family was lower middle class, but I could hide the fact that I was an immigrant. I hid the fact of being an immigrant so well at school, that I failed the immigration project. I never told my teachers that I was an

immigrant or that English was in fact my second language. I struggled mainly in English, Latin, and French classes. The grammar and conjugation of verbs always tripped me up.

But, I never told anyone that English was not my first language. That I, in fact needed help in understanding the concepts more.

There were times in school when partes of me wanted to scream out:
" Hey, I am the immigrant project. You just don't know it. Help me!" but I never
screamed out. I was turning into the Little Mermaid who had lost her voice.

I didn't receive my father's approval when I got accepted to Dana Hall and after a year at Dana, I still didn't receive my father's positive affection, rather I began to receive his negative attention full force for getting Cs. I was bringing home progress reports with comments such as: 'Diana has a hard time following instructions', this seemed to be the most frequent and prominent one. Yet through the educational struggle that made me feel like a failure, a fraud, I managed to make friends, which for me was a huge milestone. My father on the other hand made me feel like he didn't want me to have any friends. Now, I understand why, there were a lot of cultural differences in how my father wanted to raise me and all his kids and how I craved to be raised.

I rarely was allowed to go to a sleep over or have friends over, (I really didn't mind the fact in the early years of not having anyone over, it helped me maintain whatever façade of acceptance I was attempting to create), my father valued discipline and education above all else, socializing and play he found little value in.

For those instances that I was granted permission to socialize, I would need to stand ,what for me felt like over him if he were resting on the couch or shrink myself as small as I could, if he were sitting in his office by his computer, working, trembling with fear, unable to get the words out of my mouth, unable to meet his eyes, yet somehow had to ask him for permission to go to a friends house, which would turn into a presentation of sorts, he expected to know details, of why I wanted to go. What were we going to do there? The what are you going to do there question always stumped me and all I could ever retort was a mumbled "I don't know" shrugging my shoulders, looking down on the floor and shifting my weight from one foot to the next drifting way away into my secret safety spot I had built within my mind.
His "no's" were heart wrenching and frequent, my father always accused me of lying even when I wasn't. Today, I still wonder if he mistook my fear as manipulation.

Chapter 14
Dana Friendships

I sought solace in a small group of friends, whom I bonded with over school work, family troubles and numerous amounts of time spent journaling. The main struggle in middle school that I faced was maintaining my grades. Getting straight A's was no longer easy and homework would take up a huge chunk of my night, resulting in me going to sleep well past midnight to wake up at 5 am and do it all over again. At times I could feel my mind's exhaustion, but there was no time to be tired if I wanted to be worthy or loved.

Looking back, the first year at Dana Hall was a year when I learned how to make a long lasting friendship. Although I can't say I was a popular girl and had dreams of fitting in with the popular girls, the pretty girls, I felt comfortable in my friendships. I had one best friend, her name was Margie. We got each other, its almost as though, even at that young age our minds were somehow connected and linked. We felt and experienced life, it seemed through the same lens. She taught me the true value of friendship, understanding, and hope. I had never had a friend like Margie before, she embraced me as a whole.

Aside from academics there were boys. Since we didn't see boys in our every day lives at school, we would partner with other private, all boys schools for the middle school
dances. My boyfriend Bryan, was in high school and he thought I was in high school too and I never saw him. I wanted to connect with other boys, maybe have another crush. I didn't feel confident that I would actually ever see Bryan again.

It was one of those beginning of the year dances that Dana was sponsoring on a Friday night. I wouldn't even need to leave school to attend the dance. My friend's parents had already agreed on a sleep over at her house. I figured if I didn't show up at home, I could avoid asking my father for permission to attend the dance, avoid his questions of what it is that I plan to do at the dance and why do I think its important I attend. I found those questions to be humiliating. I would always wonder if he was just trying to shame me or was he, in reality just wondering what happened at dances. What I do know is that he never liked the answers I provided and most usually I wasn't allowed to attend the dance. The only way to get around that would be by asking for a sleep over at a friend's house, who's parents were trustworthy and then I could go to the dance from there. But
this Friday in particular, I had hopes of avoiding all that. I waited till the end of the day, and till the train I was meant to take back home had left. I called my mother from the cafeteria pay phone to let her know of my plans. She told me to call my father and ask his permission.
My mind screamed a huge FUUUUCKKKK as I said ok, and hung up the phone. For the

second call I mustered up all the courage I could. After all I was going to be talking to him over the phone and not in person, how scary can it be? I asked myself. Of course he won't say no, maybe I wouldn't even need to say anything about the dance, blame it all on missing the train, and I could bring up the dance if necessary, casually, I rationed in my mind.
I picked up the pay phone once again, with my two best friends on

each side of me
cheering me on. I called my father. I have no idea what I said over the phone to him. What I do remember is him saying "No, you need to take the next train home." I can still feel how my heart sank to the bottom of my stomach in that instant, and how my fingers trembeled as I hung up the phone. I told my friends that he said no. Their faces too dropped. In that instant, I decided, " Fuck him", I am staying. There is nothing he can do about it. There it was, my first rebellious act against my father and my first adrenaline high on the rebellion of knowingly disobeying.

The Dana dining hall was a two story building, the first floor was a lounge with couches, tables and the infamous payphone I used to call my father. The second floor was the
dining hall itself.

As the evening approached we all got ready in the first floor bathroom and made our way
upstairs to where all the dining hall tables and chairs were cleared off and a DJ area set up. There were streamers sporadically thrown around. We, and the chaperones were the first ones there as the music was just beginning to play. I was letting my guard down. I was letting go of my fear of my father randomly appearing and dragging me out of there when, something told me to look in the corner of the dance hall where the doors were opening, and there she was in that coner. My mother, clenching the hands of my one and half year old brother and sister, my first thought "No fucking way this can be happening." My second thought was, "I have lost my mind and I am hallucinating." I was snapped back to reality with Irine tugging on my sleeve and whispering into my ear, "Hey, isn't that your mother?"

Yes, in fact it was my mother with the twins. I wanted to die. My third thought while I was making my way to her was "how in the fuckity fuck did she get here. She doesn't even have a car!" And then I realized she got there the same way I get there every single day, the trains, and now I would need to take the train back with her. She was angry, and the rest I have blocked out.

I erased all memory of it but whatever screaming match I had with my father once we got home was going to be the first of many.

Chapter 15
Loving and Hating School

       I loved learning, I hated how I was being taught and this, I can only say now, in
hindsight. My main struggle academically was following instructions. I thought in poetry and pictures. If my Latin teacher at the moment was teaching how to conjugate words and a word, tree, just happened to pop up, my mind would pull out random pictures of trees, small trees, big trees, white trees, old trees covered in green leaves, white trees covered with red leaves, silver trees, snow covered trees, Christmas trees, all the trees I have seen through childhood, the tree I see when I look out the window and am pulled back to Latin class, where I would have missed half the instructions that followed after the word "tree". I hated learning languages, in particular the grammar, which involved following instructions.
By the age of nine I was fluent in Russian and Armenian. By the age of 12, I was fluent in
Russian and English, having barely any recollection of Armenian. In school I was learning English, Latin, and French. I hated learning French the most. It was hard and frustrating. In English class, I thrived in creative writing. All I needed to do was visualize the story in my mind and then explain the imagery I was seeing. This I did continuously in my mind already. I had the ability to play with words as a painter plays with the array of colors on a color palette. But I had difficulty explaining or defining words, or explaining why there should be a period instead of a comma at the end of the sentence or why some sentences required the use of semicolons.
I hated math, yet I was good at it. I excelled in geometry and algebra could be fun. I hated it because it required my focus and brought me away from my imaginary realm I loved to reside in. Books, were my safe haven, my escape from reality. Stories ruled my life, and math brought me back into the reality that was my life, filled with empty shapes and numbers.
I despised quizzes, tests and exams, all the multiple choice options. I always second guessed myself, never listening or trusting myself to know the answers, later to learn that my initial answers were right all along.

My father traveled a lot and for long periods of time for work. The

best way I could
explain his job at the time to my friends, was that he was a negotiator. Albeit, he was not a negotiator for the Boston Police Department or the FBI, nor was a he a diplomat, but he solved conflicts in 3rd world countries, he was the chief negotiator during the Chechen war. Although, after the mention of Chechen War, I would notice I stirred up more

confusion than providing a decent explanation of what my father did for a living. I would wonder often as to why my father didn't have a normal job, like all normal
middle-upper class Americans, and mainly my friend's parents. On the
other hand the time he was away would bestow a type of serene rhythm in the
household. My bond with my mother would evolve past friendship into a type of
partnership, in which we worked together around the house, and raised the kids. She told me what to do, and I did without question. I aimed to please. Especially after everyone found out I was a fraud, a liar and a thief. I would wonder if that was the reason my father hated me so. I brought shame into our family. I could have been deported and all for what? A sparkly sweater from Filenes Basement? Luckily I
wasn't deported, but I had to be good from now on. I understood my father's anger towards me when he was home. I deserved it. But I did feel like I was walking on
eggshells around him. I was terrified of upsetting him. I was terrified of him. When he would leave, that terror and guilt would too. I would allow myself to roam freely around our little apartment, no longer feeling the need to hide in my bedroom.
My mother and I just didn't discuss my shame, she wasn't angry with me and she didn't seem to hate me. She needed me and she allowed me to be me and that was freeing.
The best part of course, aside from feeling free, when my father was away, was the fact that I could use his computer any time as we only had one computer in a makeshift
office behind the living room couch, across from the little TV box, by the window. I was allowed to use my father's computer for school work, learning how to type, playing memory music games, writing and playing chess. That is until of course I discovered AOL or rather AOL discovered me as it swept into the 90s, completely transforming how we communicated and connected with one another.

I could message with Bryan and my friends while typing an essay on the computer,
although tying up the landline, but we didn't need it because my dad was away and my mom always busy with the kids.

I had a private chatroom for my Dana friends, there was 4 of us total in the chatroom. But when no one was available to chat and I would feel lonely, or curious I would enter different chatrooms. There were many, oh so many, and you could talk to anyone about anything. Entering a chatroom was like entering the world of the unknown. Anyone could be behind that computer screen, but I took everyone at their word. It didn't enter my mind back than that someone on the internet could be lying about their age, their life, their well, everything. I had a few cyber friends, but one stuck out the most. I met him in a chat room, and I could tell he was a hurting soul. I could connect with him through the screen. He said he was 17, and lived in Cambridge, MA and
went to Cambridge Latin High School, he was someone who didn't know me and

someone I could be honest with. I would message constantly, I felt like I could be myself. I was beginning to like him and I was beginning to like him even more than Bryan, who by this point, never called and was always away on AOL. I knew he was going to break up with me, he was in high school surrounded by high school girls and he lived all the away in Hanover.
But this boy, this AOL boy, had potential. I was beginning to crush on him. I played around with our names together and imagined what he looked like, he definitely had to be cute, and how great it would be to date someone who also lived in Cambridge and wasn't a part of the private school circle.
By thanksgiving of 1997, Bryan had broken up with me. It was over. I hurt all over. I thought someone had stuck a knife in my throat. I wasn't exactly sure what the break up meant but he said we could be friends. Weren't we always friends to begin with? As my mind pondered and tried to self soathe, my body screamed out in fear of being left
behind, rejected, and unwanted.

Jake wanted to meet. I so looked forward to our chats. I hadn't told anyone about a   random boy I met online who happens to live in Cambridge and who I can see anytime I wanted. I didn't trust to tell my friends. I was sure they would talk me out of even just talking to him. I knew I was playing with fire. But I figured "what is the worst thing that can happen if we met in a public place like Newbury Comics at Harvard, Sq.?".

If he happened to be an old man, I would just scream and run away. These thoughts pulsed through my mind as I agreed to meet him.

Prior to meeting we told each other what the other would be wearing. He said he will be wearing a black Black Sabbath tee shirt and black coat. I told him that I had brown hair, hazel eyes, and I would be wearing black tights with a denim overall dress. I even wore my first heels. They were black mary-janes, with a black strap, and one inch chunk heel bought for me by my mother from PayLess. I really wanted stiletto heels, but my mother told me I was too young. So in the end we settled on the one inch chunk heel.

I wanted to look mature, I might have told him I was 14 rather than telling him my real age, but I did tell him I was in 8th grade. He said my age didn't matter, I was on old soul and I was almost in high school anyway. I didn't bother to tell him I had also skipped a grade, and really was the youngest in my class, I had just turned 12, I hadn't even hit

puberty. I think he said he was a sophomore in high school but I also think he said he was 17. I didn't know much about Newbury Comics or Black Sabbath, I was into Spice Girls, 'NSync and the Backstreet boys. I knew Newbury comics sold CDs and I really wanted the Toni Braxton CD. "Unbreak my heart" was speaking to me deeply and I really wanted the whole album to play on repeat. I didn't own any CDs and that would be a treat for myself, I thought, and if it doesn't work out with this boy at least I would have ventured out of the house and bought a CD. I really hoped he looked like a cross between Justin

Timberlake and Joshua Jackson, dressed in black, with a troubled, mysterious soul of Edgar Allen Poe, who was going to sweep me off my feet, rescue me from my father and help me escape my own loneliness. As I left the house my thoughts continued onto Bryan and how I wished I looked exactly like Posh Spice. I bemused to myself that I would resemble her the most if my dark hair was cut into a bob hair cut. The problem was that my hair formed a weird triangle on each side of my head and my hair had no chance to resemble her straight sleek bob. The other problem was that my nose was way too big for my face. If only I was born with a small nose and silky

smooth hair. I could be pretty like Victoria Beckham.

By the time my foot had touched the entry way of Newbury Comics I had it resolved in my mind that I would go straight in search of the Toni Braxton CD. I told myself to walk with confidence and float with grace, like a ballerina. I also hoped to see if I could spot my stranger. I really hoped he would look like I imagined. A part of me told me he wouldn't. I didn't listen to that part.

I looked around the store, there were some people browsing through vinyl records, but no one young enough to be meeting me. In the back corner I saw a group of punk looking guys, one had a green Mohawk, black pants, black tee-shirt, he wasn't what I had pictured. I prayed to God it wasn't him. I didn't want to trust that voice that kept,

whispering in the back of my mind, its him.

When he turned around, my heart dropped, when he made his way towards me, my heart was in my stomach. This wasn't who I had envisioned at all. He was pudgy, he wasn't ugly, but he wasn't attractive, he looked older. I wondered if he was a metal head.

He smiled towards me, waving hi, there was no turning back. He didn't appear to be an old guy and I was frozen stuck.

A voice in the back of my head kept saying leave, but I stayed. I said "hi", we chatted. He said he came with friends but would love to just hang out with me. He bought me the Toni Braxton CD and took me to lunch. He was very nice but definitely no, not my type. I resolved in my mind he can't harm me in public, and just because he wasn't cute didn't mean we couldn't be friends. He kept trying to put his hand around me, or on my leg during lunch but I told him, I only wanted to be friends. I wasn't interested in anything more. He tried to kiss me, but I moved my head so he missed.

When the lunch was over he offered to walk me home. I told him I could

manage, I lived so close.

I left resolving in my mind, that I will never see him again, but maybe we could be AOL friends. I wondered if he really was 17, he looked older. But who was I to judge, I lied about my age as well.

Chapter 16
Titanic Hits an Iceberg

In December, and right before the release of Titanic, Bryan called me to tell me to never call him again. I will admit, I was calling him every other day, without receiving a call back. So, I increased my calls to daily, thinking he wasn't getting my messages. His mother always answered the landline and was always nice, and he was never home.

I thought we were friends. He told me he had a girlfriend and it was getting serious, and he didn't want to upset her by talking to me. And after all, what did we really have to talk about when lived in different towns and went to completely different high schools, he hadn't seen me since the summer. "This was the best." He said. I sobbed a big sob as I hung up the phone. Went in my room and blasted "Unbreak My Heart". I listened to it on repeat for a good hour. My heart was shattered and Bryan wasn't coming back to put the broken pieces together.

When the dreadful feeling of loss, began to subside I thought of Jake.

I was already on school break and could enjoy the freedom of morning and day, up until about 530pm until when my father came home from work. By 5pm I would have the computer shut off, would be logged out from all my AOL accounts, computer turned off and I would be hidden in my room. I messaged Jake, my story of woe and heartbreak. He immediately responded. He made me feel better and he asked me to a movie.

"Lets go see the Titanic movie that just came out. My treat, we can meet at Harvard Sq."

I agreed and told him I had to be home by 4pm. There was no harm in going to see the movie plus maybe just maybe I would stop hurting on the inside. Maybe my brain for the duration of the movie will forget all about Bryan, and that I could never talk to him again because he had a girlfriend and he couldn't be friends with me. In retrospect, I am not sure if it was him I was missing per se, but it was yet another loss of a friend, someone whom, I trusted, someone who I cared about. I felt completely alone, when I agreed to go to the movies with Jake.

I hoped by the time I came home from the movie, I would feel joy again. It was hard not to cry as I got ready. I missed my babushka. I wondered if she was watching over me from up above.

It was a noon showing, and I calculated if the movie was 3 hours long, I had at least an extra hour to make it home by four, and since I really needed to be home by 5pm I felt like I was safe from being caught. I told my mother I was meeting Margie at Harvard Sq, to

see the Titanic movie.
My mom gave me money and told me to enjoy myself. I met Jake inside the movie
 theater, he had already purchased the tickets. He looked different

from the last time I saw him. His hair was pressed down flat, in a weird cut, but still green. I wondered why he liked having green hair, but dared not ask him that in case that would hurt his feelings.

He reached for my hand as we walked into the show room, I let him.
I held his hand and missed Bryan even more. Something within me found Jake to be
repulsive. I tried to silence that, and told myself that I was being shallow. There was more to liking someone than just their looks.
He tried to feel for my boob during the love making scene. I pushed his hand away and said I wasn't ready. In reality, I had no boobs to feel. I hadn't even fully began to develop. I had stuffed my bra a little with toilet paper. I knew Jake was trying to be a gentleman, but all I could think when I would look over at him is that he reminded me of the Joker. Between missing Bryan and trying to convince myself to like Jake, I wasn't really paying attention to the movie. I was more consumed by my real life movie I seemed to be in.
The movie ended, and he said I seemed distant. I said I felt sad and needed to get home. He told me I should come home to his house, he had whiskey, and a drink would make me feel better. I told him I never had whiskey. He said it was a magic cure for heartache. I believed him. I followed him to the train station, and got on the Train with him. We took the red line to Porter Sq. I remember a lot of stairs. I think he kept holding my hand.
His home was big, it smelled of leather and money. I was instantly drawn to the piano. I missed having a piano. I hated playing on the keyboard, I couldn't play Fur Elise with feeling on the keyboard. I went straight towards the piano, as though it was calling my name. I tickled the ivories, as I sat down on the piano bench.
He had poured the whiskey into a crystal whiskey glass and held it out to me. The crystal felt heavy in my hand. I didn't particularly like the smell. He encouraged me to take a sip. I did it burned. I gagged. He gave me water.
He said to try again. I did. It didn't burn as much.
I felt a warm fuzzy feeling. I began to play Fur Elise.
By the time I was done playing he was next to me on the piano bench,

kissing me, trying to undress me.

"Had I really finished the entire whiskey glass?" I wondered, floating away into an abyss.
I remembered, he had the glass filled almost to the rim.

I couldn't feel my body. I felt myself slurring my no's. No, I didn't want him to undress me. He said it seemed like I needed to take a nap and would be more comfortable in a tee shirt. I said "I didn't" and I had to go home. Or at least I think I said it, it might have came out completely differently. He carried me into another room. There was a mattress on the floor he placed me on the mattress.

I wished I had a blanket. I was cold. Alanis Morsette was singing in the background.
I couldn't understand why. I didn't like her.
Everything went black.
I felt someone trying to pry my mouth open with their hands. I felt cold. I felt naked.
I couldn't move. I smelled a rubbery smell, and sweat.
Something was being shoved in my mouth. I tried opening my eyes. I wanted to see. But I couldn't open them fully. I felt myself squint. I felt pain.
I felt blood between my legs. I think there was a camera pointing at me. Jake was naked. It wasn't Jake shoving something rubbery and smelly in my mouth it was someone else.

Why where they doing this to me? This is just a nightmare. I kept telling myself over and over again. This will end.
I will wake up.
I will be home in bed.
I will be safe.
I am safe.
Everything goes dark; black and blank, after that.

Next time I try to open my eyes I am in a car. Someone had half dressed me and put me in the car. Was it a woman driving? When did a woman appear?
The car stopped and the door opened. Did she drive me home? How did she know where I lived? I saw my mom. My mom was dragging me into the apartment. I have no idea how my mother managed to get me out of the car and into the bathtub. I wasn't able to walk. I didn't have control of my body. It was limp. It wasn't

even my body it was
someone else's. I felt the ice cold water, pouring on me. I could finally open my eyes, but not for long. I woke up in my bed, in my room in clean pajamas. I jolted awake. I thought I had just woken up from a nightmare. My head was pounding. I felt a migraine coming on. I wondered if I was hallucinating.

I hid under my covers. What if it wasn't a nightmare?
What if, I am waking up into a reality nightmare?
No way that happened to me. It was just a nightmare.
I tried to hold on to the thought that it wasn't real. It didn't happen. I just had a horrible
nightmare. I stayed in bed. I couldn't face my mother. I was too scared. If she was upset with me than this was real, if she was her normal self than this was a nightmare, and life is good. I finally did see my mother. She was mad. She was giving me a silent treatment.
She later came to my room and asked me "what it is I thought I was doing." I had no answer.

She continued, "Your lucky your father had a dinner meeting and didn't come home till seven thirty. What were you thinking! getting drunk? Tu shto DURA??"
I had no answers, I mumbled sorry, I might have tried to say I would never do anything like that again. Yes, I was stupid. My body hurt. I couldn't walk. I remember crawling.
I awoke.
I wondered if I was beaten.
I went back to sleep.

My dreams were shattered overnight,
Within few hours given that
My innocence was stolen, in the darkest depth
Where monster hide throughout the day
Piece by piece I broke apart,
My soul caged in;
In outer realm, stuck on the border
Of outer banks
My voice frozen from within
The pain, the shame, the guilt
And the disgust, I felt
I inverted upon the self,
Leading up to my demise,
Where I lurked, the soul of truth
In shadows gloom, always pondering…
What if? I could have been…

Fault

*Yes, it happened to me.
I don't say it often,
For it was my fault,
I know that, as sure as day.
I should have known better
Than to trust a stranger, lurking in the 90s, Messenger maze.
Yet, I did.
On that fateful day,
I told no one
Where I went.
"Just to the movies," I said,
"With friends." My voice echoed, hollow,
As the door closed,
Behind me,
The room's shadow
Swallowed silence whole.
Off to the movies, I went.
But he was there.
I cringed at the thought of his hands upon my shoulders.
Still, It was the movie I wanted to see the most.
Titanic was showing,
After all.
Yes, the fault is mine,
And mine alone.
I didn't run— I followed. I followed him,
All the way home.
To this day, I wonder why.
No reason makes sense.
I followed him,
Dreaming of escape,
Back to my own safety.
I should have run.
But I didn't.
Instead, I boarded the train with him,
Rode past where
I needed to be.
I stayed still,
Silent as night.
Yes, The fault is mine to bear.
In that apartment,*

In the sky,

By the grand piano— Seduction was the game.
He gave me a drink I shouldn't have had.
But I drank it anyway.
I knew the toxins,
Felt disgust brew
Burning deep inside my throat.
Still, I drank.
The fault is mine.
I drank the poison,
And I alone.
Yet, in this flaw,
My fault,
My demise,
I wonder… What of him?
Where was his shame,
His guilt?
Who was he,
To hurt me so?
To lace my drink,
Steal my voice,
Throw me on the mattress,
Bare, clothe torn off.
To use me,
Abuse me,
Invite his friend,
Upon the matted floor
To pry my mouth open,
To tear me apart.
He knew all along I was a child— A mere 12, Naïve, Scared,
Alone,
Abandoned By a life that
Had given way.
Yes, I should have known better
Than to trust a stranger Lurking in the 90s' haze.

But what of him? Where is his guilt,
His shame?
His punishment?
His own demise?
For my demise
Is mine to bear.
For years to come,
Always there.

Diana Kouprina © 2024

But, it's over now, I hope.
I let it go, I broke the cycle of repetition.
I rinsed the dread out of my hair,
I felt the truth, the fault, the flaw, the failure
It wasn't me it was someone else I had tried so hard to be.
I let it go, I know my fault,
I was naïve, a frightened child with no love to feel.
I trusted easily, always believing everyone else was better off than me.
As the years would passed, rolling into one season after another,
I remained caged in, to escape the prison, I was forced to see,
My choices made of terror, had tarnished me complete.
To revert back to me, to wash the tar out off my body,
I had to see, my mistakes were mine to own,
Mine to learn from and to let go,
Only then did the windows of my prison began to open letting in an airy breeze
Within this healing road I've chosen, of loving me complete.

Andante (slow, reflective)
Remember me, this child who danced upon the wind,
Spinning, twirling, always reaching out for more.
Remember me, the one who floated upon the clouds, galloping on horses in mid day sky.
Within a breath, my voice turned into song taking on its boisterous flight.
But trauma is a thief— It has stolen me, the girl who knew no limits, whose music was an endless

remedy ballet.

Of song, of movement, of poetic infusion.
I am lost now, hidden in the fog of years,

Along with pianos that once sang under my hands—now sold, destroyed, forever lost in a world

that no longer is— their music forgotten, collecting dust.
How could I lose me, when I was me?
To see me there but not to feel me or to be me.
Remember me, the one who flew,
Who danced in the sparkle of the snow
As moonlight traced my every step.
Remember me, the dream that never slept,

My hands that reached the stars, unafraid, unbroken, living life.

Remember me, the tune I spun,
Skipping through the heart of time.
Remember me, the echo in my run,
My laughter, once bright, now a soft sigh.
My voice of song, no longer there.
I have lost me.
The girl whose fingers danced along the keys,
The girl whose heart beat with the rhythm of Für Elise—
I am a shadow, slipping through my grasp.
I do not remember how to play,
And my song, once so clear,
has faded far away.

Andante returns (slow, reflective)
But even now, in the stillness, I call upon the self.
My voice, soft as the night, reaches across time,
My angel's chorus whispers, "Remember me. Remember the beauty, the release.
Remember me, the fleeting face that once was yours."
I stand between what was and what is,
Torn by the weight of memory and the calling of tomorrow,
Listening to someone else play Fur Elise,
Headphones on, I can feel the keys,
I wonder now.... if I shall ever play again.

Diana Kouprina ©

Book II

I look around,
All I see are strange, peculiar faces.
I am told –
I am one of them.
But I know,
I am lost within them,
For I know not who I am.

Diana Kouprina ©
1998

Chapter 1
Splintered Soul

Nothing felt normal or appeared normal those days. I wasn't sure about what I felt. It felt like nothing. My mind split in two. One part was living inside the reality on auto pilot, like a robot, unfeeling, mechanical and mean to the self; the other part of me was floating somewhere above me. The auto-pilot part of me, moved my body, talked to
people, and did everything it was told. The other side was hurting and floating further and further away from me. It could not survive and live in the day to day reality. So, that other part began to create different worlds, where it could reside. I wasn't sure if I was inside my body. I didn't know which part of my brain was the real me, the one floating around different realms or the one that is making my body move?

Chapter 2
I am Nothing

The first time I had my period, I saw blood in my underwear and I told my mother. But no monumental memory of it is stored in my mind, she gave me pads, we didn't talk about what it meant, but I had known what it meant, from all the Judy Blume books I had devoured in the past couple years. All I can recall my mother saying is "Now you are a woman," as she handed me pads in the bathroom and showed me how to use them. I didn't truly grasp what it meant to be a woman. I wasn't even sure I wanted to be one; there was a part of me that wanted to remain a child forever. I didn't like the effects of puberty, the weight gain, my skin breaking out, hair growth in places like my upper lip, made me feel hideous. I despised those physical changes and I didn't know how to contain or control them. The best escape I always found was in sleep.
I liked to sleep. My dreams were my safe space, where the dream or a nightmare was even better than the reality I was living in. I could escape in my dreams, I could be back in the loving arms of my babushkas anytime I slept.

Being awake was the real nightmare.

The summer after graduating 8th grade is blurry in my mind's memory; the images almost morph together and it is hard to separate them. It is in moments like this I wish I had all my old journals that are now forever gone, destroyed.

I used to write prolifically, that was my only escape from my inner turmoil. I wrote poetry and prose, the poetry was my soul screaming out its truth, the prose was written in case

someone reads my journals as, my mother had done once, right after the incident.
That was a horrible night, the things she read in that journal must have turned her
stomach as my memories of the rape were fresh back then, a wound that wouldn't heal. She yelled at me, the only words that come to mind, still, to describe it all are that she freaked out. I got a whooping, that's all I remember.

That was also the time when someone started coming around my bedroom window. We lived in a two bedroom apartment on the first floor. I had a bedroom in the corner and I kept the window shade up for fresh air. Without a thought that someone walking by would have any interest in watching me; here, dear reader, I must admit; ***I was naïve to put it best.***
Yet, it didn't take me long to figure out I was being stalked, that someone was literally
watching me throughout the day in my bedroom and at night making a hole in the screen to slip rolled up five dollar bills through. I took the money, I kept it but I knew it was dirty and wrong. I felt dirty and wrong. But, I almost liked the dirty feeling, the wrong feeling, like I deserved it, I didn't bother to close the shade. *If my stalker wanted to kill me, well more power to him,* I would think to myself. Nothing transgressed past the slipping of the five dollar bills through the little hole that my stalker made in my window screen.
By fall I had forgotten all about it.

Chapter 3
Middle School Graduate

My next set of memories really begins with freshman year at Dana Hall, I have to this day no recollection of how I made it from failing my classes, losing myself, to graduating
middle school and to being allowed to advance to the Dana Upper School. All I knew at this point is that I had somehow made it through, and I thought the worst was behind me.

I survived the summer by sleeping a lot and blocking out all the bad feelings. Scrubbing out all memory of what had happened. But I couldn't, all I could do was build a wall around all the bad feelings.

Bryan might have visited me once or twice. My hair was finally growing back, after I
had it chopped off and looked like a boy all throughout the end of 8th grade. I never thought back to that day when I was drugged. All I knew then, was that I had to keep moving forward, I was a robot on autopilot. A part of me was ripped away from me, and I didn't even realize it.

Dana Upper School, unlike the middle school, was vast. The girls I knew from middle school all dispersed, some didn't return. I clung to my hope that Margie and I would be united and battle high school together. But that wasn't meant to be, as I was trying to survive so was Margie, during that fateful summer between eighth and ninth grade, we both lost so much of ourselves, so much of who we were before the trauma. It's funny now, thinking back to it, I can vividly see the break in my mind of what transpired.
Margie and I were always bound to the same path, but on our journeys we never crossed paths. She always will remain my soul sister, even when we don't speak over the phone, I find myself having conversations with her in my mind and for me that is enough. I know she is healing.
Margie left Dana, after a few short weeks of 9th grade, I felt alone and terrified.

Chapter 4
Upper School

In the midst of my loneliness, and loss of my best friend, I saw her in Latin class. She seemed so free, so full of life, so cool, and every time, day after day she would ask me my name, at the end of class claiming to have forgotten it. Until finally a few weeks later, as though she had a magnificent epiphany she exclaimed, Diana like Princess Di, ok I won't forget. And she didn't forget.

I found my new best friend, I wasn't alone, I had someone help me navigate through my eternal hell. What I didn't know at the time was that Stacy too was living in her own hell of her creation, and I was just a fly caught in her spiderweb. By November of 9th grade,

Stacy and I became roommates at Dana. This was my first time being a boarding student, and I loved the thought of living with my best friend over my parents any day. My father and I were barely speaking to one another, it felt as though he blamed me for everything, in his eyes I was already a failure, who couldn't maintain a 4.0 GPA. Now I think back and wonder what would have happened if I didn't board at Dana, or at least not with
Stacy. But then again I had to get away from home.

Simply put, dorm life was hell and not because it was the school's fault, quite the
contrary, I realize now it was all mine, I was trying to live when all I wanted to do was die. Luckily for me I found the perfect best friend, and roommate who excelled at
surviving without fear of dying. We had a blood sister bond; she taught me how to throw up my food, how to count my calories and starve, she taught me how to overdose on
aspirin, and she taught me how to cut my wrists.

Education was not at all a part of our survivor guide, but older boys were.

In the late 90s it was cool to have an older boyfriend, after all, age was nothing but a number, and from what I have seen of darkness, fourteen year old boys in my mind's view were dorks. Plus, I wasn't a virgin, it didn't matter to me who I did have sex with. Nothing mattered. I could barely maintain a 3.0 GPA, but I was cool after all.

It was winter when I began to spiral down completely. Somehow this is the memory that to this day sticks out vividly in my mind, I close my eyes and I am right there on that day watching it all unfold. I don't recall why I didn't want to go back to school, but it was after a weekend of being home. I had to go back Sunday, but I begged my mom to drop me off Monday morning at the dorms. I had no intention of going to class that day. I had it all planned out. By the time I would get to the dorms, they would be empty and everyone would be in class. Dorm mothers would be out teaching classes, I would be the only one. The night before I picked out a sharp knife from our kitchen, hid it in my backpack and brought it with me. I was finally going to do it.

I was going to slice my wrists the right way. I was going to get to the bone, and if I died in the process of searching for my marrow then so be it. I needed to see if I was real, I needed to write in my blood. I wasn't scared of dying, I welcomed it, hoped for it. My death would finally show everyone the truth of my suffering. I would finally rest.

Everything went as planned. I entered the dorms, went to my room. I knew for a fact Stacy wouldn't be there. I dropped my bags, got the knife out and began to slice my wrist straight down, the right way. At first I was scared, but the desperation and the determination to cut through the tendons was too much to bear.
So, I cut and I cut until I bled and bled.
I felt enthralled until terror set it in, in what I had done. I couldn't contain the blood.
I ran out of my room, straight down the hallway, at the end of the hall was my dorm mother, I knocked on her door. Luckily, she had returned from teaching class. She called 911. I was whisked to the ER. I received nine stitches on my wrist and was informed that my parents were contacted and on their way, I wouldn't be released from the ER, and that right now they were searching for any available beds in mental hospitals nearby that
accepted my parent's health insurance.
Indeed, I was fucked.

Chapter 5
Westwood Lodge
Winter 1999

The emergency room lights were bright enough to erase any shadows, but they couldn't touch the ones inside me. I was told to say goodbye to my parents, but what could I say? Their faces said everything—words would have been pointless. I watched their teary eyes, searching for something more than shame, but that was all they had to give me.
Disappointment etched deep in their expressions. There was nothing left to say. I was placed in the back of a white van like a prisoner being transferred after a guilty verdict. I wasn't cuffed, but I might as well have been.
Every mile from Newton-Wellesley to Westwood was weighed

down by the suffocating guilt of not succeeding. I wished I had died.
I wished I was dead. The only relief, if it could be called that, was knowing I didn't have to go home.
I couldn't look my father in the eyes again. I had failed, and this was the proof.
I had failed, and I was insane.

Westwood Lodge was its own kind of hell, one long, blurred nightmare. It wasn't a
hospital—it was a prison disguised as help.

Arrival felt like a death sentence, stripped of all humanity. They took everything—clothes, dignity. My body was just another thing to be searched, my naked skin exposed to strangers checking for weapons. No shoelaces allowed. That stuck with me.
Shoelaces could kill, they said. That stuck, too. This was suicide watch.
They threw me into a room barely bigger than my shame. A metal bunk bed with a plastic
mattress, stained in different shades of brown. The smell of it clung to the air, like everything there had been used up by others before me. A navy-blue blanket and a pillow that felt just as hard as the bed. No sheets. I had a roommate, but I don't remember her face. She was just a body next to mine, as faceless as the days that blurred into each other. It felt like the only thing missing was a toilet in the corner to complete the prison cell.
Suicide watch was its own kind of torture.
No cafeteria privileges.
No going outside.
No sunlight.
No human decency.
Just time—endless, suffocating time in that room.
A week and a half felt like forever.

They asked why I tried to hurt myself, and I didn't have an answer. Maybe if I had, they would've let me out.
Privileges weren't handed out. They had to be earned, or traded. Some of the girls traded their bodies for outside time, for food, for anything that resembled life. I don't know if I did, if my memories of other girls giving head, are actually of me.

There was no coping. Every day was hell, a relentless cycle of self-hate. The only control I had was over my body—over food. I found comfort in not eating, in the way starvation felt like taking back a piece of myself. The hunger was sharp, constant, but it was mine. That control was the only relief I could feel. I don't know if I did it right or not. I might have. Maybe that's how I earned privileges—maybe that's how I survived.

Or maybe life just got easier when I had privileges.

The memories slip away when I try to hold onto them. I wish I could remember. But

maybe forgetting was the only way to keep moving forward.

Chapter 6
Leaving Westwood Lodge
Winter 1999

Leaving Westwood Lodge felt less like a release and more like stepping out of the

vacuum where the world had carried on as though nothing had changed, while I was left shattered in ways I hadn't even known were possible.

I was allowed to leave under the premise that I told my father I loved him.

There was no way around it, in a family session squeezed in between both my parents and the shrink hidden away behind the desk, telling me in a strict voice,

We can't release you until you tell your father you love him.

I wanted to say it, even the first time they brought up the notion, but how do you say I love you to a man who had never said it to you before? To a man who was my father, and a man who terrified me at the same time? I couldn't say it that first therapy sessions after I was removed from suicide watch.

I couldn't say anything that first time, I was mute.

I spent three weeks in that place, learning how to package my words just right – not to say too much truth, never too little, but just enough to be let out. I focused on prepping myself in my head on how I would tell my dad I love him.

I stressed over it as if it was a huge exam I had to pass, and failure was not an option.

Failure meant hell.

So in the next family session, in a little girl voice, seeking approval for my father,

searching his eyes with mine, I said, *"I love you, papa."*

And the therapist praised me.
I was healed.
Inside my heart, I felt hate.

Westwood broke something inside
me that I hadn't even known existed, it blocked the memory of rape, as I learned there is a greater hell.

Yet, going home terrified me.

My mother picked me up in silence, her lips tight as though she feared words might
unravel whatever fragile dance we were conducting with the huge elephant following us around. We drove back to Cambridge, the weight of quiet filling every inch of the car. My younger brother and my sister sat in the back seat, their chatter oblivious, and their world still innocent. I was a stranger to that innocence now, and the silence only grew thicker with the fear of what awaited
me – what I had to face – and the shame that clung to me like second skin.

Once home, I was assigned a new therapist, and I was kept on Prozac.
It dulled the edges, numbing me in ways I didn't even know I could be numbed.

Westwood psychiatric hospital closed
By Heather Hegedus, Boston 25 News
August 29, 2017 at 7:22 pm

A psychiatric hospital has been shut down for a second time in less than a month, and this time the Department of Mental Health tells Boston 25 News Westwood Lodge has been closed for good.

The state says the 89-bed private psychiatric hospital has been closed due what a spokesman called "issues concerning patient safety and quality of care."

Last Wednesday, Westwood police tell Boston 25 news they were called to the lodge for a report of a sexual assault.
https://www.boston25news.com/news/westwood-psychiatric-hospital-closed-for-investigation-1/600158283/

Chapter 7
Therapy

My therapist spoke Russian – an absurd detail that still seems plucked from a dream – but it suited me, the perfect distance for someone who I had no intention of telling the truth. I wasn't about to reveal the rape, or the reason I slashed my wrists, or how secretly I loved the control I found in not eating, and even more so in binging and purging. I certainly couldn't admit that I swallowed laxatives like candy, just to feel something move inside me, feeling control slip through my fingers with every dose.
I couldn't admit that when I looked in the mirror, all I saw was a mess, the only way I could express it was written in a poetic format in the last surviving journal from 1999, from which I quote now to you directly, dear reader. I now wonder what it would have been like if I shared my true thoughts with my therapist at the time. What if I let her in on my secret? Would I have been saved or healed sooner?

  Or it wouldn't have even mattered at the time.

Journal entry - May 1999
I look in the mirror,
I see a mess,
I see the extra
The bulk,
The fat,
That needs to be gotten rid off,
Sliced off to the bone.
I don't want to be my father,
That's my biggest fear,
Losing the physical perfection,
Turning into a fat mess,
Turning to food for support.
Losing everything I worked for.

I put my head high up in the air,
I know I will never be like him,
Never look like him,
If I stay strong,
If I stay in control.

I couldn't say any of this to my therapist, I couldn't tell her about my true feelings.

Instead, I gave her a simpler lie: school stress, I said. Those two words would become my shield, the excuse that would slip easily and naturally from my lips.

There was a quiet shift in me after Westwood Lodge. Something essential inside me abandoned the idea of trusting anyone.

It became clear that I would have to mend myself, and if I couldn't, then I would at least learn how to pretend.

Therapists couldn't help me, no one could.

It wasn't hard to lie. School really was stressful – I was drowning in assignments, and though the teachers were kind, overly so, it did nothing to soothe the knot in my chest. I was suspended from dorm life and had to commute to school.

That worked out for the best, as the real blow came from my peers.

While I was locked away, Stacy had spread rumors. She told everyone I did it for
attention, that I didn't actually hurt myself, that I wanted to be in a mental hospital. When I heard what she'd said, it was like a switch flipped inside me. If there had been any small sliver of trust left in me, Stacy destroyed it. I stopped speaking to her immediately, but it didn't matter. The damage was done. Her betrayal solidified something in me, like a wall I hadn't even realized I was building.

She wasn't just Stacy anymore; she was everyone. It wasn't just her words that hurt, but what they revealed: that people would always twist your pain into something they could understand, something smaller than it really was. The betrayal felt personal, but it also confirmed what I already suspected—that trust was a dangerous thing, and letting anyone in would only end with them weaponizing your truth against you.

So I buried myself in schoolwork, not to move past the rumors but to drown them out. But no amount of focus could erase the shame that clung to me, or the way the rumors whispered the things I feared most. Because the truth was, maybe Stacy wasn't entirely wrong. Maybe, in some small, hidden corner of myself, I did want to be at Westwood Lodge. Maybe there was a strange comfort in being locked away, safe from the world and its expectations, and that haunted me more than anything Stacy could ever say.

Chapter 8
Trapped

I felt trapped, my release did not signify my freedom or my healing, rather it poisoned me further.

In the one and only surviving journal from that time, I wrote:

I feel so trapped.
I look out the window,
I see,
People….
Walking all around,
Smiling,
Crying,
Laughing,
Eating.
I can't feel.
I don't feel.

I don't feel the pleasure of life.

I no longer am myself,
I sit in my bedroom,
I don't think I can walk,
So, I am stuck in my room.
Inert,
Useless,
Trapped.

Chapter 9
Stacy

You were me and I, was you
But that in turn meant nothing to you at all.
Instead a game was played of Russian Roulette with my life at stake
Although I never knew it,
we all wear masks but no one told me that my life was on the line.
I didn't know you would steal my light, that burned deep within,
the light I hid from others, always feeling shame. I didn't know the mask you wore
was weaved together out of the bits and pieces of my soul.
You knew, you always knew,
But never told me, that behind your mask your pure existence was a sham,
Of exhuming power and control, of keeping me restrained within these prison walls.
Sometimes I wish I never met you, then again I wouldn't be me.
The unmasked version of the self, for the outside world to see,
The soaring spirit I was always meant to be.
Diana Kouprina ©

I broke after a month of Stacy chasing me down at school, her brown eyes wide and
insistent, saying over and over that we needed to talk, that it wasn't her. But I knew. I knew she had started the rumor. Still, somehow, it was easier to let someone else carry the blame. That was the rhythm of our friendship—no matter how much she hurt me, how far she pushed me beyond my boundaries, I couldn't cut the thread that bound us. I was tethered to her, like a drowning thing clinging to its rescuer, even though I was actually sinking. The spell held tight for 25 long years.

In reflection now, I wonder if I was in love with Stacy—a hidden part of me that I denied to myself. I copied her, placed her on a pedestal, made her untouchable. She could do no wrong in my eyes, even when her deceptions were staring me in the face. I was drawn to her like a moth to the flame. She had an uncanny ability to get any boy to like her, and I was desperate for that power, for that love. Stacy was teaching me how to navigate the treacherous waters of affection, and oh, how I wanted to be loved by a boy—any boy. That was my only mission.

When we were together, it didn't matter that others called us "Anorexic Sluts."

In those moments, I felt invincible, wrapped in the illusion of our friendship. Stacy helped me escape my father's wrath; her family provided the American warmth I craved. I didn't care that they continuously asked me what it was like to be an immigrant or how I had to explain that my father was a conflict negotiator, not a diplomat—but like a

diplomat. Eventually, they forgot that I was an immigrant, and in that forgetfulness, I found a semblance of belonging. My father was always against our friendship, seeing the danger in our bond, but my mother knew in her heart she couldn't isolate me or contain me. With Stacy, I felt free, even as I slipped deeper into a world of reckless abandon. Drinking on weekends with older boys became a welcome escape.

The parties buzzed with energy, and I was adored, told I was sexy—even though I hated it. Still, a part of me glowed under the compliments, lighting a fire of hope that I would find my Prince Charming.

I believed the only way to achieve that dream was through my friendship with Stacy, who
navigated these waters with an effortless charm I envied. As time passed, it became easier to shift the blame. Dana Hall was the culprit. The school, with its rigid rules, competitive edge, and suffocating dorm life, became the villain. It was simpler to wrap my mind around that than to confront the unhealthy bond Stacy and I had formed. I told myself it was the strict environment that had pushed me over the edge, never admitting that it was our entanglement, our obsession with each other, that had fractured me.

Life tried to pry us apart, but I clung to her, desperate, like she held the key to some part of me I couldn't lose. When she was expelled from Dana Hall, it was like the floor
beneath me crumbled. She was gone and I was left with the shame

of returning without her, exposed. I told myself it was impossible. I convinced myself that the school was to blame—that I couldn't go back, not because I was broken, but because Dana Hall had done the breaking. My father insisted I return after freshman year, believing it would be good for me to face my fears. But we fought—I fought him with everything I had,
desperate to find a way out. I found another school, made my case about Dana Hall's
rigid structure, but the truth stayed buried. I never told my parents the real reason: Stacy's sister, Sammy, would be attending this new school.

I needed that connection, a lifeline, because I wasn't ready to let go of her just yet. I poured myself into the admissions process, maintaining my GPA like my life depended on it, securing financial aid, and crafting my escape. But now, when I look back, I
 wonder. If I had stayed, if I had faced Dana Hall and the demons I was running from, would I have begun to heal? Would I have broken free of Stacy's grip? I didn't know it then, but I blamed the school for everything—Westwood Lodge, my breakdown, my unraveling.
It wasn't the school.

I see that now.

It was me—too terrified to see Stacy for who she really was, too afraid to lose her and face myself. Like Plath's Esther, I was trapped under my own bell jar, suffocating in the space between who I was and who I let her make me. Trust had become a foreign language, and Stacy was the only translator I had left. I feared everyone would be talking about me, their whispers swirling around like a storm and I wouldn't have Stacy there to help me navigate through the minefield of mean girls. It was terrifying to think of facing the scrutiny alone. But more than anything, I feared facing myself.

Chapter 10
The Journal

The irony in this specific journal from which the following text is copied from, is that it is the last one remaining and yet it is the only journal where I hid the truth completely. Every word, carefully chosen, every sentence a disguise, except for two entries written in pink ink. Those two entries stand out as if they don't belong to the rest, as though they are a quiet rebellion against the lies I wove.

I wrote this journal with a specific audience in mind: Stacy or Sammy. I knew there was a chance they might stumble upon it and read it, so I crafted it for their eyes. It became a performance, a projection of who I wanted them to think I was. The real journals, the ones in which I had poured my heart and soul—the raw, unfiltered truth—they are long gone. And yet this one remains, this hollow shell of a journal.

Most of its pages are filled with shallow recounts of events, moments twisted to fit the narrative I needed to project. Boys became conquests. Each one was assigned a role in a strategy I thought would keep me safe, keep me wanted. Plan A: the boy I liked, the one I chased but always kept just out of reach. Plan B: the boy who liked me more, the safety net, the reassurance that I wouldn't end up alone. Plan C: the boy I didn't like at all, the one who was obsessed with me, his devotion a fragile form of power I could wield.

I wrote as if I were analyzing my relationships, as though I were searching for answers or trying to make sense of it all. But the truth is, I was building a fortress—a fortress of
half-truths and strategies to protect the version of me I wanted others to see.

And yet, in the middle of all these lies, there is the pink ink. The only real, substantial thing I wrote; my broken truth.

June 7th, 1999
Around 1pm

Not a lot has happened since I wrote last. I wrote my exams, I got: B- in English, C+ in Western Civilization, C+ in Spanish, B- in Latin, and an E in Geometry, yes geometry I failed, but I can still make up the grade.
I think I did ok, well not in geometry obviously, but everything else.
My father came home yesterday, you should have seen how happy mom was when she brought him home from the airport.
Well, I will tell you I am definitely not happy that he came back. I can't help it, but I really do hate him.
All he does is criticize me, makes me feel even smaller than I

*already am. I wonder if deep inside he really hates me.
I had a two minute talk with him today, pretty much he told me
that I was stupid and I needed to study for the whole summer.
He was stuck on the idea of me going back to Dana Hall for next
year.
I am not going back, he of all people can't make me.
Want to hear a sad thing?
I am actually happy when he is out of town. When he comes
home, I get depressed as shit.
I don't think I can live with him. I really don't think I can.
I hate him so much, he said my writing sucked.
I guess that's why I got a 90 on my English story.
I wish he would just die.*

*You returned,
Turning my whole world upside down.
You think you are a great man,
But you are NOT.
You think you can control me.
But you cannot.
You think I love and respect you,
But I don't.
To tell you the truth,
I hate you.*

*I wish I never knew you.
I wish you never existed in my life.*

*You hurt me,
You turned me into a monster.
You took away my heart.
You took away my soul.
I can no longer love,
I can no longer be happy.
You destroyed me,
With your words.*

June 29th, 1999
6pm

Well, lets see, I will start with the good news first. I am going to the W. next year for sure, both the acceptance letter and full scholarship offer have arrived. I am really
excited, but it will probably hit me when I am actually packing to go away to school.
Well, now I still need to deal with the present. Yesterday, was hell for me and Stacy. Here is what happened.
She slept over my house. She needed to get away from her family. So the next morning we decided to go to Stacy's house because her eldest sister was coming over to visit with her baby daughter. I asked my mom if I could go, and she said that was fine with her, she said she needed to first pick up my dad from the airport and after that I could go over to Stacy's house with her. So when they came home, I greeted him and asked him for permission to go over to Stacy's house, just to be polite. He backfired and yelled no. He yelled at Stacy, my mom took our side about me going and he yelled at her. He kicked Stacy out of the house. I swear, I hate him. And the worst of it all, was that
Stacy missed the visit with her sister all because of my father. He was so rude, so cruel, so mean. I am so ashamed. He just wants to ruin my life.
Well, I talked to my doctor today, she said not to stress about it and instead to talk to Stacy's family about it and tell them the type of father I have. So not to ruin my r
elationship with them.
I mean I love them. The whole Benton family, it would kill me if they didn't like me.

Well, anyway nothing else is happening with me.
I cleaned my room.
I am on this new great diet.
It makes me feel great.
I swear I feel really good.

I don't know anymore….
 striving for perfection is not really easy.

Tomorrow I am going rollerblading. I haven't rollerbladed in a while,

I love it.

Well I am sitting in my clean room, thinking of what I want.
I just want so much more out of life, I really do.
I guess I am taking a step with this new diet.
I hope it really works.
I really do.
I will weigh myself in a month
To see how much I lost.
I really do need to be strict with this new diet.

Well, I gotta go. I'll write soon.
Love,
Diana

Chapter 11
Leaving Dana

This new place lies ahead of me.
Full of hope
Full of power
I take little steps
I need to achieve,
I close my eyes,
I picture lakes,
Forest,
Love,
Happiness…
What will it be like,
I try to imagine it,
If I close my eyes will I create my future?
I don't think I can,
Happiness is not within me,
Love is just not for me,
To be had,
Or felt.

I had failed Dana Hall and it seemed that nothing had changed; my scholarship remained intact, my status in school unaffected by the shadow of my suicide attempt. I was still the same girl, tethered to the same mistakes, but I felt as if I had slipped through the cracks of reality, unnoticed, invisible to those around me. The silence that surrounded my pain felt deafening and in that silence, I was left to confront the truth of my existence—a truth I desperately wanted to avoid. Every day was a battle between the façade I presented to the world and the fractured self that lay beneath. I wore a mask of normalcy, but inside, I was crumbling. Stacy had been my shield against the world, my translator in a language of pain I couldn't articulate. Without her, I felt exposed, stripped of the protection I had relied on. My mind raced with the fear of judgment, of being seen as weak or broken, and I couldn't bear the thought of their scrutiny. The irony was suffocating. My attempt to escape the pain had only deepened it, and now I found myself grappling with a reality where I was neither here nor there—caught in a limbo that felt endless. I had been labeled, branded by my actions, but those who knew my story were few, and those who cared even fewer. I wore my shame like a second skin, a burden I carried alone, and I longed for the comfort of Stacy's presence to help me navigate through it all.

After transferring to the W. School, Stacy and I didn't see each other as much, but our letters never stopped. It was like I was pouring out my soul onto the pages, diary-like letters that captured every thought, every fear, every hope. I told her everything—things I couldn't admit to myself, confessions that made their way onto paper but never into my own consciousness. We saw each other once a month when she came home, but those letters, those words, they were my lifeline, my diary disguised as friendship. I held onto her through Sammy that fall, unwilling to sever the last thread of our connection. And so the cycle continued. For years to come throughout high school, Stacy and I would find ourselves on a continuous roller coaster ride, our bond both strengthened and strained by drinking, partying, and the chaos that seemed to follow us wherever we went. It
was as though we had created our own world, one where boundaries blurred, and
consequences seemed distant.

By the age of sixteen, I was dating 25-year-olds. It was exhilarating and terrifying all at once. Stacy had a way of drawing us into these situations—boys, parties, and older crowds. She could command attention effortlessly, and I followed her lead, desperate to feel wanted, to be adored.

The older boys made me feel grown-up, like I was in control of my own life, even though I barely understood the rules of the game I was playing. But deep down, I knew that what we were doing was dangerous, that we were skating too close to the edge. Still, with

Stacy by my side, it felt like we were invincible—like nothing could touch us. As long as we had each other, I believed we could outrun the consequences.

Chapter 12
Jeremy

I met Jeremy one weekend when I was visiting Stacy in Maine, at one of those raucous parties that seemed to sprout up like weeds in the fall. There we were, all huddled around a bonfire, the air thick with smoke and the scent of cheap beer, each of us trying to forget something or other.

I spotted him across the fire—his green-grey eyes were like some kind of siren call, and I swear they actually sang to me. "Who is that guy?" I practically bounced on my toes, tugging at Stacy's shoulder like a kid desperate for a secret. "Oh, he's nobody," she said, as if she had a firm grasp on the world and knew all its players. "I don't really know him. He walks around school making dirt bike noises. You want to meet him?"

Yes, yes, I wanted to meet him. I needed to meet him. I couldn't help it. When I finally got close enough to introduce myself, he wasn't making those ridiculous noises. Instead,

we fell into a conversation that felt like slipping into a warm bath after a long, cold day. We talked about poetry and writing, sharing bits of ourselves like we were playing some kind of delicate game. He told me about his passion for Monet and skiing, and there was something about him that felt different—something I had been searching for but hadn't quite found in anyone else. I was 16 going on 17, and he had just turned 17. He was a whole universe of possibility, like a book I desperately wanted to read but wasn't sure I could understand. I didn't know it then, but he'd become a chapter I'd never forget, a glimpse of what could be amid the chaos I had come to accept as life.

That weekend, we were inseparable. It wasn't just the way he looked at me or how he made me laugh—it was deeper. We talked like we had known each other for years. He showed me how to live in moments, not in fear. We held hands, wandered through the woods, kissed under stars, and I felt love, real love, for the first time. It was terrifying and beautiful. Jeremy was everything I thought I was looking for, true love had found me; as I reflect upon it now as first true love goes, Jeremy for me was that love. I can say for
certain he loved me, I loved him the best I could, even though at the time I didn't know love, how could I know love, when all I knew was how to hate myself?

Our relationship continued, even as the distance stretched between us. Jeremy would drive four hours just to pick me up from my house in Massachusetts and bring me back to Maine for the weekend. His family welcomed me with open arms. They had the warmth, the closeness I was starving for—something my own family could never give me.
Watching him paint was like witnessing magic. He had this quiet intensity about him, this focus that made it feel like he might actually be the next Monet. I would sit there for hours, mesmerized by his brushstrokes, thinking how lucky I was to be near him.

Stacy didn't like Jeremy. She said I was becoming a bad friend, and maybe I was. The thing is, I didn't have that same desperate craving to spiral with her anymore. I didn't need to be out every night, lost in the chaos, trying to feel alive through someone else's eyes. I had found what I was looking for in Jeremy—something calm, something real. Jeremy taught me about passion, about making love in the way that didn't just involve the body but the soul.

He showed me how to dance with my hair down during summer thunderstorms, how to let go of everything and just be. Looking back, our relationship was so unique, so
extraordinary—especially because of the distance. It didn't seem to matter. We were
teenagers, but we were also so much more than that.

We believed we could conquer the world as long as we had each other. We spent one
perfect summer together, and I felt free in a way I hadn't before. I celebrated my birthday by getting a tongue ring to match his and in my teenage mind, that was the ultimate

symbol of our connection. We talked about getting married, about running away
somewhere far away from the mess of our lives. I felt whole with him, like I was finally the person I was meant to be.
But then fall came, and everything started to unravel. Jeremy had been training for the X Games, and when he got the chance to train in Lake Tahoe, everything shifted. The
distance between us became more than just miles. It became a wall. He met someone else, and that was it. He told me over the phone and it was like the floor fell out from
beneath me. I couldn't breathe. The pain was blinding, and I didn't know how to make it stop. That's when the darkness crept in. The kind that doesn't leave but stays, festering. It grows inside you, twisting everything you thought you knew into something ugly and painful. I tried to fight it, but without Jeremy, I couldn't find the light anymore. I couldn't find me anymore. And in the end, when Jeremy left, the light in me burned out with him. It wasn't just the loss of him that hurt—it was the loss of who I was when I was with him. He had made me feel whole, made me feel alive in ways I hadn't known were
possible. And when he was gone, it was like that version of me disappeared, too. What was left was a shadow, a hollow version of myself, clinging to memories that I couldn't quite shake. The light had been bright while it lasted, but when it faded, all I was left with was darkness.

Chapter 12
My Babushka Comes to America

In reflecting on the remainder of high school, Stacy remained firmly on the pedestal I had placed her on. After my scholarship ran out at the W. School it was decided that for junior year, I would live at home and attend public school. Though I didn't want to return home, the exhaustion from sophomore year weighed on me. The W. was a different world from Dana Hall—academics were less intense, and I led a double life. By day, I was a straight-A student, and by night, a popular party girl. I'd sneak out of the dorm to meet my boyfriend, living more like a college student than a 15-year-old high schooler. The summer between sophomore and junior year changed everything.

Stacy and I discovered ways to get into 21+ clubs, and soon I found myself dating men in their mid-twenties. Entering Watertown High, I didn't feel the need to fit into any groups. I was used to dating older men and lying about my age—sometimes claiming to be 17, other times 19. They never seemed to care how old I really was. I didn't realize then that

to them, I was just a party girl, only valued for one thing.

Public school felt effortless in comparison. I maintained a high GPA without much thought and partied late into the night, only to show up to class at 8 a.m. without missing a beat. Life at Watertown High didn't require the same emotional or academic investment, and in many ways, it allowed me to continue hiding behind the carefree, dual persona I had created.

When my babushka stepped through the door that fall of my junior year, the room
shifted—a palpable disturbance in the air that pulled me back to a time I thought I had left behind. There she was, a piece of home I hadn't known I was missing, wrapped in a shawl that smelled faintly of spices and something uniquely her. I wanted to cry, but the tears felt heavy, lodged in the throat I had trained to swallow emotions whole. I held back the flood, longing to run to her, to wrap my arms around her and let the years dissolve in that embrace, but I restrained myself.
Instead, I lingered in the threshold, caught between the pull of my longing and the weight of my own ignorance.

To our family, she brought a shift—a warm sun breaking through a gray sky after a long winter. My fear of my father ebbed in her presence, as if the very air had conspired to cloak me in safety. There was a freedom I felt around her, an unspoken bond that made the outside world feel less threatening. During this visit, I introduced her to Stacy and Jeremy, and for those fleeting moments, my world felt complete. But I knew I couldn't let those feelings be known; deep down,I understood it was all too fragile, too precarious. I was acutely aware that soon enough, it would
all shatter, and that impending sense of doom loomed like a shadow, ready to descend.
Her visit came before all the bad exploded—the day the Twin Towers fell, the day my world tilted on its axis, before the breakup with Jeremy, before everything I thought I understood about life

unraveled. I wish I had clung to her. I wish I had held onto every word she uttered, letting them settle in my bones like warmth on a chilly day.

If I have any regrets, it's that I took her visit for granted, blinded by the haze of youth and
oblivious to the weight of time slipping through my fingers like sand. I didn't grasp that life was truly fleeting, a series of moments strung together like fragile beads on a thread, ready to scatter at the slightest tremor. In my youthful arrogance, I believed I would die before her, as if my own existence could somehow shield me from the inevitability of loss. Her visit, I realize now, was an ironic goodbye, a final chance to connect before I spiraled into a darkness I had begun to accept as my fate.

Last year, when she passed away, it struck me that I would never see her again. In the
wake of her absence, I remain stateless, adrift in a world that feels as though it has lost its
anchor.

The echo of her laughter still lingers in the corners of my mind, but it feels like a distant melody, fading as I grapple with the silence she left behind. In those moments with her, I was a child again, lost in the safety of her embrace, yet acutely aware of the fragility of it all. Each shared laugh, each gentle reprimand, felt like a blessing I didn't deserve, a gift that would soon be wrapped away, leaving only the haunting remnants of what once was. The thought of losing her, of returning to my hollow existence, loomed like a dark cloud—a reality I chose to ignore, indulging in the delusion of permanence in a world that thrives on change.

My babushka was there the weekend that Stacy turned my hair bright orange-yellow, a decision that would haunt me the following Monday and a story I would tell later at
cocktails parties for a laugh.

My parents had gone to visit friends in New Jersey, leaving me home alone with my
babushka, my brother, and my sister. That weekend was the kind of freedom I craved, a chance to break free from the constraints of my everyday life. Stacy came over, and my babushka didn't question my plans; she let me go out with my friend. "I love you," she said, her voice warm and reassuring. "Just make sure you have fun, but be safe." Her words felt like a permission slip, a gentle nudge into a world of excitement that felt both thrilling and reckless.

And go out we did. Stacy and I slipped into high heels and painted our faces with makeup that aged us beyond our years. The night stretched before us like a blank canvas, waiting to be filled with the wild strokes of youth. We ventured to a bar, where the drinks flowed like water, and soon enough, we were drunk, laughing at the absurdity of it all.

Lines of coke followed, a reckless pursuit of more, more, more—whatever it was that would drown out the chaos swirling in our heads. In our intoxicated state, we stumbled into CVS, the fluorescent lights blaring down on us as we grabbed a box of Feria bleach hair dye. By 3 AM, we were at Stacy's house, huddled in her bathroom, giddy with

adrenaline and a sense of invincibility. I watched as she applied the dye, eager for the transformation that promised to take me further away from the girl I felt trapped as.

But as the alcohol and drugs wore off, reality came crashing back when I finally made it home that Sunday evening. I stood before the mirror, blinking at the reflection staring back at me—a shocking brightness that made me feel like Bozo the Clown. My heart sank, and the thrill of the night evaporated, replaced by dread.

I had transformed into something I didn't recognize, and I wasn't sure if I liked it. The next day, I wore my Dana Hall navy blue zip-up hoodie to school, desperate to cover my hair. I managed to go unnoticed for half the day until lunch, when a friend caught sight of me. "What happened?" she asked, concern etched on her face. Without hesitation, she approached me with a mission: to fix my hair.

To this day, her skillful brilliance with hair and makeup amazes me, and in that moment,

I was grateful for her friendship and determination to help me reclaim some semblance of normalcy. She rushed me to CVS after school and helped me become a Barbie blonde. We were all in awe of her skill; the next day, I was a blonde.

Through it all, my babushka stood by me, a quiet strength against the reckless choices of youth. Her love was an invisible woven blanket of protection, a reminder that even in my wildest moments, I had someone who cared enough to help me navigate the aftermath.

Chapter 13
Jeep Wrangler – Red

Jeremy's calls from Lake Tahoe became slowly less frequent. When he first left, he would call me every day. As the month progressed, it turned into a call once a week. I was
waiting for his call. This was before cell phones, or at least before I had one. I had a
landline in my room—white, with a thick gray antenna and caller ID.
Every time the phone rang, my heart skipped, hoping it was him. When the ringing finally came, I nearly jumped off the bed. I checked the caller ID box next to the phone—it read "California." My stomach dropped and instead of joy, I felt a cold wave of anxiety crash over me. I already knew this wasn't a good call.
But I hoped, against everything, that it wasn't bad. "Hello?" I answered, my voice thin. On the other end, his voice was muffled, distant.
"Hi," he said. The pause stretched out, too long to be comfortable. Finally, he said the words I dreaded: "We need to talk." My heart raced. Fuck.
This isn't happening. I knew that phrase, "we need to talk." It was every guy's
introduction to the breakup conversation. I stayed silent, barely able to breathe.
Then, quietly, I muttered, "Okay."
"I met someone," he continued, his voice flat and matter-of-fact. "It wasn't a big deal, but we hooked up. I'm planning to hang out with her again. I love you, but I can't do this long distance anymore. We need to take a break."
The rest of that moment is blurry. I know I yelled. I know I called him a cheating asshole. I know I told him I hated him and to never call me again. But after I slammed the phone down, my face streaked with tears, I stayed by the phone, hoping he would call back, hoping he knew I didn't mean it.
But the phone stayed silent.
I barely slept that night.
In the morning, I forced myself through the motions of my routine. I blasted Celine

Dion's "To Love You More", letting the lyrics cut through me,

cried as I washed my face, and layered on my makeup like armor. The song replayed on a loop, every note
sharpening the ache in my chest. I crouched on my bed hanging my upper torso out the window, smoking a Newport, trying to blow the smoke outside so it wouldn't settle in the room, sipping the coffee my mom had made for me in the Jazve, its bitter warmth doing nothing to soothe me.
My hands shook as I held the cup, everything felt surreal, like I was walking through a fog that wouldn't lift. Straightening my hair was next, like always. I had a towel in one hand, the iron in the other. I flipped my head forward, pressing my hair between the two, smoothing it out like I was making a grilled cheese sandwich. The hiss of the iron, the steam rising, it felt like control, something I could do right when everything else felt wrong. By the time I was ready, I had my armor on: jeans, a tube top, and my long black blazer that went down to my knees.

That blazer was my shield. I sprayed on enough J'adore to cover the lingering cigarette smell.
Today, I wasn't going to be broken.
Today, I had a plan.
Jeremy found someone?
Fine. I'd find someone too.
There was a boy at school, Henry. I knew he wanted me. He'd been watching me for weeks. Today, I would tell him he could have me. At school, I spotted Henry in the hall on my way to lunch. He was already running up to me before I had to say anything. We flirted, our words light and meaningless. I told him I'd love to go out with him. "Yes," I said, with a smile. "Pick me up today at 6 p.m."
That evening, right on time, Henry pulled up to my house in a brand new Jeep Wrangler, the headlights cutting through the dusk. Biggie was blasting through the speakers, the bass heavy and relentless, vibrating through the ground.

Biggie, Biggie, Biggie, can't you see? Sometimes your words just hypnotize me.
I climbed into the passenger seat, leaning over to give him a hug and a kiss on the cheek. His cologne mixed with the smell of new leather.
Biggie, Biggie, Biggie, can't you see? Sometimes your words just hypnotize me.
He smiled, maybe thinking tonight would be something it wasn't. He didn't know I was just trying to fill a void, trying to silence the

pain Jeremy left behind. "Where do you want to go?" he asked, but I couldn't care less.

"I don't care," I said, looking out the window, my voice hollow.

So we drove. The sun slipped lower, and the sky turned from pink to violet as we wound through streets that blurred together. Eventually, he pulled into a secluded spot.

The engine shut off, and the quiet between us felt thick, expectant. We kissed, but it felt like nothing. Just lips, just hands, just empty motions. When we had sex, it was quick and uncomfortable. His hands didn't feel right. His touch didn't make me feel anything. I was somewhere else, watching it happen from a distance, wishing it would just end.

Afterward, he drove me home. The Jeep felt colder, the music no longer filling the silence

between us. I didn't speak. I didn't even look at him.

He must have known something had shifted, but he didn't ask. When we pulled up to my house, I gave him a brief smile, got out, and walked inside without looking back. As soon as I closed the door behind me, I knew it. I didn't like how I felt. There was no triumph, no satisfaction in trying to forget Jeremy through someone else.

Afterward, a wave of shame washed over me. I welcomed it. I felt dirty and hollow, as if the act had stripped me of any remnants of my worth. It was

exactly the feeling I thought I deserved – a consequence for the love I had lost, a penance for my vulnerability. In those moments I realized just how far I was willing to go to

escape the pain of losing Jeremy, and how profoundly that pain had carved itself into my being.

This was the beginning of my senior year, and my inner world was bleak. I dove into my duality, fully embracing the two separate lives I had created. By night, I partied hard, chasing the high of fleeting connections and reckless abandon, the laughter drowning out the echo of my heartache.

By day, I studied with a determination that surprised even me. I had mastered the art of wearing a mask, flipping the switch from wild party girl to diligent student with ease.

Stacy was already at U-Mass Amherst, living out the dream we had once crafted together. We had a plan: I was going to join her as her roommate, and we would make up for lost time. I envisioned a fresh start, a chance to leave behind the remnants of my past—the

heartache from Jeremy, the shame of my choices. College would be different; I was
convinced of it. It would be our moment to redefine ourselves, a sanctuary where we could flourish together in a world that felt less suffocating than high school. But deep down, I knew I was running on fumes, filling the void with party nights and empty flings. Each encounter, each bottle of cheap liquor, only served to mask the pain I refused to confront. I was trapped in a cycle, dancing on the edge of self-destruction, and I felt a simmering rage beneath the surface. I thought about Jeremy often, a bittersweet melody playing in my mind, reminding me of what I had lost and the person I had become. In my heart, I clung to the hope that U-Mass would be the remedy I so
desperately sought. But there was a gnawing fear lurking just below the surface—what if things didn't change? What if the distance between my dreams and reality only widened?

Chapter 14
School Is Everything

After the Jeep Wrangler incident, I threw myself into schoolwork even more, doubling down on volunteer service activities and sports. It wasn't hard to do, as Stacy was away at college and my weekends were somewhat free. None of my other friends partied like Stacy; if anything, among my friends, I was the bad influence. By winter, I had built a Jeremy block and was in search of my next Prince Charming. When Stacy came home for winter break and everything turned upside down, it didn't affect my schoolwork, but it did affect my drinking. I became a pro at sneaking out of the house. My parents' bedroom was located at the far end of the house, while mine was right next to the kitchen, which had a back door. As long as I was back by 5 a.m., I went unnoticed. I pulled all-nighters where the only way to get through school was to drink. I mixed Crystal Lite with
vodka—fewer calories—and sipped on that cocktail throughout the school day. It helped my mind focus on what was happening in class and stopped my head from spinning and my hands from shaking. I had one friend in public school and she soon became my companion in the fun of chasing after the adrenaline of living on the edge.

I met Vincent that winter at Club Level. He was one of the head promoters of the club, always dressed in a suit with a dark dress shirt underneath, no tie. After a drink, he looked just like Richard Gere; he became my new infatuation. I lied to him about my age, saying I was 19 and a freshman in college. After all, it wasn't that far-fetched of a lie—I had told worse. He was 25 and it didn't seem like he cared. I got lost in the idea that maybe this was a shortcut to something bigger. The limo rides, the nightly VIP nightclubs, the parties that followed—this was it.

I was 17, living like I was in Sex and the City, and it felt intoxicating. Maybe Vincent was my Mr. Big, the one who could sweep me into a world of glitz and glamour. It was never hard for me to become obsessed with a boy; that was the easy part. The real challenge came in letting go, in stripping away the layers of fantasy to see the truth about them. I loved putting everyone on a pedestal, draping them in the kind of glow that made them seem untouchable. But as much as I loved that rush, I couldn't shake the feeling that there was always a crash waiting on the other side. Come to think of it now, Vincent never took me out on a date during the day. I never met anyone from his family aside from his cousin Larry, who was obsessed with any friend I brought around. Larry was a regular in the nightclub scene, always lurking in the shadows with a wild grin, eager for his next hit. He loved his coke, but I guess then we all did.

Our dates with Vincent were always at night, late enough that he'd pick me up at 10 p.m. or later. It was ideal for me—perfect, in fact—because sneaking out of the house was a delicate art.

His family owned a little diner in Watertown and we'd often go there. It felt like our secret world, a place where he would open it up just for us and for those stolen moments, we could pretend we were anyone we wanted to be. Inside the diner, we would drink, raid the fridge, and get lost in each other, tangled in the heat of the moment. I don't know what we talked about—maybe the music playing in the background or the absurdity of our lives—but I do remember the weight of those moments pressing against the walls.

Afterward, he'd drive me back, the streets empty and still, as if we were the only two people who existed in that universe. After winter break, I began to refer to him as my boyfriend, doodling his name in my notebooks with hearts during class. It was a silly thing, really, but it felt important—like a declaration of something that was only half real. A couple of weeks later, Vincent left for LA, and suddenly our late-night escapades were replaced by phone

calls, the distance stretching between us like a rubber band ready to snap. I never really knew if he actually liked me. It was a nagging uncertainty that lurked in the back of my mind, a question I dared not voice. But the craving for his love
consumed me. I became obsessed with the idea of making him fall for me, convinced that if I tried hard enough, I could bridge that gap. I thought I loved him and in that desperate haze, I wrapped myself in the notion that love was something to be earned, something to be won.

Everything settled once school resumed for Stacy and Vincent was in LA.

With the chaos behind me, I was finally able to focus on school, awaiting responses from
colleges with a mix of excitement and dread. It was a time when futures hung in the
balance, and mine felt particularly fragile. In this newfound clarity, I poured my energy into my senior thesis.

I chose a topic that blended my interests in film and literature, comparing and contrasting David Lynch—the director—alongside his three films, Blue Velvet, The Elephant Man, and Mulholland Drive, with John Fowles—the author—examining his three novels, The Collector, The Magus, and The French Lieutenant's Woman. My thesis focused on how both Lynch and Fowles portrayed women in their work, delving into the complex layers of female representation and the nuances that came with it. As I wrote, I found solace in the analytical process, dissecting characters, motivations, and themes. I poured over scripts and texts, scrutinizing the choices made by both men in how they crafted the women in their narratives. Each page brought me closer to understanding not just the art, but myself—how I, too, was shaping my own story amidst the tangled threads of obsession and desire.

During my junior and senior years in school, I had one clear purpose: to get into college.

That goal became my anchor, the thing that began to heal me, though not entirely. I had gotten too good at forgetting. Forgetting the chaos of late-night escapes, the blurred lines between reality and the fantasies I crafted, and the weight of everything I'd buried deep inside. College was the light at the end of the tunnel, a tangible goal that kept me moving forward, but the scars still lingered beneath the

surface, hidden by the distractions I
carefully curated. During that time, I even believed I had healed my mind. I was off Prozac, and I was certain I was better for it. I hated Prozac—it stole my light, my energy, my thoughts. It dulled everything, and increased my appetite, until the only thing it left me with was this nagging feeling that I wasn't in control of my own body. My parents weren't big believers in mental health meds or therapists, either.
They always thought I could think my way out of anything.

So, by sophomore year, I stopped seeing the therapist I had been assigned to after
Westwood Lodge. I didn't tell anyone, but I was secretly relieved. Therapy felt like
admitting defeat, and that was one thing I couldn't afford to do—not when I was so close to proving that I could handle it all on my own. I threw myself into volunteer work and playing varsity hockey, desperate for some sense of structure. By senior year, I was working as a nurse's assistant at the Mount Auburn ER, dealing with lives unraveling in front of me, while mine felt stitched together only by sheer will.

UMass Amherst, the long-time dream, started to fade as other possibilities began to
surface. Clark University became my new fixation, where I could study psychology,
maybe even figure out what was wrong with me, or at least pretend to. I told myself, "If I get into Clark, that's where I'll go." There was something about pinning my hopes on a single outcome that felt clean—like a fairytale with its inevitable happy ending. But life has a way of adding cruel, ironic twists. I was waitlisted. Then, to top it off, I found out I wasn't even eligible for financial aid because of my immigration status. And just like that, the fragile shell I'd built around myself began to crack, the pressure seeping in from all sides. The sense of purpose that had kept me upright, wobbled, like a house of cards built in a windstorm. I kept playing my part, of course—pretending I still had everything under control—but it was then, in the quiet moments, that I could hear the whisper of the lie I was living. And I was getting tired of pretending.
Acceptance letters poured in, like confetti after a battle that didn't feel like a victory. Waitlisted at two places, accepted everywhere else. I had won a writing scholarship, something that should have filled me with pride, but it barely made a dent in the

mountain of tuition that loomed ahead.

The sum was laughable, a reminder that even the things I was good at weren't enough.

I graduated in the top tenth percentile of my class with a 4.0 GPA, and yet all I could see were the cracks in my so-called achievements. I bombed the SATs, though I managed to

score in the 90th percentile on the ACTs, but none of it felt like success. I didn't see my accomplishments—I only saw my failures. And the greatest failure of all was that I had no way to pay for college.

There was still hope, the faintest glimmer, that my parents could find a co-borrower for a private educational loan. But deep down, I knew. I knew I wasn't going to college in the fall like everyone else. Like I had planned. Like I had spent years believing I would. The truth crept in quietly, wrapping around my heart until it squeezed, and all I could think was, I failed.

I was seventeen, brushing the edge of eighteen, with a Presidential Award in hand like some distant token from another life. The future sprawled ahead of me, a yawning void, its possibilities both shimmering and dissolving at the same time. College in the fall felt like a fragile dream, one I wasn't sure I'd wake up to. All the acceptance letters—pages whispering promises I couldn't hear—ended up crumpled and forgotten, except for one: UMass Amherst. That was the only one that mattered, because it was still tied to Stacy, to the delicate thread of our plan, woven from half-formed dreams of late-night talks and shared futures. It was the thing I clung to, even as Vincent drifted, ghostlike, between Boston and LA. I kept pretending he was Big and I was Carrie, that we were part of some story not written for us, something much grander, more elusive, than this.

After the graduation ceremony, my mother insisted we celebrate at Not Your Average Joe's. My brother and sister, both five, were a world apart from us, speaking in the

language only they understood, lost in a universe they had created together. My mother tried, her voice soft but too bright, trying to pierce through the haze I was wrapped in. Her eyes searched mine for connection, but I sat there, untouchable, as though already fading. The food was tasteless, the conversation muted. I watched it all like a distant observer, floating above the scene, slipping away before anyone even realized I was gone.

Later, I slipped away for real, to a friend's house where we pulled on frayed jeans and borrowed courage, ready for the bonfire at Filippello Park. The faces around the fire flickered in the dark, familiar and strange all at once, like figures from a half-forgotten dream. JP was there too, his edges soft and blurred, older and worn in a way that made him feel dangerous. He was broken, addicted, unraveling—and I saw something in him I thought I could fix. Or maybe it was just the allure of ruin. Stacy always said, "You need a plan B, maybe even a plan C." And I wondered if JP was part of that unspoken backup plan, standing there in the smoke with his half-lidded eyes and a cigarette dangling from his fingers, a question mark in human form.

It's funny how those hidden things, that you don't even talk about fester on the inside. Growing bigger and bigger, until you are right there living with your demons.

Chapter 15
College Limbo

As summer slipped away, I found myself navigating the blurry lines of my reality, a
reality that felt both suffocating and oddly comforting. The prospect of not going to
college gnawed at me like a relentless itch. It became my torment, another layer of my failure. I threw myself into distraction that allowed me to drown out the harsher truths of my life. I threw myself into parties, into fleeting moments of laughter and numbness, where the music pulsed louder than my insecurities. Vincent and JP became fixtures
in this chaotic tapestry, their presence both a balm and a source of confusion. Vincent was
intoxicating, his laughter ringing like a bell in the cacophony of the crowd, he was
Richard Gere and I was pretty woman, but it was fleeting.
When he wasn't around, JP filled the void—his charm a temporary distraction from my spiraling thoughts. The nights blurred together, each one an escape from the demons that lurked in the corners of my mind, whispering their insidious lies. I hated that I needed to be surrounded by people, but solitude was a terrifying abyss I feared more than anything. In those quiet moments, the shadows of self-loathing deepened.
I couldn't shake the belief that my parents' disappointment in me

was a reflection of my worth, a constant reminder that I was the flaw in our carefully constructed family image. With every cutting remark my father made, every silence that stretched between us, I felt the weight of his expectations crushing me. I didn't want to hurt myself, but the small pain became an anchor, a reminder that I was still alive, still fighting against the
numbness that threatened to consume me.

The end of August arrived like a thief in the night, stealing away the last vestiges of
summer. My parents finally found a co-borrower for my college loans, but it was too late for me to enroll.

Everyone else packed their bags and left for campus, their excitement a cruel reminder of my stagnation. I watched them go, a hollow pit forming in my stomach as I realized I would be left behind, a ghost haunting my own life. With the days stretching out before me like an empty canvas, I found solace in weaving a narrative about Vincent and me—a story of destined lovers, intertwined fates that existed only in my mind. I fantasized about us meeting in the twilight, our souls connected, the world fading away around us. It was a beautiful distraction, a way to escape the pain of reality, but it was also a prison of its own kind, a place where I was trapped in longing and unrequited love. As I lay in bed, staring at the ceiling, I wondered if anyone could see the fractures within me.

I earned for and craved my parents attention, but they were preoccupied with their own

lives, raising the twins and their own disappointments. I was just a shadow in their home, and that thought alone made the weight of loneliness unbearable. Would I always be stuck in this limbo, oscillating between the high of fleeting moments and the crushing lows that followed? I wanted to believe that this was just a chapter in my life, not the whole story. But as summer faded, it felt more like an ending than a beginning.

The cool air came in, but I didn't even notice. I didn't see the leaves change color, their vibrant reds and yellows blending into the background of my mind. My focus narrowed, fixated on every chance I had to jump on the bus and escape to Amherst. That's where I found my solace—in Stacy's dorm room, with its walls

plastered with photos of friends, memories, and the promise of youth. I reveled in the freedom it offered, even if only temporarily. Stacy was a whirlwind of energy, her laughter infectious and her spirit
undimmed by the weight of reality. She welcomed me with open arms, pulling me into her world filled with late-night party sessions and spontaneous adventures. I thrived in the chaos of her life, where deadlines and exams melted away in the face of reckless joy.

Chapter 16
Falling into Winter

Frat parties became my refuge, each one a riot of color and sound, a stark contrast to the
drabness of my home. I hated the ride home back on the bus, the way the world outside blurred into an indistinct smear of colors. The anticipation of returning home felt like returning to prison, where I stayed hidden in my room. My father and I lived in the same house, but I made certain our paths would rarely cross. Each return felt like a defeat, a retreat into a life I didn't want to face. I held onto the promise that I would be enrolled for the spring semester. After all, winter break was around the corner, Stacy would be back from college, bringing with her the comfort of her home and soon I would find my
footing. Or at least, I hoped.
Winter had settled in, and with it, my quiet escape. Days and nights blended into one long, cold blur at Stacy's house, where weeks slipped by unnoticed. On the nights when we were too tired—or maybe just too indifferent—to go out, we'd stay in, curling up on her worn velvet couch, watching Gentlemen Prefer Blondes for the hundredth time. I always wondered what it was about Marilyn, that sparkle she had, something I lacked. Vincent had left at the beginning of December, running off to L.A. with his big ideas and bigger ambitions. I kept telling myself he was my Mr. Big—someone to hold onto in a world where everyone else felt like a passing face—but deep down, I knew I was just another stop on his way to something more glamorous.

The men I met after were like a revolving door—faces, names, stories, all blending into one another, none sticking around longer than three weeks. Except for Vincent. He always came back, until he didn't.

Chapter 17
Holden Everlasting

I used to watch Stacy sometimes, not with envy, but with a strange curiosity. She had boys, men even, wrapped around her finger, as if by some quiet spell they didn't even know had been cast.
They chased her, bent to her whims, and I marveled at it. Meanwhile, I always felt like I was doing the chasing—waiting by the phone, checking my reflection in store windows, trying to capture that glint in my eye that others seemed to spot in her so effortlessly. It was funny, really.
The chase. The endless, futile chase. It became my uncomfortable comfort, where I wore my anxiety as a shield of armor.

The bar was laid back, with graffiti on the walls and a kind of casual neglect that suited it.
Crowds drifted in and out, disappearing as quickly as they came, like the place wasn't meant for staying. By the time "Tiny Dancer" played, the Back Bay bar had emptied. It was just us, the music, and the quiet that crept in between the notes. I'd heard the song before, but tonight, it felt different—like I was hearing it for the first time. I wanted it to play again, to hold onto the lyrics just a little longer, drawn to the way they seemed to linger in the air.
I watched them—Stacy and Ted. Watching them was easier than thinking. She was wrapped up in him, but not in the way people usually mean. No, she had him wrapped up in her. You could see it in the way she held his gaze, the way she moved, knowing exactly how he was watching her. Ted, with all his rough edges and bad decisions, was already in her orbit, like it was inevitable.

Everyone else looked at him and saw trouble, but Stacy? She saw the trouble, and that
was the point. She knew what he was, and she wanted more of it. The bad boy charm was
irresistible, not because it was dangerous, but because she knew she could pull the strings. And Ted, well, he was already halfway tied up.
I wish I could have had that—her clarity, her control. I wasn't built like that. Maybe that's why I found myself sitting next to Holden, Ted's brother, who was just about as opposite of Stacy as you could

get. Holden sat there, looking like he might collapse at any moment, his head bobbing as if he wasn't sure which direction the world was spinning.

Occasionally, he'd open his eyes, blink once or twice like he was surprised to still be here, then drift back into whatever place he was in. If there was something going on in his mind, I couldn't tell. He looked like the kind of guy whose thoughts moved at half speed, and maybe they did. Stacy had leaned over earlier in the night, right after her first drink, and said, "You should give Holden a chance. He's cute. Looks just like Justin Timberlake." I didn't say anything then. I just let the words settle in, like dust. I didn't see it—not Holden, not Justin Timberlake. Holden didn't look like anything, really.

But once Stacy said it, the thought stuck. And that's the thing about thoughts—they get in there and they start turning over and over, even when you don't want them to.

As "Tiny Dancer" bled into "Closing Time," the night started to shrink in on itself. Stacy had her head on Ted's chest, her fingers running circles on his back, and you could see it—how he was already sinking, losing himself in her. She wasn't lost though. Not Stacy. She knew exactly what she was doing. I glanced over at Holden. His head was still slumped forward, but his eyes were open now, barely. He caught me looking at him, and for a moment, there was something there.

Not much, but something. Like a flicker of light, faint but real. It was gone as quickly as it came. I looked away. I wasn't ready for what that might mean. Not yet.

The following weekend, the brothers suggested we go ice skating. It seemed like an innocent enough idea, but I knew better. It wasn't just a suggestion—it was part of another one of Stacy's plans. She was always pulling me into situations, expecting me to play along with whatever she'd decided was fun. And, of course, it wasn't just about skating. It was a double date—an excuse for her to spend more time with Ted, while Holden and I were stuck in the periphery.

As for me? I loved to skate. It wasn't just the motion—it was the freedom. The way the cold air bit at your skin as you glided across the ice, the effortless rhythm of your body pushing forward. There was a stillness that came with it—a brief moment where

everything in the world felt like it paused, and I could just breathe. In those few minutes, I could escape
everything else. So, despite knowing I was being dragged into something that wasn't my idea of fun, I was willing to try. I couldn't resist the pull of the ice, not even for a
moment. I just had to skate.

But I knew what was really happening. This was just another of Stacy's attempts to pair me with Holden. I couldn't quite figure out why. Holden wasn't rude, but he might as well have been—silent and withdrawn, as though there was a distance between him and the rest of the world. And his silence made everything feel… distant. A glass wall
between us—clear enough to see through, but solid enough to keep me from reaching him.

"Stacy, I'm not going to like him," I said, quieter than I probably should have. "It doesn't matter how hard you try. He barely talks." She shot me that look—her eyes narrowing, that almost challenging glint in them. "You're too quick to judge," she replied, voice light but insistent. "You just have to see it. He's cute in his own way." I didn't get it.
How could she say that with such certainty when Holden barely spoke? But I didn't argue. I slipped on my gloves and rolled my eyes in silence. "Fine," I muttered, and then pushed off onto the rink. The rink was quieter now, the hum of voices having faded as people left for the evening. The only sounds were the steady scrape of blades cutting through ice and the cold air that filled my lungs. It was my element. For just a moment, it felt like the world had slowed down, and I could breathe again.
Then, I caught sight of him—Holden, already on the rink, moving with an effortless grace. It was like he was made for this, for the ice, for the flow of it. His lean figure seemed to glide across the surface, his blond curls bouncing with each smooth shift of his body. He moved like a dream—fluid, unburdened, as if nothing could touch him. And in that moment, I saw him differently. He reminded me of the Little Prince, that figure I'd read about years ago—someone who seemed to float through life, unaffected by the weight of it all. Holden was like that.
There was something about the way he moved that made him seem untethered, like he was gliding through everything, untouched by time. I skated toward him, drawn without thinking.
And when our eyes met, something in them shifted. There was a

glimmer there now, something I hadn't seen before.
It was as if the ice had cracked open just enough for me to see the person beneath all the quiet. He was alive with energy I hadn't noticed until now. "Not bad, huh?" His voice was light, with a touch of something playful. I blinked, a little taken aback.
"You—talked."
He laughed, the sound low and rich, the kind of laugh that made you want to hear it again. "Is that a problem?" His grin was teasing, almost mischievous now.
"I think you've been hanging around too many quiet types." The smile that tugged at my lips was involuntary.
"Maybe I'm just used to people not talking much." Holden's grin widened, and for a
moment, I saw something else in him—something deeper, more alive than I'd expected.
"Well, I'm not like the rest."

That was the understatement of the night. He wasn't like anyone I had ever met, in a way he reminded me of Jeremy. His voice was warm, but there was also a sharpness in the way he spoke, a little recklessness, like he wasn't sure when he'd let himself speak but was glad to have it come out. And it wasn't just that. There was something about the way his words came—almost poetic, like he was saying just enough to make you wonder what

he was really thinking. As he spoke, the laughter in his eyes began to fade, replaced by something quieter, something heavier.
There was a vulnerability there, a crack in the facade that hadn't been there before. And I saw it. It wasn't just the carefree, joking Holden I had just discovered. There was a
brokenness in him too—a spirit, bruised and stitched together, waiting for someone to care enough to notice. And I did notice. I saw it, clear as day, and the impulse to help him, to heal that brokenness, swept over me like a tide. It wasn't out of pity. It wasn't because I thought I could fix him. It was because, for the first time, I understood that he needed someone—someone to see him. I didn't know how,
but I knew I wanted to try.

That winter, the four of us became something almost dangerous, caught in a rhythm we couldn't quite control. Ted and Holden's apartment on St. Germaine Street was our
sanctuary, a place too small for the things we tried to hold inside it,

but big enough to house our need to keep pretending we were free. It had the kind of space you could fill with laughter and the kind of silence you could fill with loneliness. The hum of the city outside, felt like part of the pulse we couldn't escape. Everything was lived in, every
corner a reflection of the time we were spending, and I was starting to think that maybe this—this mess—was what we had. The apartment was warm, thick with the smell of stale beer, a burnt-out cigarette, and something else—music.
Constant music. It wasn't just the beats and melodies coming through the speakers; it was the music of the life we were building. The chaos of Berklee students practicing their instruments, the scattered notes of their ambition drifting through the walls, felt like it belonged to us too. In a way, we were all practicing for something we couldn't name yet, letting the rhythm of the city spill through our fingertips like a song no one was listening to. I could feel it each time Stacy and I sank into the couch, the hours passing like they were nothing. We'd sit there, sometimes without saying a word. It wasn't a silence, really, but something deeper—an understanding we never needed to define. I could see how she was slipping through the cracks of this place, moving so easily between moments, yet I wasn't sure I understood it. When we'd leave for her parents' house, it always felt like a break, but the tension never really went away. There was an undercurrent between us, something I wasn't ready to address. It was like the apartment was a mirror, reflecting back what I didn't want to see. And still, I stayed. I was starting to understand our
dynamic, though it wasn't the kind of thing I could explain. I wanted to hold onto it, to freeze it in time, because that felt safer than facing what was coming next. It felt too
fragile, and that fragility clung to me, even when I wasn't thinking about it.

School was coming. I couldn't stop it. It should have been the dream I had been waiting for. I was supposed to go, get my life in order, move on to something else. Yet, I felt

unprepared, as though I were slipping backward, holding onto a moment that was
disappearing with every tick of the clock. I wasn't ready to leave. I couldn't imagine walking away from Holden, from Ted, from this mess that had become my world. We were the group that lingered outside the Pour House, reluctant to part with the night,

our laughter spilling into the cold Boston air. Cheap beer in our hands—Michelob Ultra Light, the drink I pretended to like when nothing else tasted right, but the need to take off the edge was a persistent piercing knife. We were always there, never quite ready to go home. The longer we stayed, the more the world outside felt like a place we
didn't belong.
On some nights, when we'd get bored of alcohol, we found ourselves reaching for
something else. Coke, the kind of high that didn't just make everything feel louder, but sharper, more defined. And Holden… Holden was always different. He would disappear, fading out, almost like he had forgotten how to stay awake. I would ask Stacy to ask Ted why Holden always seemed to vanish in the middle of everything. The answer was the same every time:
"Hard labor does that to you. Makes you tired."
It wasn't that simple. I could see the weight in his eyes, the way he pulled back when the noise became too much. There was a quiet desperation in him, like he was trying to
outrun something—something more than the fatigue. I wanted to fix it, heal whatever was broken in him. It felt like the most important thing I could do.
Then school came. Too quickly. I wasn't ready. Not for the life I had been promised. Not for the future I had imagined. It was supposed to feel like freedom, but it felt more like a cage. Every step toward it felt like a mistake. My heart wasn't in it. I had spent so many years dreaming about this moment, believing it would change everything. And yet, it felt like it was changing me in ways I couldn't understand. It didn't feel like the life I had been waiting for. It felt like the end of something—an ending I wasn't ready to face. I had started to wonder if I was running from something that had already slipped away, or if I was trying to hold onto something that was always destined to break.

We became the group who lingered outside the Pour House till the last moment, holding onto the night, holding onto something that didn't exist outside of our small bubble. Holden, with his quiet charm, with his cracked smiles, his faded eyes that always seemed like they were trying to figure something out, was always just out of reach. He was an enigma, one that pulled me closer every time I thought I understood him. I didn't want to leave. I didn't want any of this to end.
And yet, I could already feel it slipping away—each laugh, each

careless moment, fading faster than I could catch it. I wanted to stay, to hold on to this thing that felt both
impossible and perfect. It felt right, even in its mess, even in its brokenness. And yet, I was already starting to lose it.

Chapter 19
College

That year after high school graduation blurs in my mind, like a twenty-minute film where the images flicker and fade before you can fully make sense of them. There are moments of clarity, but they feel distant, like they belong to someone else, someone on the other side of the screen.
What I do remember, though, is Holden. Even when I was supposed to be starting fresh in
college, my thoughts circled around him like moths around a flame. It didn't matter how far away I was, or how many days passed in silence; I found any chance I could to jump on the bus and escape from Amherst to Boston, just to be near him. It's strange now,
realizing how hard I chased him when he barely noticed, when he never seemed to care. But back then, I couldn't see that. I just knew I needed him. I tried to separate myself from Holden, to forget him while I was at school. I went to frat parties, met boys who seemed promising at first, but it never lasted.
Some faded into one-night stands, others might linger for three weeks before
 disintegrating into nothing. It was a vicious cycle, a way to fill the void while all I really craved was stability, to be loved in a way that made me feel secure. I could love others, in my own way. But I couldn't love myself. Looking back, I'm embarrassed by my own desperation, like an addict chasing a high that never lasts. I suppose, in a way, that's what he was to me—a rush, something dangerous I couldn't control but craved all the same. Stacy saw it first. She always saw things I couldn't—or wouldn't. I remember the day she pulled me aside, her face tight with concern, her hands trembling just a bit as she gripped my arm.
"I can't keep this from you anymore," she said, her voice low like she was sharing a dark secret.
"You need to know… Holden is a heroin addict. That's why he's always nodding off, why he disappears for days. You have to let him go."
Those words, like ice, crawled down my spine, my body locking

up. I didn't know what to say. Part of me wanted to be outraged, to defend him, but another part of me—some quiet voice I tried to ignore—had suspected it all along. The signs were there, but I didn't want to see them. I didn't want to believe that the person I was so wrapped up in could be wrapped up in something else. Still, I didn't leave. Even after knowing, I couldn't pull away. Instead, it was Holden who kept pulling back, retreating into some unreachable place, while I kept chasing him into the shadows.

Chapter 20
It Happened... Again

This particular night—this one—sticks with me as if it happened yesterday. A memory, as sharp as glass, lodged somewhere in my chest. Stacy had met a boy, though she had Ted, of course, always waiting in Boston, always under her thumb, but she always had a backup plan. A Plan B. A Plan C. She was always three steps ahead. This boy in Amherst, though, was fresh—barely two weeks in the making. He invited her to a party in his apartment by frat row. He had a friend for me, a double date of sorts. We dressed, as we always did—high heels, short skirts, bare legs—and tube tops that seemed ridiculous against the March chill in Amherst. The cold air cut through my skin, but it didn't matter. Spring break was on the horizon.

The season was about to shift, just like everything else in my life. The party, like all
parties, died out by three a.m. Stacy disappeared into the bedroom with the boy who had her attention for the moment. I was left with his friend, the one who'd shown an interest in me. I told him, without hesitation, that I wasn't interested, that I had someone in Boston. I didn't feel anything for this boy. Not desire, not connection, not even pity. He was a stranger, a blur of faces and gestures that didn't belong in my life. But that didn't stop him. "I just want to leave," I told him. "I'm tired, and Stacy will be out soon."
"She won't be," he said, voice thick with some intention I couldn't place. "They're doing it."
How did it happen? I don't know. One second, he was talking to

me, the next, he was on top of me, pinning me down. I said no, but my body went limp, as though it were a rag doll, discarded and lifeless. I couldn't move. I couldn't scream. I was caught between the horror and a kind of watching numbness, like I had left my own skin. I could see it all—his body on mine—but I wasn't really there. My consciousness hovered above, an observer from the ceiling, looking down on the wreckage below. I could feel him inside me, but it was as if it was happening to someone else. My body, frozen in terror, became a vessel of time that had ceased to exist. There was no space, no sound, no reality, only the dark buzz in my head, a clock spinning, spinning, spinning out of control. It didn't last long. When it was over, I dressed in a daze, like I had no claim on my own body
anymore, like I was an alien in my own skin. I moved to the corner of the couch and curled into myself, waiting for Stacy to emerge, as if her presence could somehow
undo what had just happened. It wasn't until 5 a.m. that she finally came out. She didn't look at me, didn't ask how I was, didn't notice the emptiness that had swallowed me whole. We left, and I stumbled into the cold night air, the fog of sleep-deprivation settling heavy in my bones.

I couldn't hold it in anymore. I broke down right there on the street curb, tears burning as they fell. I cried for what I didn't have words for. I cried for the thing that I had let
happen, for the silence inside me that had somehow allowed it. And then she asked, as if it were a simple question, a matter of legal fact: "Did you say no?" I nodded through the sobs, my throat raw. "Yes," I whispered. "I froze. I couldn't fight him off." She didn't flinch. Her gaze was calculating, detached. "Then it doesn't count," she said, with the cold, logical finality that only someone like her could deliver. "Best to forget it. It was just a bad one-night stand." It was like I had never existed in her world at all. As if what had happened to me was merely a mistake of circumstance, a transient misstep in the
tangled web of our lives. Her words hung in the air, and I felt them lodge deep inside me, each syllable a weight in my chest. Forget it. Just forget. But I couldn't. I couldn't forget the numbness. The heaviness that had settled deep in my bones, in the marrow, in
the soft tissue of my soul. It was like an anchor, a weight that would never lift.
The darkness was different this time. It was not just the quiet ache

of loneliness, but something deeper, something sinister. I wanted to crawl into that darkness, hide away somewhere, perhaps on St. Germaine St. with Holden, even if he didn't want me. I
wanted to feel something real, something that could at least make me believe I existed in the world, even if that belief came from a boy who could never love me back.

 But that, too, was a dream. A fantasy. A world where I wasn't frozen, a world where I wasn't invisible. After that incident, I began to crumble, piece by piece. Staying
focused in class became a battle I couldn't win. The darkness didn't leave me; it followed me everywhere, creeping into every thought, every word, every interaction. To fight it off, I turned to anything I could find. Alcohol, ephedrine, Stacker 2 diet pills, and Adderall became my fuel. I had always loved Adderall.

I first discovered it with Jeremy, who had been diagnosed with ADHD. He was always the one making those ridiculous dirt bike noises, something I barely noticed at first but later found endearing. He said the Adderall capped his creativity, and he hated taking it, but he would give me the pills he didn't take. The focus they gave me in high school was unforgettable. For the first time, I didn't feel lost, floating away. I felt sharp, present, like the world was finally within my grasp. I'd sometimes ask my friend, the one diagnosed with ADHD, for some Adderall. Other times, I'd steal it from her—an invisible theft, as if it didn't matter. She never noticed—or so I thought.

Adderall became the lifeline I didn't want, but needed, the only thing that could silence the static in my head long enough for me to focus. I could write a thesis paper in a
matter of hours, my fingers moving faster than my thoughts, as if the pills were pulling the words from me, one by one, and stitching them together. In those fleeting moments,

the darkness receded, and I felt something like control. I wasn't floating away anymore.
But at what cost? I passed my courses, barely—Cs across the board. A success, in the world's terms. Mediocrity rewarded or perhaps just tolerated. But in my mind, I had failed. I had failed my father. I had failed to be what he wanted, what he thought I could be—something more than this hollow version of myself, an empty shell of a daughter. No matter the grades, no matter the pills that kept me upright, I couldn't escape the relentless feeling that I

wasn't enough. That I would never be enough. And that hurt more than I could ever say. Summer break came, and I have no memory of what that excitement felt

like. Holden and Ted helped us move out of our dorm room. I wanted to leave. I could go home that summer, but I refused. So Stacy and I combined all our belongings together, bundled them into chaos, and placed them in Sammy's garage for the season. How I wished I'd called my mother to come get me. To

escape the tangled web of shame and guilt. To find a breath of air, a space to heal. But I stayed. I buried myself in this black, unyielding pit. My time on St. Germaine, like a sticky, suffocating presence, began to rot the core of me. I was too stubborn, too determined, too terrified of letting go. Stacy and I planned to live together that summer, no matter the cost.

Couch-surfers in a city of lost chances. I was determined to live with Holden, whose descent into his own addiction was like the slow grinding of stone. He no longer saw me, was no longer present in the way he once had been, and I thought, in my madness, that I needed to know what that felt like. To lose him entirely, to cling to the dying thread of something that wasn't really

mine to hold. I thought I could still fix him, somehow. But I was wrong. It wasn't something I could touch or fix, and he didn't want me to. The gulf between us stretched and fractured.

Toward the end of it all, Holden and I became something else—something strange,

something I couldn't grasp fully.

We became friends. He was my best friend that summer, the only one who stayed constant in the storm, the only one who seemed to understand the weight of my world in a way no one else could. But with his leaving, I knew it was time to let go. I knew that my time on St. Germaine was up. I should have known better. I should have seen it for what it was: the inevitable un-raveling of everything I thought I could control. But you can never know things like that in advance. Not really. Not until the world has already come undone.

Chapter 21
Summer Chaos

Stacy's relationship with Ted was crumbling, as inevitable as the fall of stars. Her own emptiness was becoming palpable, and as it began to fall apart, cracks in our friendship appeared. I clung to Holden like a drowning woman clutching at driftwood. Stacy saw the shift. She felt me pulling away. I wasn't hers to push around

anymore. I had crossed a threshold into some other place. Somewhere else entirely. The longer I lived with Holden, Ted, and their sister, the more I dabbled with painkillers, those cold, quiet things that calmed my nerves far more effectively than alcohol ever had. They gave me the
confidence I had never known before. It was a regular Friday night. We were drinking, the apartment a carousel of faces. People coming in and out, a blur of smoke and half-empty bottles. I invited Stacy over, but she didn't want to see Ted. She wanted me to go out with her, but I didn't want to. I had found a new friend, a new release in getting high. Later, Stacy called me. She said she was with Vincent. She said she would sleep with him if I didn't come out with them.
She was playing a game, but it was a game I couldn't seem to grasp. B was there too. How did he appear? Why was he here? I don't know, but I knew then that there was a game being played—one that I had already lost in my haze.
B was a constant figure, obsessively driven by his infatuation with Stacy. The more she ran from him, the more he ran to her. But she would always
pull him in, offer him fleeting hope, just enough to keep him tethered to her. I never understood why Stacy would say she would sleep with Vincent. It didn't make sense. She never made sense. A few hours later, Stacy appeared at the door, her voice raw, her anger slicing through the space
between us. She was yelling at me, threatening me. I wonder now if that was a show, a performance for B, the two of them in some kind of twisted theater. I missed it all in my drug-induced haze. But I was thrown smack dab in the middle of it. "We're not friends any-more. It's over," she said, her words sharp as broken glass. I was left, crumpled on the floor, crying. Stacy had gone, but a new battle began. A screaming match erupted between Stacy and Holden's sister, their voices rising like dark, angry clouds. The escalation from bad to worse that night came swiftly, relentlessly. After Stacy left, and a few lines of coke and heroin, Holden's sister decided to take matters into her own hands, exacting revenge. Holden and Ted were on board. I begged them
not to do anything extreme. I don't know why I went with them. Was it to stop something worse from happening? Or was I just a willing accomplice in the chaos, drawn to the wreckage? We ended up parked, just down the hill from her parents' house. I stayed in the car while the three of them ran out, all of them acting like

they were gods of destruction. They found
a cinder block and decided to throw it through the bay window of Stacy's parents' house. In that moment, everything shifted. Stacy and I were no longer friends; we were enemies. That was the moment, the moment ev-erything was broken beyond repair. It felt almost like I had sent that mes-
sage to her myself, to her parents, who had become like second parents to
me. I could never face them again. Shortly after, a police detective arrived. He told me he knew it was me. He said Mr. Benton saw me. I knew this was a lie. No one could have seen me. I hadn't done it. I felt a strange, guilty relief. But then they spoke to Holden's sister. And Holden's sister… I owed it to her to take the fall. Nothing would happen to me, but Ted and Holden would go to prison. I took the fall for them, paid the price in silence. Later, I paid two thousand dollars to fix the bay window. I was
left with shattered glass and I was alone. Alone in my choices, in the ruins of the things I had once cared about.
I fell into a friendship with Holden's sister, and she taught me how to snort heroin and strip. I was already covered in shame. It was like drowning in darkness—swimming in it as though it were the only thing that could hold me. Those moments, naked on the pole, are some of the most shameful of my life. I felt no pride being naked on stage, no thrill.
Only humiliation. The only way I could do it was through heroin but I justified my addiction as, not being an addiction as I never dared to shoot it up, I told myself that was for heroin addicts, I wasn't a heroin addict I needed it to function and that's why I only snorted it.
By then, I had already seen my primary care physician, who had me on benzodiazepine for anxiety. Mixing them with heroin took the edge off. It dulled everything, allowing me to become someone else entirely.
Someone unrecognizable.
As, the St. Germaine apartment began to crumble; the cracks were beginning to show their visibility when Holden left for Pennsylvania to heal, his heroin addiction spiraling beyond control.
Ted went back to prison for breaking parole and the time had come for him to serve his sentence. Their sister, a shadow of who she once was, succumbed to all her own addictions.
It was during all the chaotic circumstances of life on St. Germaine that led me to continue on to play the game.

The Game

I was young when I began to play the game of pain.
Abandonment was its name.

He never hurt me with his hands.

I felt no pain

No broken bones, no bruises to show off my affliction, no spilled blood upon the counter.
Although my voice was lost, drowning slowly in the murky salty water.

My mind always masquerading
Tip toeing around the broken shells,
Of shattered glass upon the floor,
One wrong move,
One wrong step,
One wrong breath,

Would be a mistake made, giving reign to torment I couldn't endure.
Spiraling me into a darkness, upon which death was the only welcome door.

No he never hurt me with his hands,
A slap here or there

But I deserved it, screeching out of tune.

Who was I to yell
To raise my voice,
To think, to speak so out of turn.
After all, it was me who gave up control,
Gave him reign of power over me.
No, this wasn't pain it was just a game,
I had to, hold my breath before breathing,
To look not stare, to not disturb,
To speak when spoken to
To Always do as I was told.
A good girl I had to be,
A good wife, I was meant to make,
Hiding wounds, and tears of pain,

Hiding scars
Staying silent
Wearing heels, dying my hair,

Wearing layers of foundation, to cover up the scars that never seemed to heal,
Doubling up on mascara, layering up the lipstick, smoothing over imperfections, pulling on

the final mask of joy.

Turning myself completely into someone else,
That was never me. To appease anyone who would take notice,
Becoming an empty shell and not a person.
All the while my soul was stuck out at sea,
Screaming out for someone to please come rescue me.

NO, he never hurt me….
No sticks were thrown to break my bones,
Just words were always stinging slowly,
Seeping into me, making me believe them to be real.
Turning them into the the only words
My mind could hear or understand.
I felt it all but I felt nothing,
I blocked it all, locking up the door.

I threw away the key, keeping my soul out at sea, with parts of me screaming out for someone

to please come rescue me.
But no one ever came, my screams were silent
Never heard by anyone locked away inside my mind's abyss.

No, he never hurt me
But my soul did drawn,
becoming the mist of sea.
As words don't heal, like broken bones,
Never forgotten nor released,

No he never hurt me, my voice was just no longer there, as I became the foam of sea.

©Diana Kouprina

Book III

Chapter 1
Wasting Away

I once did dread the rain— Fearful to step outside,
The hours spent straightening my hair,
An iron and a towel in hand,
Only for it to swell at the first raindrop's fall.
Makeup so carefully applied would melt,
Mascara streaming down like blackened tears,
Revealing scars and marks beneath the guise.
The rain, exposing me as naught but a fraud,
A painted fool, perfection drowned within the storm.
Yet secretly, I did cherish the raindrops fall—
The me who cared not for straightened locks,
Nor for the marks, the scars, the flaws,
The me who danced with reckless mirth in summer's storms,
Breathing deep the scent of rain on heated stone,
Barefoot, wild within the heavens' cleansing flow.
But I lost that self; she was not fair then.
I turned her into something tame,
Something expected,
Something dead.

I Feel the pain of others— never feeling pain in me.

Pain.

Love.

Push away.

Screaming out: love me.

This and that.

Take the white.

Take the brown.

Mix it up, melt it down, shoot it up.

Spirals spinning— up and down.

The in-between screaming out in silence:

I love, I love— just love me back.

This, that, and the other.

Costumes, dressed up— diamonds, made up.

Naked, exposed, floating— hurt me, just love me.

Love me please,

Here on the floor,

Wasting away

Mix it up, snort it,

Shoot it up.

Pack the pipe,

Take a hit,

Of crystal sizzling

Burning air,

Inhale it all,

In the end

It doesn't matter,

Loneliness is pain.

Palatable— inside out.

Leave, but don't leave.

Take it all— take the bits, take the pieces.

Take it all.

But don't leave.

Loneliness is pain— it's palatable.

Cling on, hang on.

Take it all— everything I've got.

Own it, control it, torture it.

Only a body— useless,

selfish,

fat,

ugly,

slow,

unfeeling.

But loneliness is pain— that's felt. It hurts.

Make it stop.

Take it all— take everything I've got.

Just don't leave me.

Loneliness is palatable.

Don't leave me— it's all I ask.

Flesh, skin and bone.

Mind screaming in silence.

Hurt me, but don't leave me.

I wasted away in this, that, and the other.

The sting of Stacy's betrayal and abandonment lingered longer than I expected, seeping into the cracks I hadn't yet filled with something—anything—to hold me together. After her, I stopped letting anyone in, especially women. Trust had become a frayed rope, unraveling in my hands and I built my walls thicker and higher, but Holden kept finding ways to slip through. He didn't break down the walls; he simply waited on the other side, his presence becoming the only thing that felt steady in the chaos.

Holden never asked about my nights at the club, but he didn't need to. He knew. He knew me at that point better than I knew myself. I wasn't a terrible stripper; I just needed a lot of drugs to get on that stage. I needed them to numb the dread, to make the music seep into my bones, to forget the fact that I was stripping. I wasn't a girl on a stage—I was a prima ballerina, twirling in the shadows of some forgotten theater, my audience a faceless blur. For a few hours, I was weightless, floating. And then it was over. On camera, it looked like I had left with a client, and I guess, in a way, I did. But he wasn't just another man in the crowd. He was a musician on tour, a bad boy who wore his demons like an armor I somehow thought I could pierce. Maybe that's what drew me in—his familiar darkness. He didn't see me as just an act; he saw past the glitter and the performance, and for a moment, I thought I could let him in. For three nights at the Park Plaza, I allowed myself to imagine a different life. We had dinner on Newbury Street, talked about nothing and everything, and I thought, maybe he's my way out, my escape from this cycle. B

ut men like him never stay. He left, and with him went the last traces of my hope. The club fired me when they found out, and that should have devastated me, but by then, I was already numb. The pieces of myself I had given away were never meant to be returned. I wonder now why I didn't just go home to my parents, who lived only six miles away. Six miles. I could have been in my mother's arms, her hands smoothing my hair, her voice telling me everything would be okay. But fear kept me frozen. I knew if I went home, they'd see right through me. My parents would know what I'd become, and their disappointment would crush me more than any stranger's judgment ever could. So, I stayed away. I stayed lost. But then, as if the universe decided I had endured enough, my work authorization came through. It was my chance to step out of the darkness, to stop pretending, if only for a little while.

I walked into Express at Copley, and a week later, I had a new title: Customer Service Associate. It wasn't glamorous, it wasn't freeing, but it was real. And for once, I didn't feel like I had to hide. Holden was proud of me. "You're getting out of that house," he said, though neither of us could fully believe it. We still spent nights together, both of us tethered to the highs and lows of our addictions, but there was a shift. Holden had stopped shooting up, though he replaced the needles with crack on the weekends. He made me promise I'd never shoot up, no matter how bad it got. And I promised, because I had nothing left but my word.

In those late nights, under the weight of our shared self-destruction, we talked. Really talked. The drugs peeled back layers, forced us to face truths we couldn't run from. He told me his stories, I told him mine, and for once, I felt understood. Not judged, not pitied—just heard. In the hollow spaces of those conversations, there was hope, even if just a flicker.

After the musician, I stopped searching for love, for escape. I let go of the fantasy that anyone could save me. The doors to Plan A and Plan B had closed, and I didn't care anymore. The only thing I could do was survive—hold on to the pieces of myself I hadn't yet lost and pray that maybe, just maybe, I wouldn't lose them too.

That July when I worked at Express, there was this strange little flicker of normalcy. Holden and I would rollerblade along the Charles, moving over the asphalt like we were both pretending to be in some kind of movie, with the river reflecting the sky's contradictions. It wasn't anything real, though. Just a fragment of something I wanted to believe in, some peace that never lasted.

Mona, Holden's sister, ran the apartment like she had it all figured out. She collected everyone's income like it was her right, then rationed out our drugs—the crack and the heroin—as though it were something to control, something to keep us all in check.

She told me I wasn't bringing in enough money. One night she hit me, but I couldn't even tell you why. Everything was a blur—just another thing that I couldn't explain. She left me sitting outside, in the cold, like I was some stray dog. Holden came out to comfort me, but it was more like he was trying to convince himself that he still cared. Maybe he did, I don't know.

By August, Holden had decided it was time to go. He needed to heal. He needed space, and for the first time in as long as I could remember, he wasn't using. It was like   watching someone wake up from a long, dark sleep—there was a quiet kind of clarity in him, and it hurt to see. The goodbye was bittersweet. I knew it had to happen, that he had to leave. But still, standing there, I held back from saying what I truly felt, the words my soul wanted to scream.

The love I had for him wasn't just love—it was something deeper. It was the kind of love you feel for a brother, a best friend, someone who's shared your silence and your pain, someone who could see the parts of you no one else could. And now he was leaving.

So, I was left with Mona. It was worse, somehow—darker than before. My job at Express couldn't keep up with the cost of what we were doing to ourselves. I'd take on stripping gigs here and there to make ends meet, trying to avoid the way Mona's eyes followed every penny. Every dime I earned went to her. I kept thinking maybe I'd hide a little, just for myself. I put away a thousand dollars once, tucked it into the back of a drawer like it was a secret. Mona found it, of course. She just took it. "You owe it to me," she said. And I let her take it. What else was there to do?

In mid-August, I made up my mind to do something different. I thought, maybe if I gave amateur night at a strip club on Route 1 a shot, I could make enough to get out, to breathe for a minute. I'd snorted enough heroin to convince myself I was a pro. It wasn't much of a leap, considering I'd worked at a real club before. Squire was a joke next to that place. But that's how it goes when you're running from yourself. You end up in the kind of place where nothing's real, nothing matters except the next fix. The trip there was a mess, though. I didn't drive. The MBTA, that cruel thread of convenience, led me only so far.

But I made my way, the world outside blurring as I navigated the streets, alone in a world that barely seemed to exist. It took an hour and a half—long enough for a thousand thoughts to rise and vanish in the fog. That's where I met Kelley. She was one of those professionals—the kind who make it look easy. She didn't need to say much. We shared a look, then a nod, then it was like we'd known each other forever. We bonded over the heroin, and I think we both saw in each other something we didn't have to explain.

After that, it was simple—find a group of guys, take them to the champagne room, and we walked away with 2K in our hands. It wasn't hard. It wasn't even surprising. It was just how things went. The night wore on, and by the time it was over, it was too late for me to catch the train back. Kelley said her fiancé, John, was picking her up, and he could drop me off. John's black Mustang, part of the GT series, pulled up, sleek and cold like something out of a dream.

We climbed in, and Kelley introduced us like we were all part of the same broken story.She told me that if I ever needed to pick up some dope, John was the guy to see. He could get the good stuff. I didn't even hesitate. I was still high off the night, riding the adrenaline from making all that money. I didn't even remember what I'd had to do to get it, but I didn't care. I didn't care about much anymore. I was ready for whatever they had to offer—anything to keep from thinking too much.

That night, I felt free with Kelley and John. It was one of those rare moments when the

weight of the world seemed to lift, even if just for a few hours. I felt like I had scored big. I wasn't going home to Mona empty-handed. I had everything I needed: the drugs, the adrenaline, the temporary relief from the constant cycle. And yes, of course, I wanted to pick up some primo dope; I could get enough for me and Mona. It would be the least I could do. I gave John 200 dollars, feeling the thrill of the exchange, the promise of more to come. We drove to a building complex. John parked the car and left. He was dressed head to toe in Adidas sweats, his shell-top sneakers gleaming even in the dim light, a Movado watch sparkling silver on his wrist. His baby blue eyes shimmered in the night, but his lips—those lips—were like a trap, beautiful and empty, too perfect for someone I wasn't supposed to want. But I wouldn't admit it. Not tonight. Not in my men-hating phase, the one that was like a fortress I built around myself. Nothing real, nothing lasting.

I wasn't against partying with them, though. If it led to a threesome, I'd take it. The one-night stand that burned hot and quick—nothing more. John returned to the car with our bags of goodies. Without a second thought, he suggested we take the party to his place. He could always drive me back in the morning, he said. If I was up for it.

It was as though he read my mind. I wanted to party. We drove to his house. The driveway wasn't even a mile long, but the distance seemed to stretch out like a lie, a winding path to something that wasn't quite real. We went upstairs through the back door, and John greeted his dog—a pitbull that had me frozen in place. I was terrified. I'd heard their bite was worse than their bark, and the way it looked at me, all muscle and raw hunger, only confirmed my fear.

We went into the bedroom. A California king-size waterbed dominated the space, black as pitch with mirrors on top. I thought, This guy must think he's a pimp. The thought hung in the air, sharp and clear, like the screech of nails on a chalkboard. The image of 50 Cent's "PIMP" flashed in my mind, an unsettling joke that made too much sense. The two of them went to the bathroom to shoot up. I told them, as I always did, that I didn't do needles. There was no shame, just a quiet refusal.

I stayed in the bedroom, my head buzzing with anticipation, my body already crying for what I knew was coming. I broke up a line of H from my purchased stash. It wasn't the first time, and it wouldn't be the last. I didn't hesitate. I snorted it fast, and it hit like a violent kiss—a jolt of relief that sliced through my brain, leaving a sick sweetness in its wake. Euphoria laced with nausea. The familiar cocktail that drowned everything else. I lay on the waterbed, the waves beneath me rocking like the rhythm of a heartbeat, distant and cold. It was like a lullaby, but the kind that keeps you awake, keeps you alert to the shadows that always lurk. I closed my eyes, and the drug took over, but there was no peace, not really. There was only the hollow hum of waiting, the ache in my chest growing sharper. I felt the heroin move through me, the burn curling like smoke. It was always the same, but it never stopped consuming. The relief was temporary, fleeting, and it made me crave more, just like everything else in my life.

All that was left now was to wait for them to come out of the bathroom. For the next step in the ritual, for whatever came next.

They came out of the bathroom—I don't know how long they were in there. Time blurred when you were numb, when you didn't want to remember. As soon as they stepped into the room, Kelley crawled onto the bed next to me and passed out, as if sleep were the only thing she could do. But I was wide awake. As was John, who stayed alert. He kept suggesting I move closer to his side. Kelley lay between us, a barrier I wasn't willing to cross. I stayed awake, talking to him, but I have no idea what we talked about. The words blurred in the haze of the night. I know he flirted, tried to pull me in with that ease men have. I told him he had a girlfriend, that she was passed out next to him. He smiled, a half-grin that didn't meet his eyes, and said, "I'm not that John. I'm her play toy John. The one she thinks she's engaged to doesn't know about this."

I believed him. I wasn't sure why, but I did. Maybe it was the way his voice slipped into something dangerous, something like he was confessing to me, or maybe it was just easier to believe his words than question them. I don't know when I finally drifted off to sleep, but it didn't last long.

When I woke, it was to the sharpest pang of anxiety. The kind that cuts through your chest like a cold blade. My Nokia cell phone was dead. I didn't know where I was, or how to leave. The bedroom was unfamiliar, foreign, and I felt trapped. My body tensed, ready to bolt. Kelley was still there, passed out next to me, her breathing slow and even. But John was gone, and I didn't know where he went, or if I even cared. My mind was a scramble of confused thoughts, but one thing was clear: I had to leave. I needed to get out. I remembered the dog outside the bedroom.

That pitbull. I didn't dare peek out. I could still hear it—soft growls, the heavy sound of paws pacing back and forth. Suddenly, Kelley made a noise. A gurgling sound that cut through the stillness, so sharp it made my skin crawl. Her eyes rolled back in her head. Foam began to form at the corners of her mouth. I didn't know what to do. Panic hit me like a freight train. I tried to move her, get her on her back, but the noise wouldn't stop. I could feel my heartbeat in my throat. I fumbled through her things, desperate, looking for anything, anything that could help. A phone. A number. Anything to call for help, or locate John. He'd brought us here, after all. I found an address book buried deep in her purse, and my hands were shaking as I searched through it. My eyes landed on a phone—black, sleek, the same side of the night table where Kelley lay, gurgling and convulsing. I felt a flicker of hope, as if dialing would bring some relief, some answer. I dialed the number for John. A man's voice answered. "Is this John?" I asked, barely able to keep my voice steady. "I'm calling about Kelley. She isn't okay. This is an emergency."

There was a pause, then the voice muttered, dripping with anger, "That bitch did it again."

I froze. I had the wrong John. The real fiancé, I assumed. I scrambled, frantic, searching for another John in the book. This time, I dialed with a sense of urgency.

"Hi, it's Diana. Is this John?"

"Yes," he answered, his voice flat. "It's Kelley. She's not okay. She's making noises. I don't know what to do. Can you get here right away?" There was silence on the other end before he spoke, his voice sounding distant.

"I can't leave work. She'll be fine. Just make sure she's on her back." I did what he said. But even after that, the gurgling didn't stop. It went on and on, the horrible, wrenching sound growing louder, more desperate, until it abruptly stopped. I don't know what I did to make it stop. Maybe nothing at all. Maybe she was just exhausted.

But I convinced myself I'd done something right. I couldn't bring myself to get back into the bed. I stayed on the floor, my back pressed against the night table, the coolness of the black marble a reminder of the distance between me and any kind of safety. I sprinkled out the powder onto the black marble table, rolled up a dollar bill, and snorted a line. The rush didn't come. I did a few more lines. It didn't help. I waited, for him to return, for Kelley to wake up, for this nightmare to end. All I wanted was to get home.

To the safety of Boston. To the place where everything felt less suffocating, less impossible. But I couldn't move. I was trapped. And so I waited. He finally appeared. I heard the sound of footsteps—slow, deliberate—growing louder as they neared. The doorknob turned, and my heart pounded against my ribcage, as if it would break free. I prayed it was John, but what if it wasn't? What if it was someone else, someone I didn't want to face? When I saw him in the doorway, I exhaled a breath I didn't realize I was holding.

This was the rescue, the salvation I had clung to, even as I felt the sharp edges of doubt gnaw at me.

Here, dear reader, I must step back. For memory is a fickle thing, a trickster that dances just out of reach, taunting, evading, slipping through my fingers like water. I have spent two decades trying to untangle the threads of what happened that night, trying to stitch together a version of the truth that makes sense. But I cannot.

I cannot tell you if Kelley was loaded up in the car when I climbed into the passenger seat. I want to believe she was. I want to hold onto that image like a lifeline. But then, his voice, John's voice, pierces the haze, steady and cold. When he walked in, the first thing he did was check on Kelley. His eyes glided over her like she was a broken doll, a lifeless thing. He checked her pulse, his fingers pressing against her neck with a practiced calm. "She's breathing," he said, his voice flat, almost mechanical. "She's asleep. Everything's fine."

I wanted to scream, wanted to shake him, but I couldn't. I had no choice but to believe him, because I had nothing else to hold onto.

"I'll drop you off and leave her outside the emergency room," he added, his detachment settling like a cold fog in the room. I want to believe I saw him drop her off. I want to believe we drove straight to the hospital, that he rushed her to safety, and that somewhere, Kelley lived. Somewhere, she walked away from the edge of death. I want to believe that in the midst of all this chaos, I wasn't left alone with death in that room. Alone with the smell of despair. But a darker part of me gnaws at that belief, pulls it apart thread by thread. And that gnawing feeling, that gnawing, bitter truth, claws its way into my chest, tighter with each passing year.

Even now, as I write these pages—two decades later—I can't seem to grasp what happened. It's like trying to catch smoke in my hands. The truth always slips away, vanishing before I can hold it long enough to understand. What I can tell you is this: I never heard from Kelley again. Not a word. Not a whisper of the girl I spent that one night with stripping. I never even knew her real name—Kelley was a name she wore like a mask, a name that belonged to the girl she pretended to be. Later, when John and I were living together, I asked him about what had happened to Kelley. His response never left me satisfied. He said she disappeared from his life after that incident. He thinks she married the other John. To this day, I wonder if the other John was real, or if he was just another version of him. My Mr. Big. A man I would marry.

I can't remember if Kelley was in the back of the car when John drove me home that day. I try to fit her into my memory like a jigsaw puzzle, but she refuses to fit. It's funny how memory works, how I can remember him so vividly—flirting with me, while Kelley fades, erased entirely. It felt absurd. He gave me his number, and I took it, though I had no intention of using it. The strangest part was how I was amazed at being wanted, by someone I didn't even want.

I climbed the stairs of the St. Germain brownstone, exhausted. Nothing made sense, not the night, not John, not the way I felt. When I walked in, I found Mona slouched in the living room, eyes darting toward me. I told her I had a great night, even said I made money. She barely blinked, just mumbled about how all her dealers had been arrested. I felt like I'd come in like some kind of heroin fairy, floating into the apartment with   exactly what she needed.

I knew I'd have to call him. He was the only dealer we had left who wasn't in prison. The thing with heroin is, it costs a lot and never lasts. Everything I'd brought home was gone in a day. So, I called him. He said he'd be right over, and he was—like a knight in shining armor, except in a black Mustang. He had heroin, coke, crack. The night blurred into a steady high. But this wasn't just a drug deal; he came for me too. He stayed.

We did lines and smoked crack together on the rooftop, watching the city disappear into the night. Through the haze of the drugs, I could see his soul, or at least I thought I could. There was a strange beauty in him. But the more he wanted me, the more I pulled away. It felt like a new kind of power—something I hadn't known before. I was used to being the one chasing after the boys, desperate for any sign of affection. Now, he was the one leaning in, and I was the one slipping through his fingers. As tempting as this knight in black armor was, something held me back. I was still tangled in my feelings for Holden, trying to make sense of it all. I didn't want to date, didn't want to ruin my streak of keeping men out of my bed as a remedy for heartache.

The next day, Mona couldn't stop singing John's praises. She asked me what I was waiting for. He was the one, she said, and I'd never have to pay for drugs again. And to top it off, he obviously had money—the watch, the Mustang, the way he dressed. She told me I wouldn't find anyone better. I believed her, or at least, I wanted to.

So I agreed to go on another date with John. This time, it was a day date, and we were high on shrooms. He picked me up in the Mustang, and we spent the day wandering through Boston, reality stretched and warped in ways I couldn't keep track of. We walked hand in hand around Quincy Market, where a lavender purple shawl seemed to call out to me. I touched it, running my fingers over the soft fabric, and I marveled at its color. It was something out of a dream. I didn't ask him to buy it, but when I glanced up, he was already pulling out his wallet, like he knew I needed it. I wrapped the shawl around myself, and for a fleeting moment, I felt beautiful—like I was someone worth seeing.

We drove fast on the highways that night, the world blurring, spinning around us. I feltweightless, like I was flying. But we didn't have sex. I said no, and he accepted it, without question. It was the strangest thing. This was a day of firsts for me, and I wasn't sure if I was moving forward or just falling backward into something that felt too familiar, too empty. That night was the beginning of a week-long romance, though "romance" feels like the wrong word for something that was half illusion, half escape.

By the second week, I moved in with him, though I wasn't sure why. It wasn't love, not really—it was more like a slow surrender, a pulling into something I couldn't quite understand. I told myself I was doing it to have a place, to feel like I belonged somewhere, but in truth, I just wanted to disappear into him. I wanted to be swallowed up, to stop feeling the gnawing hunger inside me, the one that no amount of drugs, or money, or fast cars could fill. It was like being held by someone who didn't know how to hold, or worse, didn't care. Still, I stayed, like a moth drawn to a light I knew would burn me.

Chapter 2

Moving Out/Moving In

I didn't have a lot of things to move into John's upstairs apartment, which was attached to the family estate's main house. The space felt hollow, not just because of the bare walls, but because I was still recovering from the breakup of my friendship with Stacy. It wasn't just a fracture—it was a fire that consumed everything.

The window breaking had been the final gesture, but what followed was the true destruction. Stacy didn't stop at words or silence; she destroyed my belongings, reducing all the markers of my life to ash. The designer clothes my mother had bought for me, the patent leather boots my father had carefully selected on a trip to Milan—square toe, square heel, flawless. Coats, memories, all of it was gone.

But it was the writing that I mourned most and mourn to this day. The journals, the stories, the pieces of me that I thought would last—they were obliterated in a way that felt irreversible. It was my mother who insisted I pick up what remained. She had that way of hers, calm yet determined. "No matter what happened," she said, "you are entitled to your things." She always found a way to fix things, or at least to make it seem like they could be fixed. So she got in touch with Stacy's parents, arranged a date, and we made the trip to Winchester, where everything had been stored for the summer.

We arrived, and there was nothing. No boxes of clothes, no traces of my life. Just a mattress—pee-stained, abandoned, like a final insult. I stood there, numb. My mother tried to comfort me, but there were no words for this kind of loss. It wasn't about the material things; I could replace those. My job at Express offered me an associate discount, so I could build a wardrobe again, piecing together new clothes to make it seem like I was whole.

But the words—those could never be restored. My journals, my writing, they were the only things I couldn't afford to lose. I had to start from scratch, but the scars of losing them remained. And those invisible scars would haunt me for years to come. To this day, my mother is still distraught by the disappearance of all my belongings. She never forgave Stacy for what she did, and in her eyes, it was a betrayal beyond reconciliation. I can see it in her whenever Stacy's name comes up—an anger that never quite fades, a wound that never fully healed.

John's apartment wasn't big—a one-bedroom place tucked above the main house. It had

everything I needed. A master bedroom with an adjoining bathroom, a small kitchen, and a space that felt intimate, almost too polished for someone like me, but I learned to settle in. The dining area was anchored by an Italian white custom-made table, surrounded by

white and black leather chairs. It was sleek, almost cold, like a museum piece— untouchable, yet suffocating in its perfection, a place where I often felt like an intruder in my own life. The living room followed the same theme, with an Italian leather couch that looked untouched, more for admiration than use. A sliding door opened out onto a patio, which looked over the quiet woods surrounding the estate. The view gave me a sense of false peace, like staring into the distance hoping to see a way out. The trees stretched far, dark and tangled, mirroring the storm that never left my mind. I wanted that solitude, but it was the kind that ate you alive. John's taste was clean, sharp—black was his favorite.

Even the kitchen, small as it was, had a sterile elegance to it, as if every object was chosen not to be used, but to fill space. It felt as though life here was staged, each part choreographed, even the things that should have felt spontaneous. But what stood out the most was the PIMPed out waterbed in the bedroom, draped in black, with mirrors on top of the canopy. I had never been on a waterbed before. That is, until I met John. It excited me. John was bad. I liked it. He loved his bedroom to be all black, with no sunlight shining in during the day. The huge bed with its canopy covered the bedroom window entirely, keeping the room cloaked in darkness. It was the kind of blackness that pressed in on you, where the air felt thick and you could almost taste the weight of it. John loved his bed. He loved his flat-screen TV. The bed and the TV took up the entirety of the bedroom, leaving little space for anything else, as if nothing else mattered but those two things.

The mirrors, though—I hated them. There was something sinister about them, a reflection I didn't recognize. I didn't like to look at myself in bed, exposed like that, as if the mirrors were complicit in showing me a version of myself I had no control over. I never looked up. I imagined they would swallow me whole if I did, sucking me into a hollow version of my own skin, where I would disappear entirely. It felt like living in a strange dream where reality could slip away at any moment. The walls of the apartment, though small, felt endless, stretching into corners where darkness lingered. In those mirrors, in that bed, I could feel the void creeping in—the same one that whispered to me late at night when I couldn't sleep, pulling me under like an ocean I was too weak to swim against.

The year between 2003 and 2004 was one I can best describe as a year of healing. John had instituted a strict no-heroin policy after the Kelley incident, a firm boundary that, at the time, felt more like a lifeline than a limitation.

"I can't have you using," he insisted, looking into my eyes with a mix of concern and resolve. "It would be too much for both of us." He claimed to be clean and was diligently working the program, I couldn't shake the feeling that I was the one who needed to be grounded. I had lost so much; the thought of slipping back into those familiar patterns of

self-destruction terrified me. In many ways, his boundaries became my own—a framework within which I could start to rebuild. John's ambition for me was inspiring. He enrolled in community college classes, pursuing an interest in computer engineering, a far cry from the family business of landscaping that had defined his upbringing. I admired his drive to forge a new path, even if it felt incongruous with his past.

Each evening, I would watch him hunched over his textbooks in the dim light of the living room, occasionally pausing to rub his temples, his brow furrowed in concentration. It was both foreign and comforting, seeing him engrossed in something that didn't involve substances or the chaos of his previous life. I often found solace in his dedication. There was a certain magic in watching him learn, as if he were reclaiming pieces of himself lost in the fog of addiction. In those moments, I allowed myself to hope that perhaps we both could heal, in different ways, on this unpredictable journey.

I didn't see my parents—not until Thanksgiving. I had detached myself from my family, cocooning in the warmth of John's world, far removed from the judgment I feared. The thought of facing their disappointment was suffocating. I couldn't bear the weight of their anger for not returning to school, for stepping off the path they had envisioned for me. So, I wove a narrative to ease their worries, telling my mother I had every intention of going back to school, just with John by my side. I painted a picture of possibility, casually mentioning that he was already enrolled in community college courses. "I can get him into UMass Amherst," I assured her, my voice steady, though the words felt like a fragile thread holding my facade together. I wanted to believe it, to convince myself that this was a stepping stone rather than a detour into darkness, but deep down, I grappled with the truth: my journey felt less like a straightforward path to education and more like a labyrinth of uncertainty, where every turn brought me closer to a choice I could neither fully embrace nor escape.

Thanksgiving arrived, and with it came the burden of my family's expectations. The house was filled with the aromas of turkey and spices, memories hanging in the air like ghosts. My parents' eyes searched for signs of the daughter they once knew, while I struggled to maintain the illusion of normalcy. I sat at the table, the clinking of silverware drowning out the unspoken questions swirling around me. Each bite felt like an act of defiance against the life I had chosen, and I wondered how long I could keep pretending that everything was fine.

I began with a fierce determination to get myself re-enrolled at UMass Amherst and to secure John's admission. I took the reins, writing our essays, filling out the proper paperwork, and completing John's FAFSA, all before the beginning of December.

I remember our first drive up to UMass Amherst vividly. I wanted to show him the campus, to immerse him in the life I cherished. It didn't matter that he would be the oldest sophomore on campus; I was convinced that he would fall in love with it all. There was an electric excitement in the air, a sense of new beginnings.

The drive will forever remain etched in my memory. I wore my lavender purple shawl, designer sunglasses perched on my nose, and heels that clicked confidently against the pavement. I had found my purpose, and it felt exhilarating. The air was crisp that day as we merged onto the Mass Pike, the world blurring by us in a rush of cars and colors. And then, it all went black.

I heard my voice screaming, a primal instinct rising from the depths of my fear: "Officer, he is trying to kidnap me! I don't know him! I don't know who he is!"

Panic enveloped me, drowning out the reality of the moment. John's voice cut through the chaos: "It's me, it's John. You know me!"

As the ambulance arrived, I was disoriented. By the time the paramedics approached, fragments of memory began to stitch themselves together. I remembered John, remembered our destination—the promise of UMass Amherst. But everything else was shrouded in a fog I couldn't penetrate.

I was told I had experienced a grand mal seizure, the humiliation of wetting myself crashing down upon me like a wave. When the EMTs offered to take me to the ER, fear gripped me. I pictured Westwood Lodge, the confines of that sterile place, and begged them to let me go.

Miraculously, they agreed. John turned the car around, and we drove back into the night. I slept and slept, as if trying to escape the haunting remnants of that day. The first seizure I ever had was at the age of five, maybe six. I don't remember much except for the walk with my grand-aunt Tessa. We were returning home, and it was snowing. In Tbilisi, snow was a rare miracle; when it did fall, it felt like the world had transformed. I loved catching snowflakes with my tongue, their icy touch a reminder of childhood wonder. As we walked, I could feel the frost on my nose, a tingling sensation that seemed to dance along with the falling snow. I remember staring up at the sky, mesmerized by the flakes spiraling down, sparkling like tiny diamonds in the sunlight. The sparkles intensified in my mind, a kaleidoscope of light and color, until it all went black.

The next thing I remember is the frantic rush of an ambulance, the cold metal and sterile smell invading my senses. I threw up. I felt scared and disoriented, a child lost in a chaotic adult world. My babushka's face was terror-stricken, her usual warmth replaced with a panic I had never seen before. She held my hand tightly, her fingers trembling, as they wheeled me into the Soviet hospital. They refused to discharge me, saying more tests needed to be done.

We were placed in a large hospital room filled with other children and their mothers. As my mom put it, I was the healthiest one there. On the second day, she could barely keep me still; I was running around, trying to explore. This went on for two weeks, my restless

energy clashing with the sterile environment around me. On the third week, my grandmother hatched a plan to break us out of the hospital. With fierce determination, she paid off the doctors and nurses, whispering conspiratorial secrets as they led us through the shadowy back tunnels of the hospital.

I felt a mix of fear and excitement as we tiptoed past the ominous doorways, the thrill of escape coursing through my veins. The world outside was a snowy wonderland, waiting for us like a long-lost friend. As we stepped into the daylight, I caught a glimpse of the sun shimmering on the untouched snow, and in that moment, I was free—free from the cold confines of the hospital and the weight of fear that had lingered in the sterile air. I never had a seizure after that, but I did suffer from intense migraines that often caused me to become delirious.

There was one migraine delirium I would never forget. I was ten years old, and we were living in Central Square. My mother had discovered a newfound love for Express. I don't remember the reality of that day, but the delirium is etched in my mind. I remember being stuck in Express, the bright lights and chaotic sounds overwhelming my senses. I couldn't get out. I kept crying out to my mom to rescue me from the confines of that store. In reality, I was sprawled on the living room floor, trapped in a haze that distorted my understanding of the world around me. I might have completely forgotten about that delirium-induced migraine if it weren't for the second seizure I had on the way to UMass Amherst with John.

Ultimately, John was accepted to UMass Amherst, and I was re-enrolled. We were set to start in the fall of 2004, a new chapter unfurling before us, fraught with both promise and peril. I loved the crisp autumn air, the leaves changing color from green to yellow, orange, red, and burgundy, as I moved into UMass Amherst that fall. It felt like stepping into a living canvas. I loved the walks into town with John, the thrill of our shared existence. We had made it this far together, yet I never thought to ask how he felt amidst the chaos of college life. He was six years older than me, and I sensed his discomfort among his younger roommates, like an old soul in a world of fleeting youth. I moved into a single in Coolidge, while John was placed in a dorm in Northeast with three other roommates.

My dorm room quickly became our oasis, a secret haven where we could pretend the world didn't exist beyond those four walls. John rarely spent time in his own dorm. We bought a black futon and a small TV, cramming everything into that tiny space, creating a sanctuary of sorts.

Somehow, we both managed to fit on the twin-sized bed, clinging to each other as if our

connection was the only thing keeping the outside world from unraveling us.

I threw myself into my classes, determined to succeed, armed with the fervor of someone haunted by the specter of failure. It had stalked me before, lurking like a shadow, but this time I wouldn't let it claim me.

Yet, John was unraveling, piece by piece, in slow motion. Completely off methadone, he became a specter of his former self, a ghost drifting through the days. Each morning he looked more like a shadow than a person, thin and flickering under the weight of his own skin. He was perpetually sick, desperate for something—anything—to make the pain recede. When he began throwing up blood, it felt surreal, like watching a tragedy unfold on stage, except I was right there, bearing witness and holding him up, my heart fracturing with every heave. After he collapsed in the shared all-girls bathroom, I could barely help him back to the room. I watched him fall apart, feeling helpless and terrified. I needed him with me at UMass; I needed him to survive this, but with each passing day, I felt the fraying threads of our connection, like an old tapestry unraveling at the edges.

Around that time, he convinced himself that dealing coke could solve everything, a way to stay afloat. Coke and Klonopin kept him functioning—at least enough to attend class and not collapse under the weight of his own sickness. I watched him navigate this dark path, detached yet desperate, lost in a world that had spun out of control.

I bumped into Mindy on campus that fall. I hardly recognized her from our days at the W. She had lost weight, her form refined, an image of improvement that felt sharp against the dull ache of my existence. "I'm off the lithium," she told me, her eyes bright. "Finally got a grasp on my own reality." It was heartening to see her thriving, a stark contrast to the chaos that consumed me.

Once John left for rehab, I couldn't stay in my dorm room. The walls felt like they were closing in, the silence suffocating, every tick of the clock echoing the loneliness that threatened to swallow me whole. I struggled to function alone, the weight of isolation heavy on my chest.

Mindy had an apartment off-campus and invited me to stay with her. Without a second thought, I accepted. Anything would be better than the solitude that clung to me like a shroud in the Southwest Tower. Living with Mindy was a brief reprieve.

Her apartment was filled with light and life, a stark contrast to the dark cocoon I had spun around myself. We shared late-night talks and laughter that echoed through the walls, our lives momentarily blending together like watercolor paints on a canvas. The air was thick with youthful recklessness, and for a fleeting moment, I felt alive. Yet beneath that surface lay the reality of John's absence and the weight of our choices. Each day was a tightrope walk, teetering between distraction and despair.

While Mindy was forging ahead, I found myself entangled in the past, unable to fully embrace the present. I was living in a dream I didn't want to wake from, yet knew I had

to. I didn't go home that winter break; I stayed with Mindy while John was in rehab for thirty days. When he was released from rehab in time for Christmas, we celebrated with his family, but I don't remember much of it. There was a huge, silent elephant in the room that no one talked about, its weight pressing down on us, a reminder of the turmoil that lurked just beneath the surface, unacknowledged yet omnipresent.

When I returned to school that spring, I juggled the demands of class, with John driving up every weekend to pick me up and bring me to his house. He couldn't stay on campus with me, as each morning he needed to be at the methadone clinic picking up his daily dose. The distance became a suffocating coil around my chest; I felt torn between two worlds. By summer, the reality hit hard: I wouldn't be returning to UMass for another year. My decision not to return would only widen the rift between my father and me, especially after my parents had worked so hard to secure a co-borrower for my private student loans. Our green card paperwork was still undergoing name check, and my choice felt like a betrayal of their efforts.

John needed me at home, and the truth settled in like a heavy fog—we couldn't survive a long-distance relationship. I couldn't focus on school when the weight of our reality pulled me in another direction. As John reentered my life fully, my friendship with Mindy began to fade. The late-night laughter and escapades slipped away, overshadowed by the urgency of my commitment to John. The bonds we had once shared dissolved, leaving behind echoes of what might have been—whispers of a friendship that felt like a distant memory, slowly slipping into the void.

Through it all, Ana and Mia remained my closest companions. Their silent whispering governed the rhythm of my days—starvation as penance, binging as a fleeting escape from the suffocating void they created. The guilt, though, was always waiting, sharp as a blade, to push me back into the spiral. I could never manage to make myself throw up; something in me resisted that violent purge. But ten EXLAX, swallowed in quick succession, would bring the necessary release. The stomach pains that followed were a welcomed consequence, a reminder that pain could still break through the numbness. Only when I snorted heroin did their voices quiet, dissolving into the haze. I wasn't the heroin-thin girl I might have expected to become. The brown powder loosened something in me, and I'd find myself craving food—steak bomb sandwiches, heavy and hot, swallowed whole without Mia's voice in my ear. The heroin carved a space in me whereguilt could not follow.

As summer turned to fall, John went back to community college, and I joined him. I was just a few credits short of my associate degree, and we made plans to move out. On weekends, we'd go apartment hunting, imagining what life could be if we could just escape his parents' house. I felt imprisoned living there, suffocated by the constant presence of his family. Around them, I wore a mask of smiles and etiquette, pretending to fit into a world where I knew I was never really considered family.

Every time I bumped into one of them in the kitchen, the mask would slip into place, heavy and hollow. That year, when John wasn't home, I rarely left the bedroom. It was easier to disappear, to shrink myself in the quiet of my minds control. I would starve myself during the day, turning it into a game in my mind, waiting for the evening, when I could finally eat with him. I felt everything shift, as if the ground had fallen out from beneath us. After UMass Amherst, something in John had broken; whatever fragile control he had over his addictions had snapped. Rehab hadn't saved him—it had merely replaced one demon with another. Cocaine became his new vice.

His family's trust that he had worked so hard to establish when I met him had dissolved. Him, stealing the thirty grand, was something that was never again talked up but the consequences were felt. Under the guise of his sister's return, they took our upstairs apartment and exiled us to a cramped bedroom in the main house. I tried to hold on to some semblance of control, but my body was weary from the constant battles.

I took a job at Victoria's Secret, performing normalcy under the bright lights and glossy storefront, but at night, I fell back into the shadows. Coke made my hands shake and my mind race, but I couldn't resist its pull. It wasn't long before the seizures, once rare, became alarmingly frequent. My therapist prescribed me a cocktail of anticonvulsants, drowning me in a medicated fog that blurred the edges of reality. They never knew about the cocaine or the heroin.

John, too, was unraveling. He'd lifted his ban on heroin for me after I convinced him it kept the seizures at bay. The truth was, I still needed the Klonopins. Without them, the seizures would come, unbidden and unforgiving. But I learned to lower my dose just enough to rescue John. He was still locked in the grip of methadone withdrawals, his body craving a relief that never arrived. The Klonopins were his escape, and I could give him that. Heroin, for me, was enough to dull the edges of everything else.

In the end, we discovered an apartment that met our needs—a one-bedroom tucked within a two-family house on Clinton Ave, conveniently close to his parents. From what I could glean, John was under financial suspension from them, yet I refrained from probing deeper into our fiscal reality. I placed my trust in him, proclaiming that numbers eluded me like shadows at dusk. In truth, I found solace in the intimacy of a joint bank account—didn't it signify a bond, a tether binding us together like a couple bound in marriage? Whatever money I earned disappeared into John's hands for deposit, yet we were perpetually strapped for cash; the roar of the GT Mustang had faded into a mournful silence, replaced by the quiet resignation of our circumstances. I never fully grasped how

much John earned working for his father, nor did I decipher the complexities of our financial ebb and flow. When I toiled in the family business, my pay remained a ghostly presence, flickering at the edges of my understanding. Yet in that one-bedroom sanctuary, we unearthed our escape. It felt like a haven, an interlude in a life that often felt suffocating. The backyard, a small sanctuary for our dog, offered a semblance of freedom, while the wooden panel ceiling of the large kitchen exuded a rustic charm that whispered of happier days—echoes of youth where spaces held memories and walls whispered secrets of their own. The small living room, intimate and warm, became a stage for our muted existence, and the generously sized bedroom cradled the waterbed with its canopy mirrors, reflecting fragments of reality I chose to ignore. In that space, we wove our own reality, a tapestry stitched together from the remnants of our pasts and the flickering dreams that danced like candle flames in the dim light. I don't know how I managed it, but after a tumultuous year filled with highs and lows—seizures, the transition to our apartment, and the rigors of academia—I somehow secured a place at Suffolk University for my junior year.

I longed to be at Umass, but the thought of leaving John felt unbearable. Suffolk would have to suffice. I remained blissfully unaware of how brutal the hour-and-a-half commute into Boston would prove to be. I took nothing into consideration; all I could do was propel myself forward at an unyielding pace. That fall, I steeled myself. I told myself I would be able to focus, that I needed the drugs to concentrate, and, in part, I did. They muted the cacophony of anxiety and despair that often screamed within me, allowing me to navigate my days with a semblance of purpose. I would study at a nearby Boston bar, a beer cradled in my hand. I craved a continuous flow of alcohol and Klonopin coursing through my veins to sustain me. Heroin provided the greatest relief, yet I lacked consistent access to it. It became a fleeting treasure I obtained after John pilfered my Klonopin; he fell into a habit of stealing them. One particular incident remains etched in my memory: I was waiting for the Red Line to commence my arduous commute from Boston to home, which involved a series of trains. He called me on my cell, his voice a tempest of fury, accusing me that the dog had devoured all my Klonopin and that it was my fault for leaving them out. He insisted the dog was fine, leaving me bereft of my medication. I remember the eruption of my own voice—yelling, screaming into the phone, my body trembling with rage and confusion. A part of me refused to believe him—that PlayPlay had somehow chewed through the bottle and ingested all my pills without going into an overdose. He never produced the chewed-up remnants to prove his story.

It was then that I began to have a recurring dream haunt me—or rather, a nightmare—in which I found myself back in the dorms of Umass, single, John absent, and dating someone else. In those fleeting moments of slumber, I felt a sense of contentment, only to awaken drenched in sweat, clinging to John as if he were my lifeline. I would recount the nightmare to him, and he would dismiss it with a wave, assuring me, "It's just a dream. Nothing could tear us apart. You are my babygirl."

It was us against the world, I was his babygirl and he was my daddy. By the time junior year waned, I was utterly drained. Exhaustion enveloped me, and as senior year approached, I found myself unable to return. Defeated, I succumbed to sleep, no amount of drugs able to rouse me. Instead, I drifted into a dreamless void where nights melted into days.

Those sleepless nights turned into a cinematic marathon; I consumed movies as if they held the power to fill the void within me. I indulged in romantic comedies, convincing myself I was the heroine and John was my dashing hero. I clung to the fantasy that I was Carrie, and he, Mr. Big, while my writing spiraled endlessly in circles. I dedicated my words to John, believing that this act of devotion would somehow preserve my essence, rendering my words eternal.

Yet, beneath it all, I ached for Stacy. I bore the weight of our fractured friendship, blaming myself for the rift. I needed to find her, to apologize, to reclaim what had been lost, as if somehow Stacy could be my savior. I finally discovered her online and summoned the courage to compose a long email, an outpouring of regret, begging for forgiveness and acknowledging my failings as a friend. I insisted she must know it wasn't me who threw that cinder block through her parents' bay window. I left my cell number, hoping desperately for a response. A day or two later, she called. She reassured me that she knew I hadn't done it and that she missed me too. Our friendship resumed as though the chasm had never existed, the wounds remained unhealed beneath the surface.

Stacy came over to visit me, her arrival both anticipated and unsettling, like the first gust of wind before a storm. She lived close by, driving herself effortlessly—something I had never mastered. I had tried to learn once, but the feel of the wheel beneath my hands, the sensation of being responsible for so much, sent me into a frenzy. I would clutch the wheel as if it were a lifeline in a tempest, afraid to let go, afraid of the vastness of the open road. That day, I was jittery, waiting for her to arrive. Doubts circled in my mind like crows, dark and insistent, swooping low, threatening to tear apart any hope. What if she didn't show up? What if there was hidden malice beneath this reunion? I couldn't silence the storm of thoughts swirling through me, like leaves caught in a gust, unsettled and restless.

I shared my apprehension with John, trying to explain how much Stacy's friendship meant to me.

His reply was cool, dismissive. "You don't need her," he said, the words landing like stones.

"You don't need friends. You have me. You have family. You can always be friends with my sisters." His attempt at reassurance only made my skin prickle.

There was something sharp beneath his words, an undertone that left me uneasy. I didn't like how they sounded, how they rolled out with such certainty, as if he were narrowing the borders of my life without my consent. But Stacy arrived, just as she said she would, brushing away my doubts like cobwebs in the wind. The moment she walked through the door, the knot of tension inside me began to unravel. We slipped into conversation with ease, as if the years between us had simply dissolved. Laughter bubbled up between us, and soon we were plotting our escape for the evening—a girls' night out.

John, of course, was against it. He muttered his disapproval, but there was little he could do to stop us. Stacy carried an air of bold defiance, a kind of confidence I hadn't realized I was starving for. In her presence, something shifted. The grip I had kept so tightly on John's approval, the desperate need to please him, began to loosen. The mask I had worn for so long, molding myself to his whims, began to crack, as if it couldn't bear the weight of itself any longer.

I began working at DSW and Lancôme, juggling the two jobs out of necessity, trying to sustain the life we had built—or, rather, the life that was crumbling beneath us. Whatever money John made was always just out of reach, like sand slipping through my fingers, impossible to grasp.

But in the end, all that truly mattered were the drugs. The drugs kept us afloat, kept us moving through a fogged-up world, where everything seemed blurred, distant, and unreachable. Then there were the bad days, the ones where I had nothing—no Kolonopins, no heroin, not even a joint to numb the edges. On those days, my body rebelled. Pain crept through me like an intruder, clawing at muscles and bones I didn't know could hurt. My skin would burn and freeze all at once, my body drenched in sweat, my mind a chaotic mess. By then, drugs had become the only way I could think. Without them, the world was unbearable, a cage of sensation and need. I needed more money.

And, as if summoned by that need, Stacy reappeared in my life, like a lifeline in a sea of desperation. She told me she was modeling now, that I could join her. Her voice crackled with excitement as she recounted how she had made eight hundred in a single photoshoot. I didn't ask what the shoot entailed. I thought about what that amount could cover in expenses, I thought, eight hundred dollars—more than enough to cover my rent for the month. I was hooked before I even fully understood what I was signing up for.

With her encouragement, I created a profile on Model Mayhem. The thought of making

money while being glamorized felt like an escape from the drudgery of retail. I imagined myself draped in designer clothes, posing for high-end shoots, my life transformed into something glamorous, glossy, and untouchable. But what I didn't know—what I refused to acknowledge—was how deep a hole I was about to fall into. Any warnings that flickered in my mind were swiftly silenced, drowned out by the thrill of what might come next.

Stacy and I began to flow together in our usual rhythm, the unforgotten dance of friendship. I placed her on a pedestal and became reliant on our bond; it was the only friendship I needed.

That first night we went out, I felt as though I had returned home. The vibrant nightlife pulsed around me, the music and laughter wrapping me in warmth. I missed the connection with people, the thrill of being alive in a crowd. I wanted to run away from John, escape the constraints of our life together. But I blocked that feeling, shoving it deep down where it festered, buried beneath layers of obligation and fear. John was home, and there was no running or leaving. Plus, who could I run to? The thought echoed in my mind, an unsettling reminder of the isolation I felt. My newfound freedom with Stacy was intoxicating, yet it was undercut by the reality that I was still bound to John, my heart heavy with uncertainty. Each laugh shared with Stacy, each moment of joy, served as a reminder of the life I craved but felt I couldn't have.

Modeling wasn't what I expected, but a part of me knew that from the beginning. I will admit here, that I did have a chance to meet some amazing amateur and professional photographers who made me feel glamorous, artists who viewed photography as a form of artistic expression, rather than the objectification of the female body. One of the coolest experiences I have ever had was a nude photoshoot, in which snakes covered my body by slithering and coiling around me. It was a thrilling moment, an intersection of vulnerability and artistry that made me feel alive.

Yet, gigs like that were rare and didn't pay as much as full erotic nudes. The online

Model Mayhem industry often twisted itself into darker corners, where the line between art and exploitation blurred. What paid the most was when the photographer could have his way with you, transforming what was supposed to be a creative collaboration into a transaction that felt all too familiar. My body once again became a tool, a means to an end.

I began upping my Klonopin dose to get through the horrid pornographic shoots. Sometimes I was with Stacy, other times I was by myself. Each session felt like a disorienting blur, my mind fogged by the medication.

Stacy was planning to move to Florida, escaping from an abusive relationship, as she confided in me. She shared her big-paying clients with me, and we would double up for

shoots. All bets were off in those moments, yet I found a twisted comfort in this humiliation, almost as if I were deserving of this punishment. It was a strange paradox; the very thing that degraded me also offered a sense of control over my circumstances. John didn't seem to object to how I was making money, as long as I was bringing in income. As long as the bills were paid and our addictions were sustained, he remained indifferent to the nature of my work. It felt as though he was assuming a role of a pimp, driving me to shoots, collecting money afterward, being the body guard in case of an emergency. It wasn't discussed between us, it was understood. I was caught in a precarious dance, balancing the weight of our lives on the fragile thread of my choices, wondering how far I could fall before I hit the ground.

John and my arguments began to slowly escalate over trivial matters, like the bagel incident.

"These aren't the bagels I wanted!" I remembered sobbing one evening. "I am not eating them! Why couldn't you get what I asked for?"

"So don't eat! Starve!" he shouted back, his fury igniting a familiar guilt within me.

I ran after him into the bedroom, my mind already made up to starve anyway, and clung on to him as though I was an octopus. I wish now, I could recall the importance of those bagels, the value they held in our twisted dynamic but my mind was remains blank, consumed by the rising storm of our conflicts to follow.

The angrier he got with me, the more I wanted to please him and defy him at the sametime, as if my worth depended on his approval. I thought about how I was trading pieces of myself for survival—whether it was starving for his satisfaction or offering my body to strangers for money. It was a chilling parallel, both rooted in the same need for validation, yet both leaving me feeling emptier than before.

The night Stacy met Rob, I was there—it was supposed to be a girls' night. I left John fuming, his frustration boiling over at my decision to go out. "If you aren't back by one a.m., all your clothes are going to be in trash bags outside!" he threatened, his voice laced with anger. I assured him, promised him I would be home.

"It's just a night out; it's not a big deal, please let me go daddy" I persisted. He eventually gave in, but to him, it was a big deal, and I could feel the weight of his expectations pressing down on me. That whole night, anxiety gnawed at my insides. Instead of a bar, we went to a party—lie number one, and I knew I would be in big trouble for it.

At the party, Stacy hooked up with Rob, disappearing into the bedroom, and didn't reemerge until the next day, leaving me to pass out on the couch. When I awoke, disoriented and riddled with dread, I dialed John's number, but he didn't answer. Twenty missed calls flashed on my screen, each one a reminder of the hell I was about to walk into. I knew he wasn't answering on purpose, a deliberate act of punishment. My heart raced as I pictured my belongings strewn across the yard, unceremoniously tossed out like yesterday's trash.

Finally, he answered. "All your shit is outside in trash bags. Go fuck yourself," he spat before hanging up, the finality of his words ringing in my ears like a death knell. I urged Stacy to take me home, relying on her to drive since I didn't have a car. She reassured me, "Don't worry. John wouldn't throw your stuff outside. He's just bluffing."

But when we arrived home, my heart sank at the sight of trash bags lined up outside the door. I begged and pleaded, ringing the doorbell frantically. When he opened the door, tears streamed down my face as I explained, "I didn't do anything wrong! I just had no way of getting home."

Stacy corroborated my story, adding weight to my words. After a tense moment, he relented, allowing me inside, but the relief was short-lived, replaced by the heavy tension that lingered between us. I couldn't shake the feeling that I was dancing on the edge of a precipice, each argument, each encounter drawing me closer to the inevitable break that was just brewing waiting to explode.

Stacy moved to Florida with Rob. My loneliness returned,

I was on my own doing photo shoots,

and prostituting myself for money, under a pretense of being a model.

I quit my job at Victoria's Secret and Lancôme, sticking with part-time hours at DSW, just for the shoe discount. I've always been crazy about shoes, and I guess I still am, though these days I don't have a hundred pairs of heels lining my closet anymore.

Instead, I threw myself into modeling—if you could even call it that. MySpace became my headquarters, where I spent hours tinkering with my photos on Model Mayhem, desperately trying to create some version of myself that didn't look as lost as I felt. I took whatever gigs paid, from trade shows to promotional work—it didn't matter. The worst ones? I'd just leave my body, float out, and watch from above.

The money was enough to cover rent and most of our expenses—that's all that mattered. John worked for his father's company, the same monotonous routine every day. He'd leave early, and I wouldn't see him until after five. Most days, I barely moved unless I had a gig or had to go into the store. I started having photographers come to the

apartment instead of dragging myself out. I didn't drive, so it was easier that way—one

less hassle in my chaotic life. After a while, I hated leaving the house. It escalated to the point where I didn't even want to leave the bed, sinking into those dark purple, deep red sheets, and black blankets, disappearing into a world that felt safer than reality.

All I thought about was John. He became an obsession, the center of my universe. If he didn't pick up the phone when I called, my mind would spin out of control. Anxiety attacks would hit me in the morning, and I would soothe myself by repeating his name in my head, rubbing my feet together. The fear that he was cheating settled like a cold stone in my stomach, heavy and oppressive. Once we moved to Clinton Ave, that anxiety morphed into a constant companion, whispering that he had a whole other life I didn't know about. I fixated on it, letting it take over, drowning out everything else.

To quiet my racing thoughts, I turned to the TV, keeping it on all day long. I had a lifetime morning show routine—I watched The Golden Girls, The Nanny, Will & Grace and Frasier. Each episode became a familiar backdrop, a way to escape the chaos in my mind. Then I'd sleep, cocooned in the comfort of my blankets. After I awoke, I'd wait for John, feeling the hours stretch painfully. Sometimes, I would call him asking for his card number to order food, but really, I was calling to check on what he was doing. For some reason, I didn't have any credit cards or even a debit card at that point; I was bringing in cash, and John oversaw all of it. I preferred not eating. When heroin was hard to get, John would bring me methadone.

He had this little system—he would put two cotton balls in his mouth, and when he got to the clinic, he'd drink most of the cherry-flavored methadone, allowing a tiny bit to be absorbed by the cotton balls hidden behind his teeth. What was absorbed would be brought to me in a Dunkin' Donuts coffee cup before he went off to work. He told me soon enough he would be allowed to have take-homes, a flicker of hope amidst the struggle.

The days and weeks blurred together, turning into one long stretch of nothing. I barely left the bed, and it felt like I couldn't even if I wanted to. That bed was my whole world—the purple sheets, the black blanket, the pillows—each item a reminder of my entrapment. The TV flickered in the background, offering a semblance of normalcy. It was the one thing that kept me from completely losing it, even if it wasn't much. I'd smoke one Newport after another, just lying there, staring at the screen.

The smoke curled up, thick and slow, hanging in the room like a heavy, stale cloud. It clung to everything—just like the numbness that had settled over my life. By the time the black marble ashtrays on either side of the bed were overflowing, so was everything else. I didn't see it.

"I love you, baby girl. You are my only baby girl."

I forced myself to believe each word he said, despite the nagging doubt that clung to me like a second skin. His affection felt like a warm blanket, but it was stitched together with

threads of uncertainty, unraveling at the edges. I wanted to bask in his love, to feel secure, but instead, I felt trapped in a world where the very foundation of our relationship was shaky.

His voice echoed in my mind, sweet yet laced with an undertone I couldn't quite grasp. I wanted to believe I was cherished, that I was enough. But there were moments—fleeting yet haunting—when the darkness whispered to me that I was merely a placeholder in his life, a fragile ornament on a shelf, easily replaced. The words wrapped around me like a lullaby, soothing yet deceptive.

I was his, but at what cost? I'd watch him leave for work, the door clicking shut behind him, and I'd feel the silence creep in, wrapping around me like the dark sheets of my bed. In those still moments, I would curl up, drowning in thoughts of his promises, wondering if they were ever truly meant for me or just an echo of his own needs.

I sank deeper into the illusion of our love, crafting it into something tangible, something I could hold onto as the world outside blurred into insignificance. Each time he returned, I would greet him with a smile that felt like a mask, hoping to disguise the gnawing fear that clung to my insides. I clung to his words, desperate for validation, needing to believe that I was not just a fleeting shadow in his life but a permanent fixture.

"Baby girl," he would say, pulling me close, and I would melt into his embrace, letting the warmth wash over me. In those moments, I wished I could lose myself completely, forgetting the doubts that churned beneath the surface. But as I lay there, nestled against him, the whispers grew louder, reminding me that love could be both a sanctuary and a prison.

I loved nestling on his chest, running my fingers through his tattoos, tracing the intricate lines of a woman with bare breasts etched across his skin. It felt like I was touching a piece of his soul, each inked design a story waiting to be told. Another tattoo depicted Death and its pit bulls, a stark reminder of the darkness that lurked just beneath the surface of his charm. "Promise you will never leave me," I would say, looking up at him, my voice barely above a whisper, trembling with vulnerability.

"I would kill you before I leave you" he would respond,

"Bury me with the fishes?" I would whisper smiling.

"Yes, babygirl, bury you with the fishes." He would say kissing my forehead.

This was love, wasn't it? I would think to myself.

I would continue tracing my fingers along his bare skin, the tattoo of Death, that I could never seem to understand.

As, the words hung in the air between us, heavy with my unspoken fears. I needed to believe in that promise, to find solace in the warmth of his body, as if that alone could shield me from the chaos of my mind. He would smile down at me, his expression a mixture of affection and something I couldn't quite read always remaining constant in saying "I love you babygirl" his voice smooth like silk, wrapping around me like a protective cocoon. But I wondered if his words were as permanent as the ink on his skin or merely a fleeting sentiment meant to soothe my anxious heart. In those moments, the world outside faded into a distant hum, and all that existed was our cocoon of warmth and intimacy. Yet, as I rested against him, I couldn't shake the feeling that the darkness in his tattoos mirrored the shadows in my own heart, whispering secrets of love entwined with fear.

The thing about John was that he rarely spoke. He was always the silent observer, absorbing the world around him. But he talked to me—or so I thought. Looking back now, I realize he didn't truly converse with me; he shared stories of his past, fragments of a life that seemed both distant and unreal. He claimed he was a PIMP at one point, a boast that hung in the air like a ghost, intriguing yet unsettling. Those stories painted a picture of a man who had danced dangerously close to the edge, living a life filled with chaos and bravado. They were tales spun from shadows, designed to intrigue and entice, but beneath them lay a silence that spoke volumes. I wanted to believe I was the one he confided in, that I had earned his trust enough to hear these stories. Yet, deep down, I sensed there was so much more left unspoken, buried beneath layers of bravado and the weight of his silence.

Our relationship was stitched together by the fabric of movies, each scene a thread binding my reality to fiction. I remember the night we watched The Notebook together, ensconced in the cocoon of our bed, my head resting on his chest, his heartbeat a steady rhythm beneath me. As the film unfolded, I felt my heart constrict during the scene where the young lovers were cruelly separated by the girl's parents. Their fervent love was eclipsed by familial duty, and it struck me like a lightning bolt, illuminating the shadows of my own fears.

"That would never be us," I asserted, my voice trembling with resolve. "I would never let anyone separate us. We would face all the darkness together."

He looked down at me, his expression inscrutable, and replied, "There is no darkness to

confront; we are already together."

"When will you propose?" I asked, the question spilling from my lips as if I were challenging fate itself.

He fell silent. His quietude wrapped around us like a dense fog, thickening my anxiety, igniting my worry that he might never choose to marry me.

Despite the tender declarations of love that rolled off his tongue with such ease, I began to question their sincerity.

"I love you" became a refrain, a haunting melody that echoed in the corners of my mind, yet it felt increasingly like a brittle promise, one poised to fracture under the weight of doubt. I yearned for that ring, a tangible symbol to root our fragile bond in the midst of uncertainty that swirled around us.

I believed that if I could slip it onto my finger, everything would realign, our relationship would stabilize, as if the universe would conspire to make it so.

I was sitting at the kitchen table at his parents' house, the low hum of the new stainless steel fridge filling the quiet space between us. John was at the counter, spooning extra sugar and cream into the coffee like always. The rhythmic clink of the spoon stirring the mug felt almost calming. The sun was shining through the windows, the smell of a vanilla candle mixed with cigarette smoke lingering in the air. I wrapped my hands around the coffee cup, feeling its warmth, a stark contrast to the cold that was permanently settling in me. The conversation turned to kids, and without thinking, I blurted out, "If we have a little girl, I want to name her Polina, after my great grandmother."

The words hung in the air, unexpected even to me, as though they had escaped from a place I didn't want to acknowledge.

John barely hesitated. "I always wanted to name my daughter Crystal." He said it with that soft edge of pride, like he'd been saving that name for years. My response was immediate, almost reflexive.

"Oh God, no. That sounds like a stripper name." The words slipped out too fast, and I regretted them instantly, a bitter aftertaste lingering on my tongue. John smirked, unbothered by my remark, leaning casually against the counter. "Nothing wrong with being a stripper," he said with a light laugh. "She would rule the champagne room."

Before I could retort, Mrs. B, standing by the kitchen window, cigarette dangling from her fingers, shot him a glance. "Johnny, don't say that," she chided in her low, raspy voice. The smoke curled around her face, blurring her expression like a shroud. Silence settled over the room again, thickening the air.

It was moments like these that reminded me of the deep disconnect between us, as if we were actors playing parts in a tragedy, always out of sync. We wanted to have children. It was something we talked about openly, with his parents, with friends, with anyone who would listen.

Everyone was surprised I wasn't pregnant yet. John and I never used protection—

hadn't since the beginning. Year after year, I wasn't getting pregnant. The questions came, creeping in like shadows, curiosity edged with judgment. What was wrong with me that I couldn't figure out? I would brush it off with some half-hearted joke or change the subject, but deep down, it sat in me like a heavy stone. It weighed on my chest, making it hard to breathe in quiet moments, pressing harder when I lay awake at night next to John. I wondered what was broken inside me. There was a time when I thought maybe having a baby would change things between us, that it would pull me out of the emptiness and give me something to hold onto. But as the years went by, the idea of it became less of a hope and more of a clinging desperation, echoing in the corners of my mind. I had calendars, carefully tracking every day, every cycle, turning what used to be spontaneous moments into a calculated schedule.

I turned sex, which was already a chore to satisfy John, intoa mission to have a baby. Each encounter felt more like a mechanical layer of duty, aperformance I had to perfect to keep John satisfied and to ensure he wouldn't stray. I didwhatever he wanted, desperate to keep him from leaving me, convinced that if I could just fulfill this purpose, everything else would fall into place.

I rarely felt pleasure. It became just another task to check off, another box in the long list of things I had to do to keep everything from falling apart. The intimacy, or what was left of it, was replaced by the constant weight of expectation. It wasn't about love anymore; it was about timing, about trying to force something that wouldn't come. John didn't seem to notice, or if he did, he didn't care. He was happy to go along with it, oblivious to the growing distance between us. For me, it became a mechanical routine, and each failed month felt like another small failure, deepening the quiet emptiness that lingered everywhere I went. The cold that was settling in me only seemed to deepen, even as we continued pretending everything was fine. In the shadows of my mind, the darkness loomed larger, waiting for the day I would finally confront it.

I missed Stacy, I missed her presence. I was in continuous awe of how Stacy had effortlessly slipped into Tampa with Rob, struck by her ability to glide from one relationship to the next.

There were no pauses, no awkward breaths—just a seamless hand-off, as if love were a game of hot potato and I was left fumbling in the dark. I longed for that fluid transition, but I found myself ensnared in loneliness. Each day was a stark reminder of my isolation, even as I chased fleeting modeling gigs and clung desperately to the fragile dream of motherhood. It became my new purpose, my solitary drive. I had failed at school; I was determined not to fail at this.

My life had devolved into a cycle of pills, Klonopin my constant companion, prescribed at six milligrams a day. Yet that dosage felt like a cruel joke, an insufficient balm for the tempest swirling within me. John, too, had his hands in the bottle, feigning innocence as he surreptitiously consumed the very drugs meant to steady me. It morphed into a maddening game, each count of my pills a testament to my unraveling reality. Night after n

night, I meticulously counted, and each morning, when John left for work, I would count again. The numbers danced before me, shifting and morphing like smoke, and every time, John's denials rang hollow, a symphony of betrayal.

One day, Mrs. B called, her voice heavy with concern. "Diana, do you think Johnny is getting into your medicine? His father is worried he's high at work."

"No, no, he hasn't taken any of my pills," I insisted, the words spilling from my lips like a desperate plea.

I couldn't unveil my fears, even to her. His father had decreed he should not return to work the next day or the following months. Instead, John drifted into a job at Best Buy, navigating random hours—sometimes under the harsh glare of the sun, often cloaked in the shadows of night, long after the store had closed its doors.

"Best Buy is having a Christmas party for their employees. We're going to a restaurant," he announced one day, water glistening on his skin as he prepared to step into the shower.

"Oh, fun! Can I come? I can be ready fast. I promise." I asked, my voice brightening, yearning for an escape from the suffocating confines of my solitude.

"No, it's for employees only, and you aren't an employee, are you?" I hung my head, whispering a reluctant, "No, I'm not." He assured me he wouldn't be long, he came home in the middle of the night.

As he dressed in the Diddy sweats I had once purchased for him—two hundred dollars of my hard-earned cash, a sum he had easily transferred from my wallet to the register—I watched him spray on his Nautica cologne, that scent curling around him like a lover's embrace. Each slick stroke of gel in his hair felt like a betrayal, and to this day, whenever that fragrance finds me, I'm transported back to John. Even decades later, as I navigate the bustling streets of Boston, that familiar scent pulls me into the past, a bitter reminder of despair lingering in the air.

"We're broke," John declared flatly, announcing our financial ruin with chilling finality. He wasn't making enough at Best Buy; I needed to hunt down higher-paying gigs. Desperation clawed at me, and I reached out to Stacy, who seized the opportunity with enthusiasm. "I know a few photographers who would love to fly you out to Tampa," she offered, her voice brimming with promise. "You can stay with me for a week, and we can double up on photo shoots." John, thought it was a brilliant idea.

Within weeks, my tickets were purchased, and I flew to Tampa with nothing—zero cash,

no credit cards, not a penny to my name. The flight had been arranged by a photographer, his interest a fleeting glimmer amidst the fog of my life. I was supposed to return home with at least two thousand dollars, a small fortune to guide me through the chaos, a much-needed escape from the shadows of my existence.

I was excited to go to Florida, a chance to escape the gloom that wrapped around me like a suffocating shroud. It felt as though I hadn't seen daylight in years, each passing moment trapped in a shadowy embrace. The thought of palm trees and sun-kissed shores promised a fleeting taste of freedom. I packed a red duffle bag overflowing with lingerie, remnants of my time at Victoria's Secret. The bag was so bulging it could hardly pass as a carry-on. This would be my first flight, my first ascent into the skies since arriving in the U.S. in 1993, a memory that clung to my mind like the scent of stale smoke in a forgotten room. As I navigated through Logan Airport, I felt like a supermodel strutting down a runway.

My wide-leg bell-bottoms danced around my legs, adorned with flower gems that caught the light with each step. Those pants, a testament to my past, were one of the few remnants of joy that had managed to survive. I wore dark red stilettos, each heel a sturdy four inches, crafted from brown wood that clicked against the terminal floor like a metronome marking time. The silk top from Express clung to me like a second skin, while the ballet-style cashmere wrap enveloped my shoulders, lending a delicate elegance to my ensemble. I felt as if the world was my stage, and in that moment, I was ready to perform, to escape into the bright lights of a new beginning.

I landed in Tampa, my heart racing with anticipation and a hint of anxiety. As I stepped into the bustling airport, I was met by a short, round man who introduced himself as my photographer.

He had a jovial demeanor, but there was something unsettling about him that stirred memories of my father—a familiarity that both comforted and unnerved me. As we climbed into his SUV, he turned to me with a grin, his voice warm yet slightly lecherous. "My wife is away for the weekend; we'll have the whole house to ourselves."

The words hung in the air, thick with implication. My stomach twisted, a knot forming as I processed the unspoken message. This was a job, a means to an end, yet I couldn't shake the feeling that I was stepping into a territory I barely understood. The city unfolded outside the window, palm trees swaying gently against the cerulean sky. As we drove, I tried to focus on the sights—the vibrant colors of the buildings, the promise of sun-soaked beaches—but my mind kept drifting back to his words.

I told myself it couldn't be that bad; after all, he was Stacy's regular photographer, and s

she assured me he was nice. Maybe he really was a professional, and maybe I could be a Victoria's Secret model. The thought flickered like a flame of hope, igniting my ambition amidst the unease. I popped two pills into my mouth instead of one as we drove, hoping to quell the growing tension.

When we arrived at the house, I was taken aback. It was lavish, with gorgeous landscaping that spilled into a breathtaking pool area, the patio looking as though it belonged in a movie set. The sight momentarily captivated me, pulling me from my swirling thoughts. "I'll make us drinks," he said, his voice warm and inviting. "Why don't you go slip into your bathing suit?" I hesitated for a moment, uncertainty floating at the edges of my excitement. But the allure of the scene and the promise of a refreshing drink coaxed me into compliance. Perhaps this was the beginning of something spectacular, a chance to break free from the darkness that had enveloped me for too long.

I followed his instructions and got ready in the bedroom he showed me, relishing the warmth of the sun that spilled through the large windows and the inviting shimmer of the water in the pool.

As I prepared, I popped another pill, the familiar rush mingling with my fearful anticipation. He handed me the first drink, I took it without hesitation, drinking it down without tasting a single drop, hoping to mask the knot of anxiety twisting in my stomach. The allure of the pool beckoned me. I dove in, the warm water around me felt like a soothing warm embrace. I felt as though I could lose myself in that pool water and for a second I felt fabulous.

He pulled out his camera and everything felt professional – until he instructed me to get out of the pool and pose by the waterfall landscape. He instructed me to get naked,

"Take off your top, embrace feeling free"

I didn't feel free but the top went off.

"That's good, that's perfect, hold that. Now take off the bottom."

Look like you are enjoying yourself."

I did my best to look joyful, sensual, sexual, and erotic all at the same time.

"Beautiful! Let's do a bedroom shoot, go in the bedroom."

I did as I was instructed.

The sun was setting, casting a warm glow over everything, shifting the atmosphere.

In the bedroom, holding his camera, he instructed me on the bed.

"Look like you want me" he said snapping one shot after the next.

I tried my best, it was hard to do. "That is beautifull" he put away the camera, and stripped off his clothes.

He climbed on top of me. Pressing his heavy set, sweaty body unto me. It didn't last long, he was nice about it…. but in those seconds, my soul left my body for the weekend, floating somewhere above the chaos of what was unfolding.

No matter how hard I try to remember, to this day I can't get the full memory of the weekend. Its forever lost, replaced by a blank image in my mind. I hold on to the images of the beginning, the arrival, the first shoot but then nothing just Stacy arriving to pick me up on Sunday evening. I felt relief climbing into Stacy's car; I felt a rush of joy in seeing her. It felt like I was climbing into the safety of home. It was all worth it.

I was paid eight-hundred in cash, which I wired to John via a Western Union Money Order the next day, to pay for rent. I again was left with no money, dependent on Stacy promising to pay her back after the next gig.

This week was the beginning of many weekend trips to visit various photographers in Tampa and pay the bills.

That wouldn't be my only trip. I would take many journeys, each leading me to various photographers, some genuine professionals, while others blurred the lines of artistry andexploitation. I remember one Russian photographer, a specialist in boudoir shoots, who flew me out to his home. He and his wife welcomed me warmly, their two little children running around, filling the space with an unexpected sense of family. I was given a guest bedroom for privacy.

He never touched me; if anything, he taught me how to model, guiding me through the poses with a quiet professionalism that was rare in the industry I had fallen into.

For that weekend, I earned a mere $500—hardly enough to cover rent. John urged me to seek higher-paying gigs, his impatience like a specter hovering over my every move. In those moments, I whispered to myself that I needed a backup plan, a way to untangle myself from this precarious existence.

I began to dream of escaping to Florida, the sun-soaked coast a siren call in my mind. I just needed to figure out how to get there. Perhaps I could find another man to help me—or maybe apply to Miami University. I had one year left; I could pull it off. Nights were spent wide awake, eyes glued to the computer screen as I searched through Miami   University's application pages,

imagining a life that shimmered just beyond my reach, like sunlight glinting off water. During the day, I slept, letting my thoughts spiral back into my usual obsession with John.

Then, I connected with a photographer—young, dreamy, the kind of boy whose pictures made you forget the world around you. We began talking late at night, while John slept in the other room, oblivious. The photographer made me laugh, his easy charm lighting something in me that had long dimmed. It felt good to flirt, to let my mind wander into forbidden fantasies. I allowed myself to believe, just for a moment, that maybe he could be my way out. He didn't know about John, didn't know I shared a life with someone else. It felt like the perfect escape.

We talked for two weeks, weaving dreams of something new. He offered to fly me out for a weekend shoot, though he admitted he couldn't afford to pay me. Even covering the flight was stretching his budget, but I didn't care.

To me, this wasn't just about a job—it was my escape. I painted fantasies in my mind, believing he would fall madly in love with me, beg me to stay with him, and I would leave everything behind. I lied to John, telling him my mom needed me to help with the twins for the weekend. He didn't question it. The moment he gave me permission, I felt a surge of hope rise in my chest.

When I boarded the plane to Florida that time, I carried that hope with me, fragile as glass. That time, I believed, maybe I would finally leave everything behind.

He met me at the airport, and he was even better looking in person—his chiseled jawline, sparkling green eyes, blonde hair, and long arms that were thin but muscular in just the right way. That weekend was filled with a joy I had never experienced before. I felt free. I chose to sleep with him, and for the first time in a long while, I felt in control. We had a sensual shoot and he apologized for not being able to pay me more. We went out drinking at Miami clubs, sat together on Miami Beach, and later returned to his tattoo studio. There, he gave me my first and only tattoo.

We sat side by side, searching together on Google—this new, exciting tool—for a symbol that meant abundance, joy, and life, everything I was craving. I asked him to cover up my scars on one of my wrists with the tattoo. He did. That tattoo of the OM symbol will always remind me of him and the time we spent together. What didn't happen was he didn't beg me to come live with him in Miami. Instead, he drove me to the airport Sunday morning, sending me back home.

Home to John.

When I returned home, John transformed before my eyes—more attentive, more loving, more present. He began to bring me the foods I adored: the savory warmth of Kelley's roast beef, the indulgent comfort of pepperoni pizza, or the sweet chill of ice cream on a warm evening. We ventured out together for brunch on weekends, exploring local diners as if savoring the rediscovery of a past life, reminiscent of the John I had fallen for in those early, halcyon days.

Yet, amid this tender façade, a fleeting suspicion curled in the corners of my mind—had he unearthed the secrets hidden in my journals or stumbled upon whispers of my escapades online?

But, I quickly buried that thought, dismissing it as paranoia. After all, John loved me, didn't he? I was a fool to have considered leaving him, even more foolish for betraying him. The weight of my choices settled around me like a shroud, but in that moment, it felt inconsequential. He would never know.

That night John fell asleep early, his rhythmic breathing filling the room like a lullaby, I put my head on his chest and listened to his heartbeat. I thought of sleep, but I couldn't rest my mind, a tempest of thoughts kept swirling in my mind. I knew the code to the methadone safe, a secret I had kept like a hidden treasure. A defiant spark ignited within me as I weighed my options. My final thought: Fuck IT! He steals my pills, I know this for a fact. I am going to just do it. Sip on his methadone without him knowing. Just a tiny bit, to make him feel like he was the one losing his mind.

With quiet resolve I got out of bed, and slowly on my tippy toes crept out of the bedroom. Not making a sound, I didn't want to wake him. I crept to the safe that was kept in the kitchen on the floor by the bedroom door in the left corner. I punched in the code and sighed in relief that he hadn't changed it. I wasn't supposed to know the code, he had said it aloud by accident; I overheard, and memorized it. He must have not realized he said it aloud. I took out the little clear bottle, filled with bright red, dark pink, syrup like fluid, twisted off the white cap, peeled off the little foam like cover, which I maintained in perfect position to cover up after taking that first tiny sip.

There were two hundred milligrams in that bottle. I sipped of only ten milligrams no more than twenty. He would never notice. I told myself.

The sip warmed my throat and I knew the feeling that was to come next. I was waiting for it. I went to my computer desk, sat down in my computer chair, and pulled out the latest essay, as the computer screen illuminated my face. I was working on a piece titled Holden

Everlasting. I loved the piece, I had been working on it for years. Editing, refining the words, to make it fit into a question style narrative, where each sentence was constructed of a question, telling a story of love lost.

The methadone didn't hit, I thought I didn't take a large enough sip. I crept back to

the safe, got the same bottle as before, and took a slightly larger sip.

"No he won't even notice", I thought to myself. I went back to my computer. I began to write. Inspiration flowed. But not enough, I needed a bit more to capture the scenes forming like a movie in my mind on to the word document.

I crept back to the safe. I opened it. I took out the same methadone bottle and took another swig. It didn't seem like that much. But now I did fear he would notice.

I thought to myself, that was a bit much. Did I really drink half the bottle. I couldn't remember how I managed that. Oh well I thought to myself. I will sleep it off tomorrow. He can have my Kolonopin dose. Not a big deal.

I went into the bedroom. The euphoria I was feeling was immense and electrifying. I wanted to fly. I wanted to take control of me. I went to wake John up by arousing him. We had mind blowing sex that night. That I remember, my soul was finally inside my body. I was in control of it all. I felt powerful like Cleopatra. Afterwards, I put on my pajamas and snuggled with John to sleep. When I awoke, I was freezing cold, and   fluorescent lights were shining into my eyes.

I could hear voices, someone shouted "She is alive!"

Someone else shouted "she is awake".

I was terrified and confused, I wanted to scream but I had no voice.

I heard the voice.

Felt the movement of the room.

The fluorescent lights were blinding.

I was freezing—my teeth would've been chattering if I could move my mouth.

"Dr., she's alive!" I heard someone say.

The beeping sound of machines, rhythmic and steady, filled the room.

Terror set in. *I'm in the hospital*, was my first thought. *Where are my pants?* That was the second thought. The third—*fuck, I'm paralyzed.*

I couldn't move, but I was freezing.

"Hi there, welcome back. I'm Dr. S. I'm just going to check you for movement. Let me know if you feel something."

I felt a cold tingle glide up my foot, sharp against the overwhelming cold that gripped me. My muscles trembled from it. I managed to acknowledge I felt it. I moved my toes. Thank God, I thought. I'm not paralyzed. I must've had a seizure. My mind began to think back. Dr. S interrupted my thoughts.

"All good. You know, young lady, you're very lucky to be alive. I'll have your tubes   removed, and we'll need to ask you a few questions."

That's when I saw him.

The police officer in the corner.

Silent.

Watchful.

What the hell did I do? My mind tried to race.

Everything went black again. I don't know how long everything stayed blank. Or maybe it wasn't blank maybe something went on, but I just have no memory of it.

I barely remember the breathing tube down my throat.

How it got there and how it was removed—those memories are locked away somewhere I can't reach. The lights stabbed at my head, but not as much as the cold. I felt my teeth chatter. I tried to speak. A nurse appeared. "Let me get you some ice chips," she said.

What the fuck? I thought. *I'm freezing and they want to freeze me more?*

It was hard to say anything; my mouth felt too thick, too heavy, my throat throbbed as though sharp knives were being stabbed in with every swallow. My eyes darted around the hospital room, searching for something, anything, familiar. All I could remember was putting on my brown Velcro sweatpants from Express.

I loved those pants and now they are gone. My mind kept thinking back to my missing pants, the missing parts in my memories. I wondered who changed me, or did I come to the hospital naked? How did I end up in a hospital gown,

I must be in a hospital gown under the thin hospital blankets. What happened to me? I couldn't remember. I remembered the pants, a tee shirt, and falling asleep. Then my eyes landed on John. He looked small, like he'd shrunk into the chair he was sitting in. Tears rimmed his eyes, his face drawn and tight.

I wondered how bad the seizure was.

Dr. S came back.

"

I'm freezing," I managed to whisper. He instructed the nurse to bring me warm blankets. They layered me with blankets—thicker, warmer—but the cold still wrapped around me like a damp shroud from the inside.

"Do you know why you're here?" Dr. S asked.

"I had a seizure. I have those." I heard a voice, my voice, a voice I didn't recognize say.

"No, I'm sorry. You didn't have a seizure. You were found dead in your bed. We didn't know if you would make it. It was touch and go there for a while."

I felt a rush of terror rush up my veins, as though I was injected with a shot of venom. The words sank slowly, too heavy to fully understand.

Dr. S continued, "The police officer is here to get your statement. You had an overdose, and you were pronounced dead upon arrival. He needs to know where you obtained the opiates, we found in your system. We had to obtain a tox-screen, which shows a deadly amount of benzodiazepine mixed in with a heavy dose of opiates. Don't worry; you aren't in trouble. Your fiancée over there told us you are prescribed to benzodiazepine, but we need to know where you obtained the opiates. Your fiancée says he found you unresponsive in the bedroom when he came home at night."

Dead?

Fiancee?

Didn't I fall asleep next to him in bed?

The thoughts barely registered. I couldn't grasp anything. My mind flailed, slipping away from itself. Luckily, they didn't expect me to talk just then. John had moved his chair. He was now sitting next to my bed, holding my hand. His grip was tight, trembling slightly, like he was the one who'd been frozen.

All I wanted in that moment was my mom. I heard the voice in English: "I want my mama" and again in Russian: "я хочу мою маму."

Both languages begin to mix in together playing on a repeat loop in my mind. The need for my mother was a desperation I had never felt before, it was the only screaming heard inside my head. My mother never appeared. But Mrs. B. did.

John was sitting still next to me holding my hand. I don't know where the doctors had gone. Mrs. B, leaned in towards me and in a quiet voice, almost a begging whisper,

"Diana, you can never tell them you got the methadone from Johnny. If you tell them, they will arrest him. We can't have Johnny arrested. Tell them you don't know, you can't remember."

That is just what I did, when the officer finally asked me where I got the opiates from, for his report. I told him, "I have no idea, I went to a party that's all I remember. I don't remember getting home, I don't remember anything. I am lucky, my fiancée found me and saved my life."

When I came to fully, able to speak, a nurse entered the room.

"Hi, I'm here to remove your catheter," she said casually, like it was part of some routine I should've known about. I hadn't even realized I had one, but once she mentioned it, the dull discomfort in my lower body made sense. There is nothing pleasant about having a catheter removed. John remained by my side, his hands still clutching mine. I could feel the warmth of his grip through my cold fingers.

The nurse gave me a quick, professional smile and said, "Let's just have you spread your

legs—you're going to feel a little pinch." As she spoke, she was already helping me part my legs, the words slipping into the act as though it was a conversation. I braced myself, and then came the pinch, a strange sensation that made me wince.

I felt humiliated. Exposed. I just wanted to go home. After the nurse removed the catheter, I mustered the energy to ask, "When can I go home? I just want to go home. I'm exhausted." My voice sounded fragile, like it wasn't mine, like it belonged to someone else—someone too tired to keep fighting. She gave me that soft, knowing smile that only nurses seem to master, the kind that says she's heard this a thousand times before.

"Just hang in there a little while longer," she said. "I'll let the doctor know I removed your catheter, and if everything looks good on his final check, he'll prepare your discharge papers."

Her words felt distant, like they came from another room. Dr. S appeared again at some point—I couldn't tell how long it had taken him to come back for the final check. Everything felt blurred, like I was watching it happen from behind a veil.

I just remember the pen in my hand, shaky fingers signing the discharge papers. All I wanted was to get out of the hospital as fast as I could.

My mind couldn't fully grasp the enormity of what had happened. I was in denial, floating on the edge of disbelief.

I had died.

And then I came back.

But that couldn't be true, could it?

John and I didn't talk much on the way home. Just the usual I love you, and I was worried, and I was scared. The kind of words you say because you have to say something, but you're too afraid to dig any deeper. I wasn't ready to know the details of what had actually happened. There was a part of me—maybe a bigger part than I wanted to admit—that clung to the story I had told the officer. But even as I tried to hold onto it, I knew it didn't fit. Maybe I didn't really die, I thought. Maybe the hospital exaggerated. The words sounded hollow, even to myself.

Once we were home, I slid into bed.

The familiar feel of the black and purple sheets surrounded me, the warmth of John's body next to mine, his arm around me, but something felt off. My brown Velcro pants were missing. They hadn't been in the plastic hospital discharge bag. Somehow, I had managed to leave the hospital in scrubs—loose, impersonal, and sterile.

But those pants, my comfortable, worn-in brown pants, were nowhere to be found. I lay there, snuggled up to John, staring at the ceiling, the weight of the day finally settling in. I couldn't shake the thought. What had happened to my pants?

Finally, I asked, "What happened to my pants?"

"They cut them off of you," he said quietly.

"What do you mean, they cut them off of me? Who?"

"The doctors. You really don't remember, do you?" He paused, his voice strained.

"We had sex and we both fell asleep. I woke up to you talking in a creepy voice. In Russian. You sounded possessed."

I turned slightly, looking up at him, trying to piece the fragments together in my mind.

"I tried to shake you," he continued, "but you yelled at me, said you were talking to your grandma. And then you started making this gurgling noise. I thought you were going to puke, so I ran to the bathroom to grab the trash can." He paused again, and I could hear the tension in his voice, the hesitation as if saying the words would make them more real. "I left you on your side, like you're supposed to, but when I came back, you weren't making any noise. You were just… out. I checked for a pulse. I couldn't find one. Your eyes had rolled back, like in a horror movie."

I felt him shift next to me. His voice dropped, barely more than a whisper now.

"I didn't know what to do. I couldn't call 911—they'd arrest me for giving you methadone. So I called my mom. She got here in less than five minutes, and we loaded you into the car. We drove you to the hospital." He stopped speaking, but the silence wasn't empty. It stretched between us, thick and heavy.

"They said you were dead."

I snuggled closer to him, pressing into the warmth of his body, wanting to protect him. Feeling the steady rise and fall of his breath, feeling loved. I whispered back, "But I'm not. I am sorry I scared you. I won't do it again."

After a silence I added, "you should change the code to the safe",

and a few minutes later I added, "I can't be trusted".

John agreed.

The next day, all I wanted was my mother. I called her. Told her I'd had a seizure. That I was in the ER. Her voice, sharp with panic, felt like it was cutting through the phone. Even now, as I write this, I try to remember exactly what she said, but it slips away. I close my eyes. I go back to that moment, but all that's left is the feeling. Just the hollowness of it. I couldn't tell her I'd died. I couldn't tell her I came back. The voice inside, the one I thought I had buried, was screaming.

Tell her!

Go home!

Leave!

She'll come for you.

Just leave!

But I didn't ask her to come. Instead, I told her John wants to marry me. I asked if I should. In that conversation, the lies I told myself began to formulate like venom, spreading through my veins, becoming one with my marrow.

I didn't die. I just had a seizure. John called me his fiancée in the hospital. Therefore, John wants to marry me. So I'm going to marry him. Even though John hasn't proposed. I hung up the phone with my mother and I cried. I put one of my Celine Dion discs into the stereo. Hit repeat. Crawled back into the waterbed, into the darkness of my red, purple, black sheets, and slept. I don't know how long I slept.

Time slipped. My next memory is fall. I don't know if I died that fall.

Or in winter.

Or maybe in spring.

"If you don't propose, I'm leaving. I'll go back to my parents' house," I'd told him.

"So go. You'll come crawling back anyway. You hate your parents, and they don't even like you."

Each one of his words felt like a wrecking ball thrown at my brain. I felt the freezing cold of death. Tears spilled. I cried. And cried on the floor. I wasn't allowed to sleep in the bedroom that night. He was furious that I gave him an ultimatum. So I stayed by the closed door, curled on the floor all night while he slept soundly on the other side.

He woke at 5 a.m. The door opened. He didn't talk to me. Didn't even look at me. Like I wasn't there. The silence hurt more than the fight. He left for work, didn't come back with my Dunkin Donuts coffee. I didn't see him again until the evening.

I thought of dying. I didn't understand why I was alive. I wasn't supposed to live beyond thirty, I was already twenty three.

"Why was I alive?" was the tormenting question of the day, playing in my mind on a broken record stuck on a repeat loop.

When he came back, he said he loved me. Said he was sorry. And I was sorry too, of course I was. And of course, he'd marry me. It was supposed to be a surprise— the proposal, the ring. But I ruined it.

I ruined everything as always.

I was a master at FUCKING UP!

Chapter 3

PlayPlay (aka Playa)

I've never quite understood why anyone would name a dog Playa. To be honest, I hated it. Hated it in the kind of way that simmers quietly beneath the surface, only occasionally bubbling up in a moment of irrational irritation. It wasn't just the name itself—it was everything about it.

For one thing, Playa was a girl, and what sort of name is that for a female dog? And even if we were to entertain the idea that she embodied some canine equivalent of a "player," it didn't make sense. She wasn't conniving, charming, or even particularly sociable.

And then there was the sheer laziness of it—Playa. Not even the full word Player. As if it required too much effort to pronounce the "-er," to commit to the completion of the word. That abbreviation, that casual disregard for linguistic precision, grated on me. Why not at least roll the "r," give it some character? But John cut it short, leaving it dangling like an unfinished thought.

I nicknamed her PlayPlay, because she was playful, affectionate—she had a way of offering warmth when I felt most hollow. In the darkness of our apartment, in those days when I craved death to come and claim me, PlayPlay was there, curling beside me, a small, quiet comfort.

There were nights when I found myself sleeping on the living room floor, curled up like a pup beside her in her doggie bed. Those were the nights John banished me from the bedroom. Nights when I'd really fucked up, when I'd pushed his buttons too far. It's ironic how, when I first met PlayPlay, I was terrified of her. That first day with Kelley in the bedroom, I was too scared to leave. I thought the crazy pitbull would eat me alive.

Even after I moved in with John, those first few months felt like a cage. I never ventured out of the bedroom. PlayPlay always stayed in the living room and kitchen area when John wasn't home, her playful energy confined to the spaces I dared not occupy. I stayed in the bedroom, cocooned in my own anxieties. There was really no need for me to leave those walls in those days. The world outside felt foreign and dangerous, while the safety of the room became my reluctant refuge. As the months passed and I began to venture out, my fear of PlayPlay slowly dissipated. I started to see her innocence and warmth.

It began with the two of us finding refuge from our loneliness in that waterbed, surrounded by dark purple sheets, snuggled beneath the black blankets. I never had the chance to know PlayPlay when she was a pup or before her incident of breaking her leg after falling into the pool. When I met her, she was broken, as John put it. Her leg never healed properly, and she couldn't go for walks. Now I wonder if he simply didn't want to

take her on walks, if he resented the way she had changed. It made me think: what if I were a human, a replacement for PlayPlay? It was in our brokenness and the chained bond to John that PlayPlay and I provided comfort for one another. By the time we moved to Clinton Ave, PlayPlay was confined to the house, with the backyard being her only way to enjoy the outdoors. The backyard was fenced in, and John put three-quarter inch blue crushed stone all over one year. In her last years, I wonder now if she missed the feel and smell of grass.

There was a rhythm we stumbled into that fall, particularly after that explosive quarrel about my giving him an ultimatum. He allowed me a glimpse into his world, a sliver of the engagement I had begun to dream of, along with the ring I so desired.

"I want a wedding ring like Carmela's," I declared one evening as we sprawled across the bed, immersed in The Sopranos. "You can have your gumars, like Tony; I won't even be jealous. I just want the ring, just like Carmela's—big on my finger, like a damn lighthouse."

"Whatever you want, babygirl."

He leaned his neck down and planted a tender kiss on my forehead. In that fleeting moment, I felt whole, as if the jagged pieces of me were finally aligning.

By Thanksgiving, I informed my parents of our impending engagement. But it wouldn't be official until Christmas morning, with the grand proposal at his parents' house—words I can to this day hear echoing in my mind as I uttered them aloud to my mother over the phone one day.

I knew the ring he intended to buy me; I had meticulously selected it from Belden Jewelers—a three-stone princess cut ring that sparkled like a thousand possibilities.

"Don't tell my parents you know," John cautioned me one day, pulling on his socks. "They think this is going to be a monumental surprise," he continued on as he stood up from the bed, leaving me to admire the ring a little bit longer.

"I promise I won't say a word," I assured him giving the ring another longing look. I was amazed at the brilliance of the diamonds, the way they could shine even in the darkness of our bedroom.

I slowly slid the ring off my finger, and handed it carefully to John to place back into the black box.

We were getting ready to go to his parents' house for dinner, and John was going to give the ring to his mom secretly to safekeep, hidden away somewhere in her master bedroom.

To maintain the ruse, he told his mom over the phone, "She has been searching for the ring. I don't want her to find it."

When we arrived at dinner, Mrs. B confronted me.

"Diana, you need to trust him. Let him propose if he is to propose in his own way." I looked at her, smiling, knowing I was in control.

"Yes, Mrs. B, you are absolutely right."

I was swept up in a whirlwind of fantasies leading to the proposal, feeling as if I were the one steering this ship. Any disquieting voice that whispered against my happiness was drowned out by an extra pill or a request for more methadone. At that point, he controlled the dosage, knowing all too well that I could not be trusted. That time I broke into the safe, an act of desperation that shattered not just his trust in me, but my own fragile sense of self. The repercussions were catastrophic.

I knew then, with an aching clarity, that I had to do better by giving John control over me.

I couldn't be trusted.

Chapter 4

The Proposal

I wish I could remember more. I try so hard to step back into time, I am able to step into the slides and witness certain events unfold, but there are so many blank slides that no matter how hard I try, I can't get the imagery. It's like developing a photograph, going through the developing phases, and the last phase in the darkroom, where you await the imagery to come through clear and sharp—the imagery of my memories refuses to form. These are times where I so wish I had my writing, my journals, my old computer, all the files. But they were all stolen from me.

I will always wonder what happened to my writings. Did Stacy actually destroy them?

I can't help but turn the thought over like a worn-out coin in my pocket, rubbed smooth from years of handling. Even after we reconciled, we never spoke of the destroyed clothes, the missing journals—those small casualties that meant everything to me, but perhaps nothing to her. Our friendship was always so one-sided, so lopsided that it felt more like walking on a slant than anything steady. I was the flaw in it, the constant imperfection, the piece that never quite fit. I was always the one at fault—according to some unwritten law we both subscribed to without question. Stacy did no wrong. Her hands were clean, spotless. Just like John, who lived in his own sort of immaculate world.

It was always me—the flaw, the failure, the one with the cracked foundation, who was too this or too that, but never quite enough. And yet, there I was, letting them into the most sacred parts of me, handing them my trust as if it were unbreakable. But they—these two people I trusted with my life—continued the same familiar pattern, over and over, like a needle stuck in a groove.

They stole my written words, my thoughts. My insides, essentially. And left me wondering, as I do now, how something could be taken so completely, without so much as a sound, leaving nothing but blank darkness behind.

That morning, I had no trouble waking up at 5 a.m., a testament to the numbing familiarity of excess that followed our Big Family Yearly Christmas Eve party. I remembered attending, but the recollection felt like a fleeting whisper—a quick flash of being there, mask pulled on tightly, someone else entirely, a stranger painted over my features. I had crafted a Monet on my face, splashes of color meant to conceal rather than reveal. Each cyst, each scar, each mark was a reminder of a battle I felt I was losing. By then, I had given up any hope of clear skin. My cystic acne flared like a wildfire across my cheeks, each morning greeted by the emergence of a new, throbbing bump that brought with it both pain and a familiar sense of despair.

Every time I prepared to leave the house, I would spend an hour applying layer after layer of makeup, as though I were attempting to perfect a painting, transforming something raw and flawed into something more palatable. Each stroke of the brush was a feeble attempt at mastery, a way to mask the chaos beneath, to put forth a version of myself that felt less like a broken canvas and more like a finished piece of art. That morning, I didn't feel any of it—the usual weight of self-doubt, the relentless tide of anxiety that threatened to pull me under. Instead, there was a thrill in the air, an anticipation of the ring finally being on my finger. The significance of that simple band loomed large in my mind, eclipsing everything else.

I didn't care what I wore to the family Christmas morning gathering at John's family estate. The usual dread of choosing the right outfit faded into the background, drowned out by the hopeful hum of expectation. John's family was a lively constellation, sprawling and warm. He had three younger sisters, each a vibrant thread in the fabric of their home, weaving in and out with children of their own, boyfriends, and husbands in tow. His youngest sister had already married, a mere year younger than me, her laughter filling the space with an air of ease I both admired and envied.

It was a tradition to gather in the living room, everyone drawn to the huge Christmas tree, its fake branches heavy with ornaments and memories, overflowing with presents that sparkled under the lights. But this year, amidst the chaos of bows and wrapping paper, there was only one present that truly mattered to me. It was my ring. It was the proposal. It was what would cement me to the family, a tangible symbol of acceptance and belonging that I so desperately craved.

I pulled on my new pair of Velcro pants my mom had recently purchased for me, a replacement, her token of love. Though I liked the idea of them, they didn't feel as comfortable, didn't wrap around me the same way the pants had before they were cut off at the emergency room.

A wave of discomfort washed over me, an echo of that night, filled with confusion and fear.

Why did they have to cut off the pants? Couldn't they have just taken them off me gently? Had I soiled myself?

Those thoughts played around in my mind, bouncing off the walls like a pinball, each one sharper and more jarring than the last as I skillfully applied foundation that morning. The mirror reflected a face I barely recognized, each stroke of the brush a reminder of the battle I fought daily. I didn't care about styling my hair that morning; I let my frizzy long curls sleep in their hive atop my head, a wild testament to my indifference. It didn't matter. This was a pajama roll-out-of-bed type of morning, a brief reprieve from the expectations that seemed to suffocate me.

I felt light that morning, buoyed by the knowledge that I had only popped one 2-milligram pill of Klonopin. Just one. The soft haze of calm that settled over me felt like a gentle embrace, a comforting cushion against the weight of the world.

The next scene that is embedded in my memory is a clear picture, vivid and unfading. I am sitting on the couch, the familiar fabric beneath me worn and comforting, and John is on one knee in front of me, holding out a small box. Oh, how I loved that box; it was finally mine, a treasure that shimmered with the promise of forever.

"Babygirl, will you marry me?" I still hear John's voice, clear and sharp, cutting through the fog of uncertainty that often clouded my thoughts.

"Yes! Yes! I will marry you!" My words burst forth, echoing in my mind, ringing like church bells announcing a joyous occasion. My dream come true, the culmination of all my hopes and desires wrapped in that tiny velvet case. This was the moment I had waited for, the moment I had dreamt of. I belonged—or so I told myself, a mantra meant to drown out the whispers of doubt lurking in the corners of my mind.

Chapter 5

To pee or Not to pee?
(Whose pee is really, in my fridge?)

"Diana, do you want a spring wedding or a summer wedding?" I can still hear Mrs. B's voice inquiring, a gentle nudge that pushed me further into a world I wasn't sure I was ready to inhabit. I was still riding the high of the proposal. I wanted the wedding but I had no idea of what I wanted the wedding to look like. No image, no wedding dream.

"Babygirl, my mom needs to know the date for the wedding. Wanna get married in the spring?"

I hear John asking one morning as he was getting ready for work and the methadone clinic. His mom was on her way to pick him up, the air heavy with the unspoken weight of urgency.

"Spring is so soon, we won't have enough time to plan a wedding."

"What's there to plan, we will have it at my parents house." He said giving me a kiss goodbye as he walked out of the bedroom. I thought I had choice of venue and in that minute, I realized I didn't.

John had lost his take-homes, failed a drug test that showed cocaine in his system. Just the week before, he'd been passing those tests with ease, relying on someone in the clinic to provide him with their clean urine samples. He needed urine from someone on methadone, and only on methadone.

As I write this now, I wonder who it was that felt such a bond to him, someone willing to provide continuous urine samples for months on end. It was a bizarre kind of loyalty, twisted and tangled, much like our relationship. He kept the urine in the fridge, warming it up in the microwave before heading to the clinic. The image is seared into my mind: a bottle of someone else's life, kept cool and concealed, a life he was passing off as his own. Now, I'm left wondering why he failed that drug test that jeopardized his take-homes.

"The guy's pee was no good. He told me he didn't mess with other shit, but they found coke in his piss. I can't use it anymore. I need to find someone else." Soon after, he did.

Who was this guy? Who was the other guy he found? I think back now, and none of it makes sense. John had no friends, and that is not an exaggeration, but rather a stone cold truth. Or so I believed. But he obviously had friends, people he saw outside of our bedroom, people I didn't know and would never meet.

Who were these people so dedicated to peeing into a small container just for John.

And Why?

"Babygirl, I gotta meet the dude. Gotta get the clean pee for tomorrow. He's picking me up in a minute. I gotta go," he said, urgency lacing his words.

"Don't leave me," I pleaded, coiled around his body, his Nautica cologne enveloping me like a warm blanket. He was dressed in his white Adidas shirt, jeans, and those familiar shell-top sneakers, the uniform that made him feel like my anchor in a sea of chaos. His Motorola phone rang, a jarring interruption.

"I am coming now," he answered, flipping his phone open with a practiced ease that felt oddly detached.

"Babygirl, I gotta go," he said, pushing me off of him gently. I felt the loss of his warmth like a chill sweeping through the room. He kissed me on the lips, and I wasn't ready to let go. I clung to him, my knees wobbling on the waterbed beneath me. My arms were wrapped around his neck as he stood up, a lifeline I didn't want to lose.

"Don't leave me," I whispered, the words slipping out like a plea. He kissed me again, soft yet tinged with a sense of finality, before he unclenched my hands from around him.

"I will be right back. I'll pick up a present for you."

With that, I let go, reluctantly releasing my grip. As he left the room, the door closing behind him felt like the slamming shut of a vault, sealing away whatever fleeting sense of safety I had.

Now, I wonder why I didn't get out of bed to go see who this dude was picking John up in the darkness of the evening. Instead, I reached for my bottle of pills on the bedside table, my fingers trembling as they grasped the familiar container. I took one, letting it wash over me like a wave. Thirty minutes later, I took another, seeking refuge in the numbing embrace of the substance. I don't know when he came back. I can't pinpoint the exact moment he reentered my world. But when he did, he came back with clean pee and heroin for me, the double-edged sword of my love, my high functioning addiction.

Chapter 6

*Boobies and Bootie*s

John loved looking at other women. Every time we went anywhere, he would beam, his voice a triumphant trumpet in the symphony of our mundane outing.

"Babygirl, look at the boobies on that one!" he'd declare, as though he were unveiling a masterpiece in a gallery. The ways his eyes lit up, was a jarring contrast to the way I felt inside a steady hum of unease threading a spiderweb through my mind.

Once we were engaged, the veil of pretense slipped away completely. His excitement for other women had transformed from a secret thrill to an open invitation.

"We should have a threesome," he would pursue and push daily, with a glimmer of mischief in his eye. His eyes danced at the thought of other women, they had a hunger he had long lost for me. Or at least he no longer looked at me with those eyes; only when he was entertaining ideas of inviting another into our bed did he look at me with those sparkling, dancing, blue eyes. His gaze would always dart from one woman to the next, as though we were window shopping for ornaments or clothes – trivial, unimportant, easily discarded.

"Look at those titties! Do you like the booty on that one. That booty is better than Jlo's!"

Did I like the booty on that one? Was it better than Jlo's? I didn't know. Did I even find women attractive? Each glance he cast at another was a dagger, severing the delicate thread of my self-worth. Each woman was a competition, with their perfect curves, flawless sin, and small button noses, there to steal John away from me.

I feared him leaving me for another more than I feared death.

John had a small nose. I loved his button nose; it seemed so perfectly tailored to his face, like the gentle arc of a bird's wing. Back then he looked just like Leonardo DiCaprio, even my mom agreed with me.

Of course everywoman wanted him. And he let them know he wanted them with his eyes, his smirk. I saw it and that would make me shrink more into the obsession of changing me. I was an ugly hag, My reflection haunted me, a witch with a large nose, distorted and cruel in its honesty. If only I could get a nose job, I would think to myself, allowing the spiral into the depths of my insecurities rush through me, turning my veins into ice. Starving myself expanded the cold, the hunger was a feeling I cherished to control. I allowed John to control, when, how, and what I ate, mainly it was what he ate. I needed to be controlled, but the feeling of hunger and the purge after the binge was mine to control. My secret thrive, another high.

"You know, babygirl, you can't be trusted. You set little fires everywhere you go," he would say to me, with a strange mix of affectionate teasing and accusation in his tone.

And of course he was right. I did set little fires, bright and chaotic, consuming everything in their path.

Beneath the surface however, I secretly yearned for the very thing that made me tremble. I wanted a threesome. Did John read my mind? Did he already know my deepest darkest desire? Although I didn't want it for his delight, I secretly earned for the soft female touch. There was a secret craving I had, for the warmth, and comfort of another woman.

My relationship with sex was always tangled, a curious blend of yearning and trepidation. Sex had always been for me a means to an end, a solution I wielded to keep John satisfied, to ensure he wouldn't leave me. Without him I was sure to die.

"Look at those titties bouncing up and down, don't you just wanna squeeze them?"

I really didn't it, that sounded so intrusive.

"Yeah, she has some great tattas,"

I would chirp trying to match his enthusiasm, hoping to deflect any brewing storm. It was a delicate dance, one that often ended with me curled on the floor, tears pooling at the edges of my vision, a desperate plea for mercy that would never come.

It was always better to agree with him, to nod along with his whims, even as I felt the weight of each agreement pressing down on my chest, suffocating my voice. In those moments, I was less of a partner and more a pawn, caught in a game I didn't know how to play. It was a different type of chess games, where no one had bothered to explain the rules to me.

Chapter 7

Sex with John

I always hated switching sexual partners. It was the most painful part of a break up – getting used to a new body, new penis, new way of movement, the way they touched you. Every time felt like tearing off a layer of skin, the penetration felt as though I was being raped all over.

John and I, by the time he proposed, had been together for six years. His fetishes slowly became mine, like second hand smoke creeping into my lungs. I began to enjoy the pain during the sex portion he called Fucking. John loved porn, cocaine and sex. He loved to penetrate and thrust, until I felt like my insides were ripping apart. He loved shoving random dildos inside of me, asking me it felt good. I always moaned and said it did. The making love portion of sex, I loved most but rarely felt. I never experienced a true   orgasm. Sex for me always felt like I was being raped again and again and again.

"You know what adidas stands for babygirl?" He asked me one night after the fucking type of sex.

"All day I dream about sport?" I responded, wondering if I had memorized the acronym

correctly, lighting my Newport in bed.

"That's what they want you to think, really it stands for all day I dream about sex."

John is the one who really introduced me to porn, he made me watch it, made me enjoy it. You need to "enjoy it" I still hear his words echoing in my mind. He loved having sex with the screen flickering in the background, bodies twisted in impossible angles, moaning from somewhere that wasn't us. I didn't really get it, but I learned how to fake it.

Wasn't porn something you watched alone? When you didn't have someone? I would always wonder, but never dare to pose the questions aloud to John. He loved it, and he made it part of our ritual. Eventually I stopped posing those questions to myself. I let it blend into our routine the way you let something inevitable just happen, like rain on a day you didn't bring an umbrella.

The only other time, I'd ever seen porn was back at the W. I was the manager of the Varsity boys soccer team. The only girl. It was Thanksgiving break, and the dorms had all closed, except for one wing where the team and the coaches stayed. I was the only girl left, provided with a single room in the boys' dorm. We all hung out together anyway, crowded into someone's room, eating snacks, watching whatever was on TV.

One of the guys – I can't even remember who – popped in a tape and smirked.

"Guys, you ever seen fat porn?"

A chorus of disgusted groans, my voice included filled the room.

"FUCK NO!" we all yelled, but no one moved to stop him.

"Well get ready to see some shit you'll never unsee," he said jamming the tape into the VCR. The static crackled, and then there it was, right in front of us – flesh spilling over, sweaty bodies, something grotesque and absurd all at once. Ten minutes of this. Ten minutes of my eyes not believing what they were seeing. The boys laughed, throwing comments like darts. And then Coach C. walked in. He was the hot coach. Only twenty five. The kind of guy all the girls secretly liked and openly gossiped about. He sat down, joined in with the jeering, at first. But then, after a minute, his eyes locked on mine. I was there, silent, the only girl. His face changed.

"Guys, turn it off. We've got a girl in here!" He barked, like it was something that just then dawned on him. One of the guys shouted back, "It's just little D. She don't care. This is some crazy shit!" I shrugged my shoulders, maybe I didn't care.

Coach C. Stood up then, and said, "Now, I am serious shut that shit off. We have a big game tomorrow!" And with that everything went quiet. Everyone dispersed into their dorm rooms.

But the damage to me was done. To this day, I can't unsee those ten minutes. The flashes of hanging skin, the guys laughter that filled the room in disgust. The way it made me feel, like something had been peeled back inside me, something I didn't want exposed. So when John said, "Let's go to the porn store," all I could think about was that tape. My fifteen year old self, sitting on the twin sized bed, surrounded by a bunch of guys, ranging between the ages of seventeen and twenty, plus one hot coach who a little bit too late realized, that I was there.

Chapter 8

Life with John

"You always need to answer when I call you, babygirl," he would say, with a tone that seemed to hover somewhere between a command and a plea.

And I always did. If I missed his call during the day, perhaps because I was asleep, I knew he would be upset. It was a certainty I could feel creeping in, even before I dialed back, an anxiety settling deep in my chest. I would have to make it up to him, somehow. The guilt that followed me, a shadowy presence at my shoulder, was always there. I still feel it, a dull echo, when I think of missing one of his check-ins, his "I love you" calls.

Yet when it was I who needed to check in, he was rarely around. Never there, always too busy for me. I remember the way my hands trembled when I had to dial the main company number. My heart would race, almost leaping out of my chest. His father might answer. Or B. Either way, I'd come off as the needy girlfriend. Either way, it would bother John.

He was sensitive, you see, in a way that made me feel as though I were navigating around glass. I walked through his emotions like I was stepping on eggshells, careful not to crack anything. There was fear, but I mistook it for love. Perhaps, at the time, I had to.

This is not to say that John didn't bring me presents. He did. Flowers, shoes, watches—whatever I wanted, truly. He made sure I wanted, or rather, he believed I deserved. His gestures of affection were constant, unrelenting, almost like a ritual we both performed. After all, I was to be his wife.

Of course, my favorite moments with John, the ones that stand out, were when we walked to Barnes & Noble together. We had this on-again, off-again tradition, especially when the weather was nice—sun shining, crisp air,—where he would suddenly announce,

"Let's go for a walk, my babygirl deserves a book."

And I'd feel something loosen inside me, even if only for a moment. I loved losing myself in the aisles, the smell of new pages, though, if I'm being honest, what I missed most were the old books, their musty scent and forgotten corners. Still, I never went without him. Never ventured anywhere without John, except for work or school. Even the library felt out of reach unless he was by my side.

After we got engaged, life seemed to flow more easily, though in retrospect, it was less flow and more a current I had resigned myself to. John bought me more gifts. He would leave money for me, telling me to get my nails done, to go tanning. It seemed, to me, that

this was how things were supposed to be. The shift came quietly, like so many shifts do.

"I don't want you to fly to Florida for photo shoots anymore," he said one day. "You're going to be my wife soon, and you shouldn't be traveling without me."

And I, in full agreement, responded, "No, daddy, I shouldn't be traveling without you." Relieved, in fact, that I wouldn't have to feel another sweaty body on top of me.

Chapter 9

Lightly Shattered

      I love my father, I can write it now and accept the fact that I always will. Although, throughout my childhood, my teens age years, my twenties, I hated him. I was consumed by hate for him, and the fear of him. It has taken me over thirty years to acknowledge the fact that, there is no way around it, no escaping the fact that he is a part of me, intricately wired into the mechanics of my mind. We think alike, he and I—our thoughts twist and tangle, overlapping in ways that feel inevitable.

And so, to love myself fully, I have learned that I must also love him, this man who has shaped me in ways both clear and elusive, this man with whom I have had the most complicated relationship of my life.

Still, I can't help but wonder—did he ever feel love for me?

I've never heard him say it aloud, not once. I catch flashes of him in my mind, those early memories from the Soviet Union, a towering figure always busy, always studying. When he would visit my mother, it seemed his only purpose was to correct me. Discipline became the language between us. I will never forget the tears I cried, pressed into the corner between the wardrobe and the window. The wardrobe's door swung open just so, blocking purposefully the outside world away from me. All that was left was my reflection, ghostly in the windowpane. I shook with sobs, the kind that stole the breath from my lungs, while my babushkas pleaded with him, begged him to let me go.

Their words clashed with his anger, and I feared—deeply feared—that his rage would spill over onto them. He would yell, they would fall silent, and I would cry harder. I felt, in those moments, that I had failed him.

"She can't memorize a simple Pushkin poem! She has no drive!" The words thundered in my ears, though in truth, the original Russian was even harsher.

No matter how hard I tried, I couldn't memorize the poems perfectly, not in the way he demanded. My mind would slip, betray me by changing a word or skipping a line. I wasn't trying to defy him; it was simply beyond me.

But I could never make him see that. His punishments were precise, predictable. If I couldn't recite the poem flawlessly, I would stand in the corner. No friends, no play. Just stand, still and silent, for at least an hour.

But I couldn't do it without crying.

How could I explain to him that I had tried, truly tried, with all the force of my will, but my mind had other plans? Even now, I struggle. Words escape me at the last moment, my brain twisting them as if on purpose, breaking from the script.

But I've learned to mask it.

My mind is faster than it appears, correcting itself before anyone notices. Back then, though, all Iccould do was cry and call myself stupid. A failure. At five years old, that word had already lodged itself deep in my chest.

"Do you always expect praise?" my father had asked, his voice cool and detached, as if praise itself were something beneath contempt. He made it clear that to seek praise, to crave it, was wrong. The way he said the word—praise—made it sound like something dirty, shameful.

"No," I had replied, instinctively denying the hunger I felt.

But inside, I was screaming.

Yes! Yes! Yes Please!

I wanted praise. I longed for it, craved it like water in a desert. But admitting that was unthinkable.

My father, a genius in every sense of the word, was not a man to be trifled with.

His accomplishments were vast—full scholarship to Yale as an immigrant, a lead negotiator in resolving the Chechen War. But at home, he was distant, always working. I doubt he ever truly wanted a family. We pressed on him like an unwanted weight. When we moved to the U.S., my childhood fears of him only deepened. He became an immutable authority, his word law. As I grew older, I began to rebel, quietly, subtly. If he said no, I would find a way around it, but only so he wouldn't notice.

"You need to tell your father you love him," the shrink had said, her voice firm but soft, coaxing me from behind the veil of my silence. My father sat to my left, my mother on my right, and I had edged my chair farther from him, terrified of what those words would mean.

"If you tell your father you love him, you can leave today," she added, dangling freedom in front of me like a lifeline.

Didn't she see? Didn't she understand that being in this place, this psychiatric ward, was already enough to shame him? How could I tell him now that I loved him, when I had never heard it from his lips? My body was frozen, the words stuck somewhere deep, unreachable. But as I sat there in that heavy silence, I chewed on the inside of my cheek, as if searching for a place where I could still move without being seen. My teeth found that hidden spot, gnawing at it while the rest of me remained paralyzed. I could barely breathe, my eyes flickering toward his, unsure of what I would find. In that brief, stolen glance, I saw something I hadn't expected—a tearful glaze, like a thin layer of mist over his eyes. It caught the light, bringing out the full green in his hazel eyes. In that moment, it seemed as though he wanted to say something, or maybe feel something, but the silence remained unbroken.

I wanted to speak, to tell him I loved him. But I couldn't. I couldn't even move my lips to shape the words. The room closed in, and I sat there, trapped. I spent another week and a half at Westwood

Lodge.

To this day, I can't remember if I actually said the words. But I must have, because they released me.

My father and I have learned to live in silence. Our interactions now are void of words, as if we have tacitly agreed that language would only complicate the vast space between us. Or perhaps it's just him—perhaps he simply has none left for me. As for me, I am full of words, swollen with them.

They sit heavy in my chest, pressing against my lungs until I feel like I might burst from the weight of them. But I can never utter them, and I never will. Those words, those desperate, aching questions—what would they even change? They feel too raw, too wild to be spoken aloud. There is a part of me that is learning, slowly and painfully, to let them go. It doesn't matter if he loves me. It doesn't matter that he has never said the words, not

once in all my years of waiting.

Love doesn't have to be spoken to exist, does it? You don't have to like to love.

But still, the thoughts linger like a shadow: it doesn't matter that he will never understand me. Because to understand me, he would first have to face his own demons, the ones he's buried so deeply that they've become part of the foundation of who he is. He assumes he knows, when in truth he doesn't. He has never seen me, the full picture of me.

I don't think he ever grasped, the fear I felt of him. But I know he felt the hate, he is a master at reading people, emotions, body language, but he always misread me.

I've tried to unearth those demons, not for him, but for myself. In some strange way, understanding him feels like the key to understanding myself. We are more alike than I'd care to admit, and sometimes I wonder if my battles with my mind are really just echoes of his.

But when I search for answers, I find only silence. There was a time when I would have given anything for a glimpse inside his mind. To know what he thinks of me—if he even thinks of me at all.

Does he see me as the child who failed, the one who couldn't recite the Pushkin poems perfectly? Does he see me as a reflection of his own shortcomings, someone who could never live up to his expectations? I'll never know. And slowly, I'm coming to terms with the fact that I don't need to know. His approval, his love—these are things I once craved with every fiber of my being. But now, as the years stretch between us, I'm realizing that they are not what define me.

I am more than the daughter who stood in the corner, more than the girl who couldn't say "I love you" when it mattered most.

Our silence, in a way, has become our language. It's the only language we share or are able to understand.

I love my father, although I am not sure if I could utter those words aloud to him, not even today.

But I am able to write them, and for now that is all that matters.

I tried to gather myself together, piece by piece, like patching up a broken mirror where the cracks still show. The engagement ring on my finger felt like proof I was doing something right, like it meant I was whole or getting closer to being whole. I applied for a management position at Things Remembered, and it came as a strange comfort when they hired me that same week. A steady job to hold onto.

But no job, no ring could stop the days from bleeding into each other. They gelled together into this viscous loop of nothing. I still took modeling gigs, the ones I could get without losing my grip on the last bits of sanity I had. Time for print, or if I was lucky, fifty dollars here, a hundred there.

The high-paying gigs were usually shady, and I was done with those. Stacy was too far away, I couldn't take on the shady gigs without her. I couldn't handle the humiliation of being naked and touched and probed, all the while being told I looked hot. With her at a distance, I was able to find some grounding, set a boundary to my brokenness.

My mind? It was still broken. I couldn't function without a high dose of Klonopin, and more often than not, I didn't have them. John kept me going with methadone, smuggled from the clinic in cotton swabs, like it was some backdoor treatment plan for living in this limbo.

The seizures, they were worse. I was having one every other month, sometimes more. Lucky, they'd say, that I wasn't breaking anything.

But I remember the time I did. That horror, the way it's still there, lodged in me like a thorn that can't be pulled out. I was working at the Square One Mall, but I can't remember which job it was—Victoria's Secret or Lancôme. Those details slip away, the way memories sometimes do when trauma erases the margins.

What I do remember is being on break. I walked up to Dunkin' Donuts on the second floor. I had fifteen minutes, just enough time to grab an iced coffee.

My usual: large, vanilla iced coffee with extra cream and sugar. I remember feeling something coming, a shimmer, like when a light bulb flickers before it goes out. I stepped onto the escalator, clinging to the black snake like moving rail, and that's when everything went black.

When I woke, I was staring at the blinding fluorescent lights of the emergency room. The disorientation, the sheer panic of waking up in a hospital bed after a grand mal seizure -it's a fear I can't put into words. It's like dying, and then coming back to life knowing that your mind had been gone, disappeared, failed you. It's like the world happened without you, and you're left trying to fill in the blank space where you used to be.

They told me later what happened. I had stepped onto the escalator, and as soon as I did, the seizure took over. I went flying down the steps and smashed my head against the

mall's marble tile flooring. I cracked my skull, lightly they said, as if there's any light way to break your skull. Seven staples.

Seven little bits of metal holding me together. I broke my collarbone too, and that pain—it was endless. I numbed it the only way I knew how, by snorting Heroin.

John brought me what I needed, the same way he'd bring the methadone. It all blurred together into one long haze of pain and escape. I couldn't even shave my legs, the simple act of caring for myself.

John took over that too. He'd bring me into the shower, and I let him, let him run the razor over my skin, smooth away the hair I could no longer reach. At the time, I thought there was something tender in it, some reflection of love or care. Now, I'm not so sure. Maybe it was just another layer of control, another thing I couldn't do for myself.

      The only weddings I have ever seen firsthand were wedding ceremonies in Tbilisi. A traditional Georgian wedding ceremony looks nothing like a traditional Catholic wedding ceremony in the US. The wedding costumes, the dancing, and the slaughtering of the lamb are in no way accepted Western traditions of a wedding ceremony.

When I was little, before the move to Armenia, I must have been six. It was in our Tbilisi apartment; my great grandma had kept the wedding pieces of her own wedding. She had a traditional Russian wedding, which also differs from Western weddings and Georgian weddings. She would tell me stories of her dowry and the traditional sacrament of marriage. She had the veil saved and would let me wear it. I would pretend I was a bride walking down the aisle. The veil itself was beautiful; it was made of silk tulle, with exquisite embroidery. I wanted to wear that veil on my wedding day. But that veil was gone, destroyed and abandoned as all our other possessions, everything we had in Georgia, died with my great grandma, Polina.

I wasn't excited to plan a wedding. I had no idea how to even go about it. My family was tiny in comparison to John's, a mere collection of souls against the overwhelming expanse of his lineage. It was just me, my dad, my mom, my brother, and sister. We had no relatives in this country, an echoing silence that filled the empty spaces in our lives. I didn't even know how to appreciate my family then; all I could do was try to run away

from them, into a dream family I created first in my mind and then projected out into the real world—an illusion wrapped in a fragile veneer of domestic bliss.

By all Hallmark card expectations, John's family met the standards, glossy and idealized, yet beneath that surface shimmered the danger of ties to the mob. John loved The Sopranos. It was his Sex and the City, a strange juxtaposition of suburban glamor and the violent underbelly of organized crime.

He idolized Tony Soprano, and I, in turn, idolized Carmella—her poised exterior masking the turbulence beneath. It was through The Sopranos that he began to push the ideas of a threesome or of him having other women, a script I was beginning to willingly sign up for. I had given up my dreams of being someone, to becoming a trophy wife without a voice. John, to me, was Mr. Big mixed with Tony Soprano, an intoxicating blend of charm and menace, enticing and terrifying all at once.

But as for wedding planning? I was in the dark, a flickering candle in a vast, unyielding night. I had no idea what my expense budget was, but I knew we didn't have money, just a patchwork of dreams stitched together with imagery. Whatever was decided upon was expected to be paid for by John's parents, a burden I didn't carry, merely a spectator in this grand production. My parents were willing to contribute, and it was decided that they would pay for my wedding dress and the wedding cake, sweet offerings amid the chaos.

There was a relief with John's mom taking over. I had no idea or the strength to please all his relatives, an army of expectations that loomed large over me. His mom knew how, a seasoned general navigating the treacherous terrain of family dynamics. I was happy to float along for the ride, surrendering my autonomy to the currents that swept around me. I gave up all wedding ideas—or any I could have had on my own—to her. She did it all, even planned out a bridal shower that included around twenty close female family members of John's, my mom, my sister, and me—an overwhelming tide of faces, laughter, and unspoken judgments.

Chapter 10

The Bridal Shower

Mrs. B. organized the whole bridal shower down to the seating arrangements at Kowloon. It was her event and she ran it like a perfectly oiled machine. We were seated around a massive table, the kind meant for family style meals, laden with Pou Pou platters that overflowed with every possible fried delight – egg rolls, chicken wings, beef teriyaki, crab ragoons all of which Kowloon was famous for, and the family was known for ordering the large Pou Pou platters for family dinners when Mrs. B. didn't feel like cooking.

My mom sat silently, her posture straight and stiff. I could tell by her body language that she wasn't sure how to handle herself in the middle of all this, I was wedged between my sister and one of John's sisters, feeling detached from the swarm of loud conversations bouncing around me.

The room was a buzz of excitement, laughter ricocheting off the walls as relatives who hadn't seen each other in years caught up over greasy finger food and cocktails. It wasn't exactly my crowd, but I had masterfully learned how to navigate through the hum of it all. So, I plastered on my smile, chugged my long island, and tried to absorb the moment. I had long resigned myself to float through this kind of family affair – always the outsider, but present in the role I was supposed to play.

Suddenly, I heard, a boisterous shout cut through my absorption of alcohol process like a knife,

"Now that you're getting married, you're going to need to keep it sexy in the bedroom."

Keep it sexy? I let the words sink in like an old, wanted tip. As though I hadn't been playing that part for the past five years, as though that is not what got me a ring on my finger. The unspoken expectations of my future as John's wife started to feel heavier. Maybe a threesome was what it would take to keep it spicy.

Keep it sexy, but I couldn't entertain the idea yet. He hadn't said "I do". He could still walk away.

One by one, the presents were passed my way, each unwrapped to reveal an array of see-through lingerie.

If they only knew about my two, already stuffed drawers with Victoria Secret lingerie, or my nude photos. Would they still give me these presents?

I can still recall myself musing then, to myself. as I unwrapped through tissue paper each piece of lingerie, each gift.

One of the presents was a delicate, turquoise, babydoll piece, almost sweet in its appearance, until I noticed the nipple slits and the underwear that seemed to forget its purpose entirely. Just strips of lace missing any semblance of modesty.

Was my sister ok to see this? I was thinking in that moment…

I didn't have time to process, as I heard someone shout, I bet it was John's aunt D,

"Oh, that's a fun one! He can fuck you and suck on your nipples as the same time, and you don't even need to take the damn thing off!"

I could feel the heat rising in my face, burning with the kind of embarrassment I thought I'd left behind in adolescence. I chugged the rest of my second Long Island Iced Tea, hoping the alcohol would dull the sharpness of the moment.

I thanked God I couldn't see my mother's face. I couldn't bear to meet her eyes, to know what she was thinking, sitting through this charade of raunchy jokes and ill-timed comments. What about my sister? She was only eleven. Should she be hearing this?

I voice jumped around my head, bouncing around the walls of my skull like a tennis ball. As I tried to contain myself on having any reaction, other than excitement of joy to the present I had just received. I thanked God my father wasn't there. I could only imagine his reaction if he had been. This event was light years away from the polished political events that my parents attended, where university professors and politicians mingles with foreign dignitaries and members of Congress.

Those circles, with their wine-fueled cultural debates, and intellectual sparring now felt like a distant universe. John's family operated in an entirely different stratosphere – sharp contrast to the bourgeois world I had grown up in.

Chapter 11

Spike Photography

The wedding date was decided on in the months of spring, when the air still had a chill, and there was a desperate need for warmth. A lingering cold that clung to everything, making the idea of July feel distant, like a mirage of heat and sun that would somehow melt away the frost still settled in my bones. It wasn't my idea, not really.

"Maybe we should just get married on my birthday: July 30th? That way I can celebrate my birthday and wedding anniversary on the same day. My wedding is like my rebirth?"

I was saying to John, snuggled up to him, craving the heat of his body, a familiar refuge against the cold I couldn't shake.

"No, that wouldn't be right. A wedding date needs to be separated from your birthday," he responded, his voice always so firm, as if the world could only be held in place by his rules.

"Well, I don't know then. I don't have a date in mind," I murmured, my uncertainty mixing with the chill in the air, leaving me unsure of anything, of everything.

"It can still be July, just not on your birthday."

And so the wedding date was set for July 19, 2008. A day chosen not for meaning, but because it was convenient, because it was close enough to a day that mattered to me, but not so close as to threaten John's sense of order. The spring air still had its teeth, biting at me, making July feel impossibly far away. But it was settled, like so much else in our lives, a decision that left me half-frozen, half-warming to the idea, never fully sure which.

During this time, I had become friends with one of my photographers. Spike. He was young, close to my age, and had an effortless way about him, like the world hadn't yet sunk its claws into him. He had mastered the art of natural light photography. And unlike the others, he didn't care about getting me naked, didn't need to strip me down for his lens to find beauty. He cared about the art— the play of light on skin, the shadows curling around form. There was something pure in that, something that didn't leave me feeling hollow after the shutter clicked. I loved working with photographers who were driven by more than just the need to capture a pretty face, or worse, to possess it.

Spike was like that. His drive was magnetic, pulling me toward something bigger than myself, something beyond the confines of what I'd been taught to expect from the world. With him, it wasn't about what I looked like, but what I could be.

"Ok, hold your shoulders back. Now stretch your neck back, then slowly bring your head

forward. You'll feel it align," he would say. His voice was steady, grounding. Even now, I can hear him in my head, as though his words were written in the air, a quiet instruction that lingered long after the session ended.

He taught me how to model, how to find my center in the chaos that swirled around me—how to inhabit my own body when it felt like I had forgotten how. I use that trick to this day. Whether in front of the camera, speaking to strangers, or simply standing alone in a crowded room, I straighten my shoulders, stretch my neck, and realign. It's a small ritual of survival, something to hold onto when the world feels too sharp.

But outside the shoots, Spike and I didn't hang out. John wouldn't have liked it. He didn't like me working with Spike to begin with.

"Why are you doing shoots you aren't even getting paid for?"

John's voice always had that edge, the one that cut into me, questioning my every decision, reminding me that everything had to have value, a price tag, or it wasn't worth doing.

"It's good practice. I'm actually learning something. I'm learning natural light photography," I said, trying to soften my words, trying to make them palatable to him. My voice felt small, as though I were shrinking inside my skin.

"Plus, Spike agreed to photograph our whole wedding. Private photographer, free of charge! Private wedding photographers are expensive," I added, desperation creeping in.

"Fine, but after the wedding, you're done with the monkeyspank Spike!" John snapped, dismissive, as though Spike were nothing more than a name to be ridiculed, a person reduced to a single, crude label. I felt the sting of that comment, the way it hollowed me out.

John always had a way of reducing things, people, until they fit into the narrow space he allowed for them. He couldn't stand the idea of anyone, especially another man, being in my life if they weren't under his control. But for now, I had Spike, at least until the wedding. I held onto that small rebellion, even if John didn't understand it. Spike would photograph the wedding—our day, my day, the day I was supposed to be reborn. And yet, I couldn't shake the feeling that I was fading. Fading into something smaller, something quieter, as though each step toward that wedding day was a step away from myself.

Chapter 12

John's Foot

John had bought me a collection of Sex and The City DVDs one day. It was the collection I dreamt of—hot pink box, velvety to the touch, each season nestled perfectly inside like little secrets waiting to be unraveled. I went on daily, weekly binges, watching and rewatching the episodes, sometimes with John beside me, though it wasn't really his thing.

"Oh please, let's watch this episode together. It's the one where she wears an Oscar de la Renta dress to McDonald's with Mikhail Baryshnikov! Just this one episode? Please, daddy?" I pleaded with

John.

Baryshnikov. How I adored him. I had fallen in love with him from the moment I saw White Nights, his escape from the Soviet Union to America playing out like a fantasy I wanted to be part of. His body moved like water, every muscle and line a stroke of genius. I would have give anything to be in any scene with him, real or imagined.

"Ok, babygirl. But then we're watching Prison Break."

"Deal! I just love the episodes with Baryshnikov. He's no Mr. Big, but he's an incredible ballet dancer in real life."

"So, he's a Ruski fag in tights?" John said, half-laughing.

"No, he's not!" I snapped, the joke landing sour.

"Ok, babygirl, I'm just kidding."

We snuggled into bed as the episode began. Carrie, ever the dreamer, floated across the screen, her life impossibly glamorous and, in that moment, deeply unrelatable. I watched the scene unfold, half-wishing I could trade places with her, just for a second.

"I want to wear an Oscar de la Renta dress to McDonald's," I said wistfully. "I wish I was as beautiful as Sarah Jessica Parker. But maybe I am—she has a big nose too."

"You're way more beautiful. She looks like my foot."

John lifted his socked foot, up to the screen, blocking Carrie's face.

"That's mean, don't say that," I said, smiling. But I wasn't smiling on the inside. My face wore a smile that wasn't real, a mask I had crafted over time, so tightly wound it felt fused to my marrow. The mask held the pain back, separated it from the surface, hiding the insecurities that rattled inside me. My thoughts ricocheted around my skull like wild bullets, uncontrollable. If he thinks Carrie is ugly, then I am hideous.

I am nothing more than his foot.

My reflection would later take on the shape of the words he spoke, seeping into the cracks of my self-worth. Every time I looked in the mirror, my nose long, sharp, staring at me, looking like John's foot, his big toe, misshapen out of place.

I couldn't help but wonder if he saw me the same way—flawed, misshapen, just a body part lying next to him, not worth the Oscar de la Renta dress or even the fantasy of it. Inside, something sharp twisted. I sat there, invisible in my own skin, as John laughed, unaware, unaffected, as if his words hadn't left bruises.

Chapter 13

Maid of Honor Comes to Town

I was counting down the days and hours until Stacy's arrival, clinging to the thought of her like a life raft. I had placed her high up on a pedestal, my fairy godmother, my sister in all but blood. There was no wrong she could do, not anymore. The bad—whatever had happened in the past—was buried deep, forgotten, never to be unearthed again. Water under the bridge, as Stacy's mom would say. The plan was that Stacy would stay with me in the apartment while John moved into his parents' house for the week. That separation increased my morning anxiety attacks even more. I would wake up, as usual, my morning ritual, before the drugs, heart pounding, body feels like its shaking, although I am not sure if it is or not, I am trying to soothe myself by rubbing my feet together, one over the other a rhythmic motion, but the pounding of the heart increases and begins to swell up in my throat. Next a round of dry heaves would take over and without a choice I would bolt out of bed to the bathroom, I would hurl over the toilet seat. As though I was trying to throw up my heart, but only mucous would come out.

Was he really going to stay at his parents? The question stalked my dreams. Was he   really just going to sleep there, like he said? What about his bachelor party?

He hadn't told me a word about it—no details, no plans, just that his dad was going to throw him a party.

Was he hiding something from me?

These questions lingered like smoke, swirling just beneath the surface.

Making my way to the bed, I would take the bottle of Kolonopin off the night stand, pop one in under my tongue, letting it slowly melt into me, the medicinal sweetness, the numbness of the pill was like warmth of love I needed, like I needed air each morning.

With the pill melting under my tongue I would crawl in between my sheets

…..and wait.

Wait for it to take its full effect to push the anxiety down, deep inside, burying it beneath my skin where it could only come alive in the mornings, before my daily methadone intake. Each morning, John handed me my measured dose of methadone, carefully doling out every milligram, like some tender act of devotion. He had the take-homes again, a small blessing.

"Let's honeymoon in Florida," I had said to him a few weeks prior to Stacy's arrival, my voice lilting with the excitement of the fantasy.

"I've always wanted to see Nana and Papa's mansion in Fort Lauderdale. It just sits there empty all summer. You've got the take-homes; are you sure your dad won't give you a week off for the honeymoon?" John had sighed, his face a mix of guilt and resignation.

"You know how he is. He won't give me more than three days. We can go to New Hampshire. Summer is the busy season. You know this."

New Hampshire. The words tasted flat and gray. My heart had sunk like a stone, but I had pouted anyway, trying to keep the mood light, playful. Still, I couldn't help the tears that gathered in the corners of my eyes. New Hampshire wasn't what I wanted.

I wanted more. I wanted the glittering lights of Miami, the soft pastel hues of Fort Lauderdale, the languid afternoons spent in Nana and Papa's empty mansion—just John and me, cloaked in the luxury of a life I'd only ever dreamed about. But that wasn't going to happen. Instead, I was left clutching at the edges of a dream that was slipping further and further away.

The morning Stacy arrived, I woke to the same hollow ache in my chest, the familiar knot of unease coiling tighter. But underneath it all was the bright spark of her visit, the hope that maybe, with her here, things would feel different. I had placed so much weight on her presence, as if she could magically make everything better, as if she could fill the cracks that had started to show between me and John. Her text came just after she landed, and my heart lifted. She was finally here.

As I waited outside for her cab, my mind raced. What would she say when she saw me? Would she notice the lines of worry etched into my face, the weight of my uncertainty? Or would she see only the version of me I so desperately wanted to present—the version that had it all together, who was excited about the wedding, who was happy and in control?

The yellow cab pulled up, and there she was, stepping out with her usual grace. Stacy always looked perfect, like someone who hadn't known a day of struggle. But the truth was she knew struggle, the torment of the mind with insecurity embedded in her DNA. She wore it well, though, her hardships wrapped up in a cloak of resilience and charm, so much so that anyone who didn't know her like I did would be fooled. Stacy's life hadn't been easy, but she carried herself with the kind of confidence that only comes from enduring and surviving. She smiled, that same wide, effortless smile, and in that moment, I envied her. We hugged, and it was like no time had passed.

"God, I missed you," she said, pulling back to take me in. "You look incredible." I smiled, trying to mirror her ease, but it felt fragile, like if I exhaled too hard, the whole facade would crack.

"I'm so glad you're here. I missed you so much!"

Inside, we settled onto the couch falling into familiar patterns. She talked, and I listened—about her and Rob, the break up how really it had to end. In the end he was just another asshole. She was going through a whirlwind of drama of her own. Stacy's struggles had always seemed more poetic than mine, like she'd somehow taken the chaos of her life and spun it into something glamorous, while I was left stuck in the mud of my own worries.

"So, how are things?" she asked eventually, her tone caring. "How's everything going with the wedding?"

I hesitated, getting off the couch going over to the fridge to grab a beer before lighting my cigarette, as if the answer could be found in the depths of a nicotine and alcohol concoction.

"It's good. Just… a lot, you know?" I said assuming my seat on the couch, close to her that I could smell her Victoria's Secret Angel mist, far enough to keep the black marble ashtray wedged safely between us preventing it from spilling over on the leather couch seats.

"Yeah, I bet."

She leaned in, reading me the way only she could.

"And John? How's he handling everything?"

I shrugged. "He's been busy. He's staying at his parents' this week while you're here." Her eyes sharpened, a slight frown creasing her forehead.

"Wait, he's staying at his parents'? Why would he do that? I was planning on staying at my mom's in Boston anyway."

I shifted uncomfortably, trying to downplay it.

"He thought it'd be easier, I guess, plus you know the premonition, husband shouldn't see their wife before the wedding day. There is also a bachelor party he said his dad was throwing him. I don't know, he hasn't really told me anything about it. He said he was going to go there and sleep."

Her frown deepened. "He hasn't said anything? Not even plans for it, like it just going to be him and his dad doing what?"

I shrugged my shoulder, feeling the familiar knot of unease tighten in my chest.

"I don't know. But it's fine. I mean, I trust him."

Stacy's expression left unchanged, but I could see the wheels turning in her mind, always three steps ahead. She reached out and touched my arm, her voice gentle but firm. She lit a Camel cigarette, as I reached for my pack of Newports, an ashtray was wedged between on us on the black leather couch.

"You don't have to act like everything's fine with me. If something's bothering you, just say it."

The floodgates opened. "I wanted us to go to Florida for the honeymoon," I confessed. "To Nana and Papa's mansion in Fort Lauderdale. It's empty all summer, just sitting there. But John's dad won't give him more than three days off, so now we're going to New Hampshire."

Stacy leaned back, her face showing a flicker of disbelief.

"New Hampshire? For your honeymoon? You deserve more than that." I swallowed, feeling the weight of it all pressing down on me. "I know. I just… I thought Florida would be perfect."

She squeezed my hand, her voice steady.

"Diana, Listen TO ME. You deserve perfect. You deserve everything you've been dreaming of, not some half-hearted compromise."

I blinked back the tears that threatened to spill over, ruining my makeup. Stacy's life had been full of its own struggles, but she'd always had this way of cutting through the bullshit, of reminding me that I didn't have to settle. Not for John, not for anyone. But she didn't understand; that I did have to settle.

As she edged further away from me to take a call, my mind began to process her arrival.

Hearing her talking to her mom, it all felt like a piece of home arrived to my rescue.

Chapter 14

Month before the Wedding

During the sweltering summer months, Spike and I fell into a rhythm of Gloucester Rockport photo shoots. I loved the thrill of climbing, the salty air tugging at my hair as I posed on the rocks, feeling free in my bathing suit, the sun warming my skin. Each snap of the camera felt like a release, a fleeting moment where I could capture a piece of myself amidst the crashing waves. I even felt inspired enough to take a few nudes, trusting Spike completely—an innocent exchange of art and friendship.

But John hated that trust. His insecurity wrapped around us like a noose, echoing and suffocating us.

"I don't understand why he needs to take so many pictures of you. He's not even paying you,"

John snapped one evening, his voice thick with suspicion, turning his ocean eyes black.

"But this is payment for him agreeing to photograph our wedding," I replied, my voice wavering beneath the tension.

I will admit here and now, dear reader, that when I first said Spike would photograph our

wedding, it was a lie, an instinctive maneuver to diffuse the situation. I wanted to make it

seem like we owed Spike something, anything, so I wouldn't lose that connection. But as the month progressed, I found myself asking—no, begging—Spike to photograph my wedding. I told him about how he could use the images to promote his photography business. How this could work to both of our advantage, and of course I would remain his number one go to model, in exchange for TFP. "And wait till you meet Stacy! You're going to love her!" I can hear myself saying, as though Stacy could magically fix all the brokenness, magically like the fairy god mother in Cinderella with her magic wand.

Ultimately, he agreed, turning my initial deception into truth. So it wasn't a lie anymore; it hadn't been for months. But this conversation, this particular one, we had dissected it too many times, its echo clinging to us like the salt and sand, after a day spent at the beach.

"Spike has no interest in me. He doesn't want me. I think he's gay," I said, forcing a flirtatious giggle that felt brittle and thin. That last line was a stretch; I recalled Spike mentioning a woman he'd been dating, but it felt safer to believe in the benign rather than confront John's dark jealousy. Stacy was supposed to come for the wedding, and I clung to the hope that her arrival might sidestep the Spike conversation, if only for a few days.

All hope was on Stacy. That kept me going.

Until the unexpected blow came, like when you are walking in stilettos on cobblestone, and you feel like you have the pace, and the spacing all maneuvered with each click of the heel, confident that you won't slip into the cracks, comes an unexpected crack invisible to the eye on the cobblestone, so unexpected, that it jams the heel, twisting the ankle making you fall forward. This was that moment. It was my fashion roadkill moment at its best, if I were walking the runway. In a way I was walking the runway, a runway I had crafted in my mind made of cobblestones.

"My parents want you to sign a prenup," John said, his voice steady, as if discussing the weather. The words hit me like a side blow I hadn't even considered.

"Why would we need a prenup if we're never getting a divorce?" I shot back, frustration bubbling beneath the surface.

"It's just in case we do and you decide to go after their money, they have millions in businesses and they need to just make sure it remains safe." he replied, his words felt empty, and calculating.

"Why would I decide to do that?" I pressed, confusion twisting in my gut.

"You wouldn't. It's just a safety precaution," he insisted, as if reciting a script he'd rehearsed a thousand times.

I remembered in that instant watching an episode of Sex and the City with John, the one where Charlotte had to sign a prenup.

I had turned to him, my voice playful yet earnest.

"Promise you will never make me sign a prenup. It's so mistrusting."

"My baby girl will never sign a prenup. I promise," he said, his eyes serious as he placed his hand over mine, kissing my head.

"Pinky promise?" I asked, running my finger along the tattoo on his stomach of death, with its pitbulls, running my fingers up his belly to his chest where his second tattoo was of a bare breasted women, a barbie with bare breasts.

"That's me, right?" I had teased.

"Yes, baby girl, that's you."

"When we get married, you should tattoo my name below her breasts."

"No, that would be wrong," he replied, his tone turning firm. I wondered why, but didn't dare voice the question aloud. I was too fearful of his answer.

"I don't want to sign a prenup," I declared, my heart racing as the weight of his expectations pressed down on me.

"Okay, I'll tell my parents you don't want to sign," he said, his tone clipped.

Days later, after relaying my refusal to his parents, John confronted me again, his determination turning into an ultimatum.

"Babygirl, you need to sign the prenup. The wedding is in 19 days. If you don't sign, there is no wedding. We have an appointment scheduled with my parents' attorney. They use him for everything. He can be like your attorney, too."

"But why should I be thinking about divorce at all? I don't want your parents' money. I want you," I replied, my voice breaking, a fragile thread hanging between us.

"If you don't want their money, you shouldn't have an issue signing the prenup. I promise, babygirl, we will never get a divorce. You and me forever."

He kissed me.

The words twisted in my gut, a promise laced with uncertainty. The next day, in an attorney's office in Newton, I signed the prenup. I signed with trust—but a trust I didn't feel. Each stroke of the pen felt like an act of submission, a hollow promise. I wanted to escape that judgmental

office, to run, to flee from the weight of the decision pressing down on me. I could almost see myself bolting out the door, hiding beneath my covers, where the world couldn't reach me. But instead, I stayed. I smiled and I signed away my worth, hoping that maybe, somehow, this would all make sense.

Chapter 15

The Bachelorette Party

"Please, please sleep over," I begged Stacy, my voice reaching a higher pitch than I wanted it to. "I don't want to be alone wondering what John's doing." Borderline whining and pleading.

Stacy's eyes flickered with something between amusement and pity.

"Why do you have to wonder? Just call him."

I shook my head. The thought of calling John filled me with a quiet dread.

"I can't. He gets mad when I call too much. And I've missed you. Please stay."

There was a hesitation, a slight pull away from me, but she resolved.

"Okay, but I have to stop by my mom's eventually."

I exhaled, relieved, rooting myself to solid ground as though I could fly away any second,

somewhere far away.

"Tomorrow you can meet Spike," I offered, trying to brighten the mood.

"I'll invite him over. John's just supposed to swing by in the morning to bring me my Dunkin' coffee."

Stacy's lips curved into a mocking smile. "Aww, that's sweet."

Sweet. Yes, sweet. John would be bringing my methadone with that coffee, the little lifeline I needed to get through each and every day. I'd been rationing everything so carefully. I had already handed over twelve of my two-milligram kolonopins to him. The stash was running low.

I felt the panic flutter in the back of my mind, what if he doesn't show up in the morning, but I kept my smile fixed, pretending everything was fine.

"No worries, be happy" I heard a voice sing in my head after popping another pill in thebathroom, away from Stacy. My bachelorette party was a half-baked idea, thrown together in the last-minute chaos of everything. It was just me, Stacy, and Spike. No extravagant plans, no wild nights out in Vegas.

Our version of fun was simpler, rawer—Fanueal Hall, hitting up the old bars Stacy and I used to sneak into before we'd even turned twenty-one. Those places held memories, sticky and stained, like the floors we used to dance on.

As we prepped for the night, Stacy and I applied our makeup like old times, side by side, catching each other's eyes in the mirror. It felt familiar, a ritual that bound us together through the years, like threads woven into the fabric of our shared history. The air was thick with the scent of lipstick and the faint hint of our favorite perfumes mixed together, and as we worked, laughter bubbled up between us, a sweet reminder of simpler days when our biggest worries were what outfits we would wear or which bar we'd hit first.

Later that evening, as we popped open a couple of beers and put on our favorite playlist, the atmosphere brightened like the sudden dawn after a sleepless night. We talked and laughed, slipping into our old rhythms as if no time had passed. I felt a flicker of hope—maybe this night would help me shake off the weight of my worries, even if just for a little while.

Spike was always on time, but this time he was fifteen minutes early. When he showed up, I invited him in, grabbed a beer from the fridge, and told him to relax—we were running behind as usual.

He settled onto the couch, casual but watchful, his eyes scanning the apartment as if trying to piece together the fragments of our lives scattered around the room. Stacy peeked her head out of the bedroom, a quick flash of acknowledgment.

"Hey, Spike," she called with a smile before retreating back inside. She was mid-dress, pulling on something tight, the kind of dress that highlighted every curve of her perfectly sculpted body.

I saw the way his eyes lingered on the spot where her head had bobbed out of and I could feel the shift in the air, the atmosphere thickening like smoke. He was already hooked, just like I knew he would be.

As we headed out to Faneuil Hall, I watched them fall into easy conversation, Stacy laughing at something Spike said and I trailed behind, pretending not to notice the way they pulled into each other's gravity, like celestial bodies caught in a delicate dance. At the bar, Spike ordered us all shots of tequila and we threw them back like we were still

those wild girls, sneaking into places we didn't belong, clinging to the thrill of it all, chugging one shot after another.

But I wasn't feeling wild. The alcohol burned going down, a fierce reminder of my growing unease, but it didn't smooth out the jagged edge of what I was seeing. Not even after four shots. I felt alone and jealous and somehow alcohol was making me feel worse. But, I refused to show it.

Spike kept leaning closer to Stacy, finding reasons to brush her arm, and she wasn't exactly pulling away. The night wore on, and it was clear—what was supposed to be a celebration of me had turned into something else entirely.

They were lost in their own orbit, while I stood there, feeling the distance between us grow wider with every laugh, every glance exchanged. I had thought this would make things better, that it would give me the peace I needed with John. But standing there, watching Spike and Stacy, I felt like a bystander in my own life, an uninvited guest to my own celebration. I had built the scene, orchestrated the moment, but now I was on the outside, pressed against the glass, watching them from a distance. I clung to my drink, wondering when exactly I'd lost my grip on the night, the plan—on everything.

We all returned home to my apartment, the night's laughter still echoing in my ears, but the buzz was fading, replaced by a nagging sense of disquiet. I gave my bedroom up for the lovebirds, a reluctant sacrifice that felt like it came straight from some ancient script of friendship.

"You two can take my room," I said, forcing a lightness into my tone. "It's fine, not a big deal. The couch is already set up for you. Take the bed; it's more fun. It's a waterbed with mirrors, how can you resist?"

Stacy flashed a grateful smile, her eyes sparkling with the remnants of tequila and excitement.

"Are you sure? I don't want to kick you out of your own bed."

"I love you, have fun." I said giving her a hug, and moving to put blankets on the pulled-out sofa bed, the cushions molding into shapes that echoed my own confusion of myself.

The hum of silence outside enveloped me as I settled onto the couch, the world outside a distant murmur. Inside, I heard the soft whispers and giggles of Stacy and Spike, their voices intertwining like a melody I couldn't quite catch. I closed my eyes, hoping to drown out the rising tide of feelings threatening to pull me under.

I awoke to John kissing me on the forehead.

"Wakey Wakey eggs and bakey, I have your hot French vanilla with cream and sugar" his mouth left my forehead, and in my ear he whispered "with special medicine."

John disappeared as quickly as he had appeared. I drank my "special medicine" hoping to nod off back to sleep.

It was still early in the morning, John had just gotten out of the clinic, it was around seven am, and I had fallen asleep sometime after three am.

I counted the hours in my head as though counting was an antidote to the pangs I was beginning to feel of a hangover headache, not the methadone that I knew soon enough would take its course through my body, with each sip of the coffee.

Chapter 16

Days Before the Wedding

Stacy and Spike awoke sometime that morning, tangled in each other like two lovers who'd drifted in from a dream. The kind of dream that stains the sheets and leaves the air thick with last night's sweat. We all shuffled into the living room, eyes half-open, cigarettes lighting one after another, a lazy rhythm to the morning after. Spike, ever the gentleman of low-grade chaos, ordered breakfast for everyone, like it was part of some unspoken ritual.

I popped a pill, washed it down with a gulp of Bud Light, the bubbles rushed down my throat. The pill hit my bloodstream like a warm, slow wave, just enough to keep me hovering above the day. This was good. This was the kind of good that made you forget where the bottom was and hope you never found it.

"You guys should stay another night," I said, the words floating out of my mouth, barely tethered to reality. Spike took a bite of his breakfast sandwich, chewing with a mix of thoughtfulness and indifference.

"Man, I wish I could. I'd do anything for another night with Stacy, but I got family stuff," he said between bites, glancing over at her. "I can drop you off where you need to go."

Stacy, curled up on his lap like a satisfied cat, chimed in. "Yeah, I gotta go to my mom's in Boston," she said, wriggling just a little, that perfect blend of innocence and seduction she carried without even knowing it.

"I wish you could stay longer," I confessed, my voice betraying more than I meant. "I hate being by myself."

She turned, eyes sparkling, smiling like the world was made just for her. "Don't worry! I'll be back tomorrow. And then it's the big day! Yay!"

Her excitement felt foreign to me, like it belonged to a different species, one I couldn't quite touch.

Spike smirked, his fingers dancing on her ribs. "Well, maybe we can stay just a little longer," he said, his voice teasing, already knowing the answer.

Then they kissed. It felt like slow motion, their lips meeting with a kind of gentle passion that oozed out of them, as if the rest of the world had dissolved.

Were they already in love? It felt that way—like something deeper had already taken root between them. I watched them, unable to shake the thought. Are they getting married next? The idea wasn't so far-fetched; they moved together with an unspoken bond that seemed to deepen by the minute.

Stacy leaned in close, her lips brushing my ear, her voice a whisper so sweet it could rot teeth.

"Do you mind if we go use your bedroom one more time before we have to leave?"

"Of course I don't mind," I heard myself say, hollow, mechanical, as if it wasn't even me

speaking. "Go have fun."

They giggled like children and disappeared through the kitchen into the bedroom, the echo of their laughter fading into the walls. I was left alone and the loneliness I felt, was palpable. I sat there, still, staring at the blinking cursor on my screen. My fingers hovered over the keys, but there was nothing. I was empty. Jealousy crawled under my skin, making me itch in places I didn't want to scratch. I wanted what they had, even if it was fleeting, even if I knew better.

A bad friend, a terrible friend. I should've been happy for them. I should've smiled and cheered them on, but instead, I was drowning in my own want, my own loneliness. I grabbed my beer and downed the rest, the cold liquid doing nothing to soothe the heat rising inside me.

The day stretched ahead, long and bleak, and when the door clicked shut behind them, the silence that followed felt like a punishment I'd earned.

The next days gelled into ones of me floating around in the high mixture of kolonopins,methadone, and alcohol.

Fairy Tale

I was asleep for years,
Before I met him,
Put under a spell,
Like sleeping beauty I had fell,
Dreaming of a prince to enchant me with his spell,

I lived in terror of my dreams,
A fear of a witch upon me loomed,
As tales are told of witches roam,
Casting spells to own the souls,
Stealing voices to self preserve!
But there he was, to my surprise,
My prince dressed up in shining armor, gallantly appeared
Galloping to me on a tamed wild white mustang, reaching out his hand
To lift me up atop the horse, without a second thought,
I reached up to him convinced his love would bring me back to life,
Thus, off to we went to his castle that he made.

Alas, I didn't awake but dreamt of him throughout the day.
He gave me medicine to take,
Telling me it would be of help,
As time went on, he kept me cribbed
Within the castle walls that he had built.

As to further on his sted of stealing me,
Charming brought me to specialists', to see
Telling them of my paralysis and sleep,
The doctors of the mind did give,
Pills of various, shapes, and sizes, hues array,
I took the capsules with gleeful hope
That my heart would melt into a whole.
Instead the drugs turned me trape,
Sending me into a daily haze of muted sleep,
I never felt.

The fear of witches roamed deep within me, still
Suffocating me in my nightly sleep,

As time stood still, within this castle he had built.

Within my unsightly sleep,
I couldn't see the witch, that hunted me,
Was me!
Hunting me with warnings from dusk to day,
That the prince was cunning,
He was nothing,
But a wolf hidden inside sheep's clothing,
Cheating his way, to be.

I clung on still, unwilling to see.
The truth behind the cunning wolf,
The prince there still, always, smirking back at me
Alas, no happy ending upon my sight,
As my mind remained torn between the dreams of day,
And of a secret life I could not grasp, hidden inside this nightmare's realm.

Although eventually the spell did break
Once charming had fulfilled his lust and drank me dry,
His seven year itch, began to itch,
Love for another the prince had found,
That's when he discarded me, like dregs found inside of yesterday's trash.

At last! I did awake by seeing the truth of me and him,
The darkness he had cast upon our souls
A tumor bred, poisoning the drinking water of our well.

I wonder still, why I refused to heed,
The warnings I had felt, from deep within,
The truth, behind the witch that I had met,
Were always me, and me alone,
No prince could ever rescue me.
Why did I than, refuse to see,
The truth, the power of me,
Casting myself into a slumber made of ice,
Within this fairytale dream's demise.

Chapter 17

The Wedding Day

I awoke early that morning, excitement jostling with fear, the twin jesters of my mind stirring me at five a.m. The house was quiet, the air thick with the kind of anticipation that makes every breath feel fragile. I stepped out onto the patio, a cigarette in one hand, watching the curl of smoke disappear into the dawn as PlayPlay wandered the yard, oblivious to the weight of the day. John brought my methadone coffee, the sweetness grounding me just enough to function.

I could see the anxiety in his face, reflecting my own, as he waited for me to pack my makeup, to gather my defenses for the day ahead.

When we arrived at the house, it felt almost too grand, a place built for someone else's happiness, not mine. Mrs. B had outdone herself. Pink, white, light green, white and champagne-colored decorations spilled from every corner, as if they could dress up the truth of it all. The outside patio shimmered, the pool like a mirror that might break if I looked too hard.

And the tulle tent—God I loved it, it was the replacement of a veil for me, the way it hung so delicately, swaying like something alive, something that might swallow me whole. It was where we'd say "I do" in just a few hours.

The thought of it felt like a weight around my neck, and yet, there was a seduction in it too, in the finality, in the way it called me to step inside and become someone else. I stood there, staring at that tent, feeling both drawn and repelled. Was it calling me to my future, or was it trying to warn me?

Stacy was my maid of honor and should be arriving shortly. She and Antonia were part of the "get ready" crew, along with my mother and sister. Stacy despised all my friends who weren't her. None more than Antonia, my best friend from public school. There was one night I thought we could all be friends. I invited Antonia out with me and Stacy for a night of clubbing at Club Level. Antonia got smashed, her head lolling on her shoulders by the end of the night, begging for water like it might save her.

I could still hear her slurred plea, "My head is spinning, I'm going to puke. Please, can you get me some water?"

Stacy, quick as ever, jumped in, eager. "I'll go grab some from the bar," she said, with a grin I should've questioned but didn't. She came back with a plastic cup filled with clear liquid and passed it to Antonia. "I wasn't sure, so I got them to load the water with lots of ice."

Antonia didn't think twice, just chugged it. But it wasn't water; it was vodka—vodka with ice. The way Stacy laughed, her eyes gleaming with delight as Antonia's face twisted in confusion, still haunts me. I carried Antonia out of the club that night, and Stacy was supposed to drive us to our respective homes. But Antonia was too scared to go back to her house, smelling of vodka, puke, and cigarettes, so we dropped her off at a park, where she slept it off under the rising sun on a bench.

After that, Antonia hated Stacy. I couldn't blame her. Stacy had crossed a line, and I had let her. So when I saw them today, standing stiffly in their mismatched dresses—Stacy in her skintight hot pink magenta number, and Antonia floating in lavender—it made sense that they would clash, that they'd carry the weight of that night with them. Their resentment was stitched into the seams of their dresses.

But none of that really mattered. What mattered was getting through the day. I had to get ready to say, "I do."

Nothing else matters. Smile on and get through the day, that was as the mantra playing in my head on repeat as I applied my foundation in the bathroom, the sentence almost developed a beat, which went along with snaps of Spikes camera, who had arrived notably early to photograph the wedding, and document "the bride getting ready", as he put it.

I didn't have a makeup artist, nor did I want one. What was the point? No one else knew the angles of my face, the ways to hide the scars that ran deeper than just my skin. I had mastered the art of concealing, of creating a smooth surface over the chaos beneath. It was mine alone to control.

John's sister, May, a hairstylist, had agreed to do my hair. She had planned an updo—something glamorous, something I wasn't sure I could pull off. But she exceeded my expectations, though I hadn't anticipated how much pulling and tugging it would take to shape my hair into something presentable. She wove in extensions with mechanical precision, turning me into something polished, something ready for display.

My family arrived later than planned, as they always did. My mother, ever the picture of elegance, looked stunning with her blonde hair styled into soft waves, a light green silk-layered dress that rippled when she walked. My father, in his dark suit with a matching green tie, was her shadow, a silent guardian.

My sister, standing out in her champagne-colored dress, was only twelve, but today, she was part of the show. Her dress didn't fit her as well as it should have, barely grazing her ankles when it should have flowed gracefully. It seemed she, too, was dressed in a costume, one that didn't quite blend with her. Her innocence shone through, though, despite the awkward fit. Her brown waves framed her face perfectly, but I knew she had wanted to have her hair done by May.

There hadn't been time for that. We were all rushing toward the inevitable. As I slipped into my wedding dress, the fabric clung to me in all the right places, but it felt like a   foreign skin, something that didn't belong to me. Mrs. B had taken me to a tailor, desperate to make it fit, but I was down to ninety-five pounds, and even the size 00 I had painstakingly ordered online was too large in the waist and bust. Still, we made it work. We always did. And now, on my wedding day, it fit as though it had always been meant for me. But it wasn't.

The tightening of the corset was the final touch, pulling me into this day, into this role, until I could barely breathe. The dress, the shoes, the hair—it was all a costume. The waiting of the guests, the stepping into this version of myself—it felt like a scene unfolding in someone else's life. Like I was watching from a distance, detached, not really part of it. My heart wanted to jump out of my chest.

What if he doesn't want this? Just hours ago, he had made a huge stink about wearing a suit and black shoes that weren't Timberland. First of all, he didn't own a suit, nor did he own a decent pair of men's dress shoes. Second of all, he refused to rent a tux. And lastly, he had no choice but to settle for one of his dad's old suits, a light grey one that was too big for him. John wasn't a small man, but in his father's suit, he looked shrunken, almost as if he had disappeared into it. He felt wrong in it.

And the shoes—those hideous black shoes that looked like they belonged on broken feet—made the whole thing worse. I couldn't help but wonder if that feeling was mutual.

Did he feel like he didn't belong in this moment either?

Was he shrinking from the weight of it all, the way I was?

Chpater 18

Achoo Much Ado About I Do

Guests slowly gathered one by one. I didn't see anyone come in or take their seats. The world inside the house, where I was getting dressed and pampered, was a flurry of activity. Champagne flowed freely as I gulped down the bubbly liquid, letting its effervescence carry me momentarily away from my anxiety.

My mom and Stacy, dusted me with golden sparkles, while Antonia helped me clasp the pearl bracelet that coiled around my left wrist. Every few seconds, the camera would snap, the clicking sound becoming a rhythmic beat for me, helping me keep my mask in place.

Stacy and Antonia almost moved in rhythm, their silence looming like an invisible elephant in the room; heavy with unspoken tension. The way they traded glances spoke volumes, each trying to outshine the other, as if this day were a contest rather than a celebration of love. But I appreciated them nonetheless for being there, for showing up, for standing by my side, for being my friends.

John had no one to guide him through his wedding day. Yes, he had his father but his father wasn't his friend. They didn't have that friendship bond.

I had asked John why he didn't have friends. His response always left more questions than answers:

"I don't need anyone but you, babygirl." He had a way of kissing my forehead as though he was soothing my concerns.

"But doesn't it feel lonely? Didn't you have friends? I mean besides Frank,"

"I did, we all did drugs together. We aren't friends anymore."

"But what about that guy I met? He said he wanted to spend more time with you. The one at Frank's funeral. He said we should visit him in Fort Lauderdale."

"That was just talk, babygirl; he isn't my friend. You are so smart when it comes to books, but not so much when it comes to street smarts. I have you, baby girl."

He had me. There was no denying it, and he was about to have me forever.

Then the music changed. "Here Comes the Bride" began to play from the speakers. We all aligned—first the flower girl, then Antonia, then Stacy, my mom, and finally, me and my dad.

This was the closest I had been to my dad in years. My hand rested atop his, a

ceremonial gesture of the traditional father giving away the bride. As I walked, memories of my father and I floated through my mind, the fear of him both intensified and subsided. I told myself I must be doing this right.

I looked into my father's eyes, seeking his approval, his pride, but I couldn't see past his plastered smile—his own mask for the day. My father guided his hand with mine atop John's. John took my hand, one in each of his. I was passed over from one man to another. I couldn't meet John's eyes. I felt like crying; emotions threatened to spill out of me, ruining my makeup. I couldn't look him in the eyes.

"Do you take this bride to be your lawful wedded wife?"

When I heard "I do" from John, I finally met his eyes. He had tears in them. This would be the second time I saw John's eyes swell up with tears.

The first time was when we found out Frank had passed away. It was a cold, icy phone call John received that consumed him with guilt.

We had just seen Frank.

He came over, interrupting our romance, bursting through the bedroom door as John had me bent over the bed. I remember yelling at John to get Frank out, scrambling for my robe.

"It's nothing I've never seen before," Frank had said, his casualness adding to my embarrassment fueling my anger.

John pushed Frank out, their voices muffled as they talked outside. I could hear snippets, but I was too flustered to make sense of it. A moment later, Frank left, and the door closed behind him with a finality that sent relief washing over me.

"Thanks for kicking him out," I had said, turning back to John. "We would have had to hang out with him all night." I felt the atmosphere shift, the tension dissipating. "But now it can be just you and me." I said leaning into him, slipping off his matching bathrobe.

The ringing of the phone had woken us up.

John answered. It was about Frank.

Frank was dead, it was an overdose.

Things took a turn for the worst,

Paramedics didn't get there in time.

When we saw Frank he seemed fine, talkative, and gleeful almost, and hours later he was dead.

We later found out he had gotten high—his own mother supplying him with the benzos that ultimately took his life. She hadn't known he had just shot up heroin in the bathroom, he had been clean for year. He had told her he was anxious and needed a few Xanax.

After the call, John cried, the sound breaking something inside me. The next thought in my mind began to fester inside me like a slow growing tumor.

Was it my fault, that Frank died?

If I hadn't told John to kick him out, he would still be alive. This one was on me wasn't it?

Did John know it was my fault? Did he blame me?

I held John's eyes in mine, I saw the swelling of his tears after he said "I do." I told myself it must be love. I didn't kill Frank.

"I do," I said.

As soon as I uttered those two words…

….out of nowhere, on that sunny, hot midday of July, water sprayed the tent—the side where my family and bridesmaids were standing.

Someone said the water came from the top of the tent.

"It must have accumulated overnight" I heard another voice say, but from where?

It hadn't rained the night before. That amount of water felt like a bucket thrown from the sky at that portion of the tent. "Water is a bad omen," someone started to say. "No, water is a good omen," someone else interjected. I tried to forget that it could be a bad omen. It came from nowhere; it had to be a blessing.

This was my forever. Maybe it was Frank playing a prank on us.

John kissed me, and I felt comfort in that kiss; making us husband and wife, until death doth us Part.

Chapter 19

Husband And Wife

  We kissed, and the crowd erupted—cheers ricocheting around us, hollow yet deafening. It was a moment suspended between the public and the private, a secret on display. The delicate tulle tent had promised some kind of sanctuary within its sheer walls, a place for family, for intimacy, but there we stood, at the center of everything. It felt like we were caught under glass, actors on stage, and the world watched through the slits in the fabric, their eyes on our every move.

They saw the water, how it appeared like a trick of the light, pouring out of nowhere, drenching the backside of my bridal party. I wonder what it looked like for them; the guests, the audience, now. The sky was light blue that day, the sun shining, the heat was felt. We all agreed it was an omen, but was it a good omen or a bad one no one could establish clearly. It was up to me to conclude the meaning behind the water, to uncover the sign. But, I refused to see.

"It was Frank playing a prank from heaven", I told myself repeatedly to believe.

We said I do.

All was forgiven.

I was married.

I still couldn't believe it, no matter how many times I repeated it in my head.

It didn't feel real—like a dress that didn't quite fit, as if the seams could split open any moment. We moved out of the tent like we were following a script, a slow, careful procession. John and I led, fingers laced, though my hand ached from gripping too tight. My feet throbbed with each step, a dull reminder that this was just the beginning. I needed something—something to numb the edges, to blur the lines.

"I need a little medicine," I whispered to John. My throat felt tight, like my words were pressing against something lodged deep inside.

"I can't breathe. I don't know how to dance with my father."

I hadn't danced with him before—I hadn't danced with him ever.

What if I stepped on his feet, stumbled, faltered?

I imagined his eyes, quietly assessing, a father weighing his daughter's worth in those small, calculated ways.

The rhythm was out there somewhere, just beyond my reach, slipping through my fingers.

I caught sight of his face—his smile stretched too thin, plastered like a mask.

I could see the cracks beneath it, the strain.

I needed the noise in my head to stop.

To JUST STOP.

"Sure, baby girl, let's sneak off. We've got to go through the house for family pictures anyway."

"Wife, not baby girl," I reminded him, the word twisting in my mouth.

"Can you believe we actually did it? We're married."

"Yes, wife," he said, his lips brushing my forehead, soft, almost too soft. "We did it."

"That we did, husband." I said gripping his hand even tighter, leaning my weight into him as we circled into the house, in full view of the seated guests on the patio. We walked off the invisible stage with the invisible curtain closing behind us.

Inside the house, I found my way to my makeup bag, my fingers shaking as they closed around the bottle of pills. One slipped under my tongue, dissolving slowly, sweetly, like a promise I knew too well. The world tilted, just a little, enough to make room for air again.

"Here," I heard John say behind me. He held the liquid dropper between his fingers, with magenta liquid methadone gleaming in the light.

"Open your mouth and say 'ahh,'" he said, but it felt more like a lullaby than a command.

I parted my lips, the cherry-flavored syrup mixing with the pill under my tongue.

The relief was subtle, slow, like fog rolling in, thickening the air but making it easier to breathe. Then a wave of panic gripped me—sharp, sudden.

"John, we're right in the hallway, blocking the bathroom! Didn't anyone see just now?"

My voice was taut, trembling with the fear that someone had witnessed what they shouldn't.

"No, no one's in the house. Chill." His voice was calm, unfazed, like this was the easiest thing in the world. But my heart kept racing.

I couldn't have anyone knowing about the methadone.

No one knew.

Not even Stacy knew.

I'd kept it from everyone, buried it deep. This was my other secret, and I clung to it like a

lifeline, it was another part of Ana/Mia; of me. Control was slipping away, and I fought to pull it back, throughout the wedding party pictures, before father-daughter dance I could barely face.

Chapter 20

Daddy Daughter Dance

Reflecting now, it feels like I was dancing with myself. I barely felt my father's hand holding mine, as though the connection between us was more symbolic than real, a placeholder for something we never truly shared. The steps were easy, but unrehearsed, as if my body moved out of habit while my mind drifted elsewhere.

I wondered if my father was proud of me for knowing the basic box step, or if I was simply expected to know it.

Perhaps the real freedom, the real discharge, would have come from messing up—showing, in some small way, the truth of how awkward and ill-fitting this entire moment was. But then, I would be repeating the same old pattern of failure.

The dance of failure, my father and I knew how to dance quite masterfully:

it went something like this….

He restricts,

I rebel,

I sneak,

I fail.

He punishes,

I rebel,

so it goes….

And…

He thinks to himself,

I know this one is the failure.

Click. Click. The camera went off again, Spike's presence hovering at the edge of my vision. The smile I wore was automatic, the same rehearsed expression Spike had trained me to perfect during our endless natural light beach photo shoots.

It had become second nature now, a mask I could slip on without thinking, my face serene and composed, even while my insides twisted. His voice echoed in my head, reminding me to relax, to lean into the pose, to make it look effortless. But none of this was effortless. It was all performance—layered upon layers of unspoken roles and obligations.

As we moved in those slow, deliberate circles, I could feel the space between us

—my father and I— growing wider, though we were only inches apart.

His hand on mine felt weightless, detached, and I wasn't sure if he was leading or if I was. It didn't matter. We were simply moving through the motions, locked in a fragile choreography that would only last as long as the music. I glanced up at him, searching his face for some sign of pride or approval, but there was none.

His movements were deliberate, efficient, but empty of affection or pride. In the quiet space between us, I could feel his judgment pressing down on me.

She cheated, I could almost hear him thinking, as his breath held a steady pace. There are no shortcuts. This isn't the moment. This is her death, not her rebirth.

And though we didn't say a single word to one another, I could hear his voice in my head throughout the entire dance. It was the same voice I'd heard all my life—unyielding, stoic, unsatisfied, with a hint of sarcasm. Almost mocking me, as if every step I took was an unwelcome surprise. Somehow, despite the silence, we flowed together in the steps and movement of something we had never rehearsed or practiced, as if we had been destined to perform this strange ritual.

But as I moved in time with him, I realize now: I wasn't dancing with my father.

I was dancing with the weight of who I could have been.

Chapter 21

Husband and Wife Dance

John had just finished his dance with his mother, and now it was our turn to dance for the first time as husband and wife.

"Diana, he is so stiff, see if you can get him to relax a bit on the dance floor," Mrs. B murmured as we passed each other.

And stiff he was. John had always said he couldn't dance, but this was extreme. He looked like a middle school boy at his first dance, feet planted firmly, swaying awkwardly back and forth, a suit that was too large on him, a marionette with tangled strings.

The song began.

The beat,

the melody, Bryan Adams' raspy voice echoing in the air like a memory refusing to fade:

"Look into my eyes, you will see, what you mean to me." The words hung between us, a fragile bridge across the awkwardness, beckoning for connection.

"Search your soul, search your heart, and when you find me there, you'll search no more."

John wrapped both arms around my waist, his feet stubbornly rooted to the floor, pressing his lips against my forehead as we swayed.

In that moment, I was instantly pulled back to middle school, to that first dance between Dana Hall and St. Sabastian's, a time when innocence and expectation mingled like shadows.

"Will you dance with me?" a boy from St. Sabs had asked, his hand extended, a fragile promise.

"Yes," I had replied,

As Bryan Adams wove through the air:

"Don't tell me it's not worth trying for. You can't tell me it's not worth dying for."

We swayed, his hands held out uncomfortably wrapping around my waist, I was caught in the ebb and flow of bittersweet nostalgia, swaying in the rhythm of that boy. An instant of love from a boy I would never see again.

My wedding dance was no different, a mirror reflecting past and present, desire and disappointment. I've never claimed to be a professional dancer, but I always loved it—ballet especially. I could feel the rhythm, moving with the beat, slipping between it. At Dana Hall, I took advanced ballet classes, dancing alongside girls already performing at a professional level with the Boston Ballet.

I was self-taught, a solitary figure in a world of polished talent. But I quit, just like I quit Dana Hall. Always feeling like I wasn't enough, like a bird that had lost its way, flapping against an invisible wall.

Now, at my own wedding, my husband wouldn't and couldn't lift his feet. He couldn't even move his mouth, his lips were glued to my forehead as though my head was leading the sway, I tried counting, softly humming the song, trying to anchor myself in this moment.

"You know it's true, everything I do, I do it for you."

The lyrics wrapped around us, binding our hearts even as the moment felt heavy with unspoken words.

"Look into your heart, you will find there's nothing there to hide."

In this dance, I longed for acceptance, to be seen.

"Take me as I am, take my life, I would give it all, I would sacrifice."

I could feel the weight of my choices, the sacrifices I had made.

"Don't tell me it's not worth fighting for, I can't help it, there's nothing I want more. You

know it's true."

"Everything I do, I do it for you. There's no love like your love, and no other could give more love."

I felt an instant rush of love, the kind that brings out tears, I felt the depth of my commitment, the complexity of love that wove through every note.

"There's nowhere unless you're there, all the time, all the way."

This song, this was it! It was my testament, my song to John:

I had sacrificed for him,

I had lied for him,

I had died for him,

I would keep fighting for him,

He knew everything I did,

I did I did it for him.

All he had to do was keep me in his heart of hearts, to love me.

He had to love me.

He said "I do".

He would do for me as I did for him.

I sang to myself, with John's lips pressed to my forehead,

I sang along with Bryan Adams.

Chapter 22

Costume Changes

Throughout the day, I went through three dress stages. The first was the ball gown Cinderella look—the white dress flowing, Swarovski crystals sparkling in the sun on the bodice. I felt like a Victorian princess in that dress. Each step I took seemed to rustle with centuries of delicate, forgotten elegance, like I was a part of something ancient, something out of reach.

I wished it had a long veil, an old-world veil that would have cloaked me, made me unseen, invincible, for just a moment. But the veil's existence died with my babushka Polly, never making it to the US from the Soviet Union. I still can recall the delicacy of that veil and the simplicity. I remember wearing it around our little apartment in Tbilisi. "Up to the stage is Diana Kouprina," my babushka's voice echoes clearly in my mind, in Russian. I would come into our makeshift living room, dining room, piano room—all in one—and I would walk the little aisle, dancing in the veil. When I was done, my babushka would clap, and I would take a bow, curtsying.

"Диаточка, ой ты, ой ты моя молодец, талантливая умница," she would say, holding out her hands. I would run to her for a warm embrace.

I still dream of the veil, of my babushka Polly.

We had made it through the first dress change. After the dances and the pictures, I had another dress—long, flowing, simple, elegant, clinging to the body. It was Sammy's old prom dress, something borrowed. I loved the fact that I could fit into it. I was finally as skinny as Sammy. I felt confident in that dress, like I was in a supermodel costume. The married woman everyone was there to celebrate—me.

I took another dose of methadone. Just a tiny droplet. I didn't even have to beg John for it. He gave it to me happily in exchange for some of my little pills. John didn't drink. He didn't like how alcohol made him feel, but the high of opiates, benzos, and speed? He lived for that high.

I wanted to stay in that dress for the cake-cutting ceremony. I was starting to feel my character more and more. I was Снегурочка. My grandmother felt within my reach. The way it hugged my body made me feel like I was still that little girl, but also something more. But John wanted out of the suit. He had his outfit ready—his grey Adidas crew cut, wifebeater, and those grey sweatpants. His Adidas shell top sneakers, too. I watched him clean those sneakers earlier, scrubbing them carefully with an old toothbrush and toothpaste. He'd learned the trick in prison, how to keep his shoes clean and white.

The toothpaste worked wonders on the shell top sneakers, making them shine like new.   I still use that trick.

Toothpaste, when combined with the scrubbing effects of a toothbrush, works wonders not just on Adidas but on Converse and even Crocs. It's one of those things you don't forget: practical, simple, and oddly effective.

John seemed more himself in his Adidas, moving around the reception like he was already out of the ceremony, like he'd shed the pretense along with the suit.

I don't think anyone noticed how quickly he made that transition, how fast he was to return to who he really was. Maybe that was his way of staying grounded, too.

The cake was cut, and while we were feeding each other, John thought it would be funny to smear the cake over my face, smashing a big piece into my mouth. I tried to open my mouth as wide as I possibly could, desperate to avoid the frosting getting anywhere near my face. My makeup—I had spent hours applying it, if the sticky white frosting touched it, I'd have to start all over again. The thought terrified me.

But everyone thought it was funny. What a cute little prank. Pictures were snapped, capturing the moment as I tried to keep smiling, while internally I was fighting the panic of smeared makeup and sticky frosting. It felt like a loss of control, but the laughter around

us was too loud to protest. It was what people expected—fun, lighthearted, harmless. I smiled for the cameras, but inside I just wanted to wipe it all away.

The third dress change was the bathing suit portion of the wedding – the part where everyone jumped in the pool. That part I don't remember. Was my father there? He must have been. There is a picture of me, my mother and my sister. My mother is in the middle of my sister and I in her stunning light green dress, my sister and I both in bathing suits, I have that smile plastered on my face but my eyes are bloodshot red, this was my "I am fucked up face."

Was my father sitting watching me, feeling horrified for me? Or was it just all lighthearted fun, a celebration.

This was acceptable.

I was an acceptable amount of fucked up.

I must have been, I had to have been.

Stacy had on a skimpy two piece bathing suit on that barely provided any coverage to her new breast implants; which she complained of hurting throughout the wedding.

Which became the center of conversation amongst John, papa and his father, they all mused how glorious Stacy's boobs appeared to be.

"I want a boob job" I said to John, in my drunkedy drunk voice, floating on a mixture of benzos, methadone and champagne.

"We will get you one. You will have nice tatas like Stacy."

"No, I want better ones, hers were only three thousand, I want ones for twenty thousand."

"You will have even better and bigger boobies, for twenty thousand, babygirl."

"Not babygirl, wife." I corrected him.

"Wife." He repeated.

"Husband." I kissed him.

The three of us posed for a picture together. A thought popped into my head: did John want to fuck Stacy? But it disappeared as quickly as it appeared.

Even if John wanted to, Stacy would never. One thing our friendship had never faltered in was that. We had complete opposite taste in men. I never found anyone she dated attractive and vice versa. It was something I didn't need to worry about.

How I ended up in our Honeymoon suite in New Hampshire? I don't remember.

Chapter 23

Honeymoon Suite

We had three nights to our honeymoon in Lake Winnepesaukee, New Hampshire. How I ended up at the motel was a mystery, one that still lingers in my mind today. John had driven, and I must have dozed off, lost in a fog of post-wedding euphoria.

Had we said goodbye to all our guests? Who had caught the bouquet my parents had lovingly chosen for me—those delicate baby pink roses entwined with sprigs of baby's breath? And where was my bouquet now? I wish I hadn't thrown, wonder who the lucky gal was who caught my bouquet? I could have dried it and kept it forever, but now it was gone.

As I crossed the threshold into the motel honeymoon suite, those thoughts swirled in my mind like confetti in a breeze, bright and fleeting, yet heavy with unspoken questions, I didn't dare voice aloud.

The motel itself felt like a time capsule from the '70s, a relic that clung stubbornly to a past that seemed both vibrant and decayed. The honeymoon suite was awash in shades of Pepto-Bismol pink, an oasis of excess with its heart-shaped pink, red Jacuzzi nestled in one corner, and a large pink bed dominating the center of the room.

It was a bizarre blend of garish and nostalgic, a place where style and kitsch collided like the shards of a broken dream, akin to some fever dream mixing "Pulp Fiction" with a tacky wedding planner's worst instincts. Ironically enough, "Pulp Fiction" flickered to life on the TV as we entered, the chaotic energy of the film matching the tumult within me. John had immediately flipped on the screen, the familiar strains of the soundtrack enveloping us.

I found myself drawn into the scene where John Travolta and his boss's wife danced, her black pants and oversized starched white shirt creating a stark contrast against the vivid backdrop. My body began to sway to the rhythm, my feet aching as I let the music guide me toward the bed, even as a whisper of protest echoed from my sausage swollen toes. Those silver strappy sandals, cruel in their beauty, had turned my toes into little swollen sausages, unrecognizable and throbbing with pain, like the memories of this day pressing on me, relentless and suffocating. I had swapped them for low heel wooden wedges only during the swimsuit portion of the day.

Now, as the throbbing intensified, I realized my feet were not the only things hurting; my

hair felt like a heavy crown of thorns, pulling painfully at my scalp. I stood at the crossroads of discomfort—should I untangle my hair or rub my aching feet first? The choices felt trivial, yet monumental, like the choices that had led me to this moment, this surreal tableau of love and confusion.

John had already flopped onto the bed, clad only in his boxer briefs, a picture of relaxation amid my chaotic whirlwind of thoughts. I glanced down at myself, confused; when had I changed into these jeans? It hardly mattered.

My fingers moved almost instinctively toward my hair, desperate to free it from the prison of bobby pins and extensions. It felt as though I were peeling away layers of an identity I barely recognized.

As the night wore on, John's love for the jacuzzi came to the fore, his favorite pastime being underwater pleasure. I learned how to hold my breath, how to synchronize my movements, all while satisfying him in the warm, bubbling embrace of the water. Those moments felt secretive and sacred, shrouded in the mist, where pleasure intertwined with the lingering ache of my exhaustion—a strange dichotomy of vulnerability and control.

The days gelled into one long stretch of indulgence and hedonism. It was our honeymoon, and I craved that euphoric high, that fleeting feeling of liberation. One day, I think it was joy—though perhaps it was merely the methadone coursing through my veins—we rented a boat, and John let me steer the wheel. I could barely drive a car; the thought of it frightened me. I would always grasp the wheel as if clinging onto it for dear life.

But there, on the boat, the wheel felt like an extension of me, a part of my very being. Was this joy or freedom, or perhaps a mix of both? I didn't know, but it was a glorious few hours, untainted by the heavy clouds of uncertainty that usually shadowed me.

As the day faded and the sun dipped below the horizon, I realized I had left my brand-new white- rimmed Dolce & Gabbana sunglasses on the boat—an extravagant gift from John just a month before. I had begged for them, I loved them, their sleek lines and glamorous aura, but now they were lost, drifting away like a memory that had slipped through my fingers. When I remembered I had left them behind, they were already gone, whisked away by the tides of chance and forgetfulness.

The rest of the honeymoon felt dimmer without them, each day marked by the absence of that small piece of joy, a reminder of something beautiful that had been so easily lost. In that pink-hued suite, time seemed to stand still, each moment stretching into eternity. I lost myself in thehaze of a honeymoon that was both intoxicating and disorienting, where every touch and every taste melded into an exhilarating blur. And as I surrendered to the rhythm of our days, I knew this was just the beginning of a journey neither of us could fully comprehend, still wondering how we had found ourselves there in the first place,

the answers as elusive as the fading echoes of a laugh that once rang true.

Chapter 24

Immigration

We returned from our honeymoon, and for the rest of the summer, I floated on a strange high. It wasn't just that I was married—it felt like I had won something far grander, a Pulitzer, maybe even an Oscar. As if the simple act of becoming someone's wife had catapulted me into a world of accomplishment, something highly revered and celebrated.

"We need to change your last name. My wifey needs to have my last name," John had said, smiling, his hand running through my hair as we lay tangled together. I agreed. I wanted it too.

My maiden name could still live on as a middle name, a vestige of who I used to be. A rebirth, after all. That's what marriage was supposed to be, wasn't it?

So we went to the Social Security office, filled out the paperwork, and I became a Mrs. John Big.

It felt monumental.

Not long after, my parents received a letter from the Department of Homeland Security. The letter glowed with good news—our family had passed the name check, and we were on track for permanent residency.

Finally, after years of fingerprints, interviews, paperwork, attorneys, more paperwork, the light at the end of the tunnel was near.

But there was a small catch: the government wanted information about my arrests.

From the time I got caught shoplifting in Filene's Basement to the incident with the bay window, and then, the third one—the one my parents had no idea about. One I had told no one about. Only John's parents knew. This was how John had lost his takes homes, around the time I died and had come back to life.

It's shameful for me to even acknowledge it to you, dear reader. To tell the story of my criminal activity.

As I write this I can hear my mom's voice on the other line, "What is this third arrest? You are a criminal! What if you can't get your green card now!" She shouted in Russian, I felt her anger, her stress across the phone line, choking me, my words.

"Ma, its going to be fine. I will handle it. It was nothing and the case is closed."

"Why did this happen? What were you doing?"

My mom's questions felt like a knife stabbing me, each question was another stab. I couldn't answer her questions. All I had for her in return was my guilty, shameful silenece. I couldn't tell her it was because I was an addict, because John stole my medicine, and there was never enough pills for the both of us. I couldn't tell her that it happened before I died.

He was working at Best Buy at the time, he had finally got his takes home. It was a methadone infused time period for me as John loved my pills, and methadone for me seemed like a good substitute for my pill. Yet, there was still never enough, my monthly prescription of two milligram kolonopin three times a day was not enough for the both of us and would vanish within a week. Thus, John being John developed a forgery habit. He began forging my benzodiazepine prescriptions, masterfully; I couldn't tell the real from the fake. He was so good at it that we would drive from pharmacy to pharmacy, scattering the forgeries across different towns, where the scripts where always filled.

We were Bonnie and Clyde of forgery.

I would soothe my guilty conscience by convincing myself I needed them. I couldn't live without them.

The bottom line was: I needed my medication.

Without it, I'd suffer seizures. There was just no way around it, I had tried to be off the benzos, not by choice but by the lack of medication, and every time I went over a month without them just self medicating with methadone and heroine I would have a grand mal.

The end justifying the means. Over time I would wonder if John needed the pills more than I did. Did he love them more than he loved me?

Was he addicted to them? Maybe more than I was.

It was a huge risk, but John assured me I'd be fine. "If we ever get caught, I'll take the fall. It won't touch you," he'd say, his words like a security blanket, but one that was threadbare and fraying at the edges.

"I can't get arrested, my immigration would be all messed up."

"Nothing will happen to you babygirl" he reassured me. I wanted to believe him, it was easier to believe him than to acknowledge the truth of my addictions, my secrets.

But then came the day that everything unraveled. I was working at Things Remembered when John dropped off a forged script at our local CVS.

A few hours later, I got a call at work, asking me to come by and pick up my prescription. My stomach knotted immediately, a warning signal I tried to bury. I knew the script was fake, and yet I convinced myself it would be fine. I was wrong. The second I stepped into the pharmacy, my anxiety sharpened.

A man approached me, and before I could react, he asked, "Are you Diana Kouprina?"

"Yes," I said, my voice wavering, too soft for what I felt inside.

"Can I see your ID?"

I handed him my work authorization card, " I am sorry but I don't have a drivers license, I don't drive, I have siezures" I said my voice already coming out shaky, and that's when I saw it—the badge clipped to his belt.

"Where are you from?"

"I was born in Georgia…"

"What country are you from?"

"Um, I don't know Russia, Soviet Union."

My heart slammed into my ribs.

"Do you know what this is about?"

I shook my head NO!

"No sir, I don't know what this is about."

Yes, yes I did know what this was about. This was it.

"This is about your prescription," he said, the words hanging in the air.

Of course it was, I already knew that.

"Do you know what I'm talking about?"

Fuck.

The word reverberated through my skull, like a drum beat growing louder, faster.

This was it. John had told me to keep my mouth shut if we ever got caught, that he'd handle it, but here I was, cornered.

"I don't know what you mean," I lied, the words spilling out like bile. "I'm just here to pick up my medication. I'm prescribed this by my psychiatrist."

His eyes hardened. "Your psychiatrist didn't write this prescription. I spoke to him thirty minutes ago."

Double fuck.

There was no escaping now. I was cuffed and walked out of the

CVS, my mind a riot of panic, screaming at me over and over again, y*ou are a criminal, jail and deportation, that's where you're going next.*

We drove across the parking lot to Best Buy, where John was arrested. We were kept separate. I watched him get shoved into a cruiser, his face drained of color. He looked weak being handcuffed with hands behind his back. I was placed in a holding cell, my hands shaking uncontrollably, my mind racing, spiraling. Anxiety gripped me so hard, I thought I might die from it right there. My chest tightened, my breath caught in my throat choking me. The walls of that cell were suffocating, the bars felt icy cold to my already cold touch.

Eventually, we were released on bail. His mom posted it. A court date was set, but I can barely remember it.

It's all a blur of terror and shame. I remember sitting in the courthouse bathroom, poppingKlonopin just to steady myself, just to survive another minute.

We were put on probation, John and I. For six months, we had to submit to daily urine tests, our futures hanging by the results of those tests. To fail the test meant prison time, for me it could mean deportation, which for me was worse than prison time, it was prison time plus loss of country.

The problem with both our urines was that we both had drugs in our system we should have and drug in our system we shouldn't have had. My urine was supposed to test positive for benzodiazepine only not for opiates, that would include the methadone, for him vice versa. John resolved to finding clean urine, he didn't seem to have a problem with that. But for me there was no urine available. He told me he knew a trick.

It was simple and it worked, it was just gross going down. All we needed was Epsom salt and gallons of water. The concoction was simple to make, it required between two to four cups of Epsom salt mixed into the gallon of water. I had to chug the gallon as fast as I could.

I did it anytime John gave me methadone.

I chugged that gallon like my life depended on it, and in a way it did.

I passed the drug test every time, as did John without fail, the case was dismissed after the probation period ended. No one ever had to know about my shameful felony.

But now, the Department of Homeland Security wanted the paperwork, the details of every arrest. Every screw-up. Every scar hidden inside the foundation of denial.

John and I went to the courthouses together, collecting all the necessary paperwork. I gathered every document they asked for, and even some they hadn't—just to be sure. Along with the arrest records, I added our marriage certificate, carefully compiling everything into a neat folder for USCIS.

A month later, my parents received their green cards. I, on the other hand, received a denial. And it wasn't because of my arrest record; no one seemed to care about that except for me and my parents. What they cared about was the marriage certificate. By getting married, I had become ineligible to receive my green card with my parents. The denial notice urged me to file for the I-130 visa—the only way now to get a green card through marriage to a U.S. citizen. Just like that,

I had to start over with immigration.

New petitions, new timelines.

I told myself it wasn't a big deal.

I could handle this.

All I had to do was file the new petition, and everything would work itself out.

It had to.

Chapter 25

Intermission

After we were married, something had shifted even more between John and me, like a tide receding and leaving behind an unfamiliar landscape. In bed he always preferred the fucking portion over making love, but even that was becoming rougher than usual. On the nights we would get high, he on cocaine and I on methadone or heroin, on those nights he began to develop a habit of choking me. Not enough to leave a mark, but enough for me to feel the loss of breath, gasping for air. Other times he enjoyed putting a pillow over my head and pressing down with one arm so I could feel being suffocated. For me sex had become three things, sex was pain, sex was an obsession to have a child, and sex was necessary to keep John.

As fall settled in, my desire for a baby turned into an obsession that wrapped around me like a blanket protecting me from the chill settling in the air. But John, wasn't interested in nurturing that part of us. We managed one fertility consultation, to test ovulation. The test showed I ovulated, my eggs appeared to be functioning fine. The doctor wanted to test John next, but he refused, crossing his arms with a familiar stubbornness, that without a fail always told me he would have his way and there was no point in pressing the matter further.

"No one is probing my wiener or my nut sack." He had said as we were leaving the doctor's office and that was that.

I kept myself busy during those fall months with the hope of getting pregnant by taking natural fertility boosters, I attempted to track my periods, and with every period I would have a break down, as each month I would hope, fingers crossed, that it was the month I would get pregnant. My periods were irregular to begin with, so on the months I did miss my period, I would hold on to the hope, trying to convince myself; that I could be pregnant.

But then the painful cramps would start, the pain unbearable not even methadone could ease it. It felt as though something inside of me was exploding, the flow itself would come out in red chunky globs.

To soothe myself through my distress, anxiety and depression, I would lose myself in house hunting online. John's parents had offered to cover the down payment and be our co-borrowers on our mortgage application. I scoured listings in New Hampshire, the one place that felt like a compromise. John liked the idea of a small house in the woods there, and the prices were low enough to tempt me into dreaming with rose colored glasses on. I printed out the listings, organized them in neat piles, and pleaded with him over and over again.

"Please, can we go to an open house? It would be fun." I still hear myself begging him.

His response was always the same, "Maybe next weekend."

As next weekend rolled around, he would be tired, or busy working for his father. After all, I had to accept the fact that fall was a busy season in Landscaping, and John had already taken three days off in the summer for our honeymoon. He would have more time in the winter. I would tell myself, fiddling with my wedding bands, growing confident with the lies I told myself.

This was also the time where John was trying to convince me we should buy a boat instead of a house. His parents were after all going to give us thirty thousand dollars, why not just buy a boat. We actually went one weekend to look at boats. He had managed to find the time for that, although deep down I knew his parents wouldn't buy him a boat.

"We can have threesomes on a boat. Like in the porn, you like."

"But I don't know if I want a threesome. Porn is porn, what if you fall in love with the other woman and leave me?"

"I would never do that…you are my babygirl-wifey."

John's push for a threesome was a constant, where before it was a subtle joke now was a persistent conversation which was slowly turning into a guilt trip.

"I married you." He would say, like I owed him this. "I've done what you wanted."

His words would sink into me slowly, twisting up the lines between desire and obligation,between what I wanted for us and what he was now demanding. It wasn't a request anymore; it was a debt he expected me to pay.

I told him maybe for his birthday in March, hoping it would buy me time, hoping I could string it along, or that something else would distract him.

If we had a baby he wouldn't be thinking about a threesome. I would tell myself.

Chapter 26

Crepes and Pancakes:

The bedroom was steeped in darkness, a void John demanded and needed. No light crept through the cracks; even the early morning sun was shut out. The huge water canopy bed, with its reflecting mirrors, mirroring our movements in bed, seemed to be the only thing he still loved.

John was sprawled out, limbs heavy and still, oblivious to the day starting without him.

He didn't have work that specific morning, where the memory of it unfolds clearly in my mind as though it just happened; its clarity striking in comparison to all my other memories I try to untangle, just to understand.

That morning, I'd wanted to surprise him with breakfast.

I wanted to bring back something simple, something soft, something that reminded me of my childhood. My heart was set on making crepes, like the ones I grew up eating. I hadn't had them in years and never really even made them.

But I wanted to make them for John. Maybe food could bring us back to the days when I believed he loved me, and that seemed like enough to hold us together.

I picked up my phone, went into the little living room and called my mother.

"Ma, how do I make crepes?"

Her voice crackled through the line warm and familiar. There was excitement, like she had been waiting for this call.

"How many do you want to make? Well, start with a small portion. You will need three eggs, two cups of flour, one cup of milk, sugar, salt. Mix it all together very well. No clumps. Heat up the pan, and you know babushka Polly had this trick. She would pour a little vegetable oil in a dish, take a potato cut it in half, and would grease the skillet with it, spreading the oil evenly."

"Thank you, Mommy," I had said hanging up the phone, feeling a smile tug at my lips.

Outside, the world was drenched in light. A clear, crisp day, the kind that made you want to believe in possibilities again. I wish there was grass, I thought to myself as I looked down at the ground. The backyard was fully covered with ¾ blue crushed stone, a decision John made with the landlords, in exchange for paying rent one month. I wondered if the crushed stone hurt Play Play's paws every time she walked out in the yard, like it hurt my bare feet every time I tried to walk across without shoes or slippers. I let her out, watching her trot carefully across the stones, tail wagging despite the uneven ground.

I crushed my cigarette out on the outdoor ashtray and turned back inside. The kitchen was

waiting for me, a quiet area of sunlit peace I could control, if only for the next few minutes. I cracked the eggs into a bowl, whisked them together with milk, sugar, salt, flour, feeling the rhythm of the recipe settle into my hands, my bones, feeling my babushka near.

Bubushka Polly's trick made me smile, as I sliced the potato in half, dipping one half into the oil dish, and gliding it across the frying pan. The sizzle of the batter hitting the pan was a small triumph, a sound that reminded me of mornings back in Tbilisi, before life had become real, complicated, grown up.

I poured the first ladle of batter, watching it spread thin and delicate, knowing soon it would bubble, flip and become something whole: something simple; something that might bring us back even if it were only for just one moment.

I heard my babushka's voice: "Deanachka, wait for it bubble, when you see the bubbles flip."

I felt her guidance in a task I didn't know to maneuver with ease. We made the crepes together, her spirit crafting the crepes through me.

John wandered into the kitchen, bleary-eyed, walking over to me to kiss me on my forehead.

"Good morning, babygirl-wifey," he said in his sing-song, higher pitch than normal, joyful voice.

"Coffee's ready," I said to him in return, beaming with joy.

He went over to the coffee put, taking out a cup from the cupboard above and pouring himself coffee, the fragrant smell of Folgers hit my nostrils. He stirred in his, extra cream and extra sugar and went to sit at the little table by the kitchen wall across from the stove where I was standing.

"I am making, blinu, almost done. They are like Russian pancakes." I said, feeling his eyes on me from across as I flipped the last one messing up completely. I turned off the stove, and brought over the plate with thin crepes, layered one atop one another, to him; presenting them to him as though they were medals.

He blinked at them, "my babygirl cooked,"

Was he surprised?

I smiled at him, placing one thin crepe on his plate.

He took a bite,

He chewed,

I waited for praise.

After what felt like a forever silence, he said:

"These aren't pancakes."

"These were the pancakes of my childhood," I replied softly, defensively, my voice retorting to a child like whine. "My babushka made them for me all the time. Every morning I can remember I remember her making me blinu, I loved eating them with sour cream."

"Babygirl, Russian food is just not for me." He said putting down the crepe he was holding in his hand like a sheet of paper, on his plate.

"Well, guess we are going out for some real American pancakes, with lot of syrup, just how my babygirl likes it."

"Yeah, ok," I said feeling small. Like a child that failed once again.

"I didn't make them right anyway. It was my first time. But I get an A for trying."

"That you do babygirl. A for effort."

And just like that my crepes were degraded, and thrown into the trash.

Outside, the sunlight kept pushing its way through the morning, though none of it touched me. I couldn't feel it. I was somewhere else entirely.

Chapter 27

Black to Blonde

I had long, curly, luscious hair, which I dyed black for years; my go to color after being blonde back in 2003. I loved the black hair on me, as opposed to brown my natural color or bleached blonde, where the bleach ate away my hair; the black took away from my most prominent features, cloaking them in an alluring darkness. The day I married, I wore my black hair like a crown, a testament to the persona I had cultivated.

It was time for a change, to mark my rebirth; once again.

And as fall descended casting a veil of change over everything, I found myself craving blonde hair. It was a persistent, obsessive craving, an ultimate solution to my problems.

I envisioned it short and bright, like Carrie's in Sex and the City, where she gets a new hair cut and a new job at Vogue, making 80 cents per word. That transformative moment a fleeting dream of reinvention seemed within my reach, yet so far away.

I wished I looked like Marilyn Monroe, a sire whose essence seemed unattainable. But I knew that to resemble her, I would need a nose job, which I desperately craved and breast implants which John desperately craved for me, even then my bony body would never match her voluptuous allure, plus I didn't want to be voluptuous. The closest celebrity I could resemble was Carrie from Sex and the City, a character who danced between worlds with effortless grace; a grace, I could never seem to attain.

I can't recall the exact moment when I fixated on the idea of sporting a curly blonde bob, but it felt like a necessary rebirth – a shedding of the skin I had worn for so long. It was a desire to transcend, to emerge from the shadows of my past as Mrs. John Big.

I begged John daily to see when May was available to do my hair. She was the only one I knew who could masterfully transform me. Besides, she was his sister, and she did my hair for free or for a huge family discount, I am not quite sure of the logistics.

John handled the finances.

It was early winter when May finally had a day with a clear schedule to take me in at the salon. The air was crisp, filled with the promise of change. I watched, entranced as she deftly turned my long hair into a braid before severing it, a symbolic act of letting go.

After she cut it, she held the braid up for me to see, its entirety a cascade of darkness. "This hair will make someone very happy. It's perfect for wigs," she said her voice mindful and steady.

The idea that my hair was perfect for someone else made me laugh, quietly in my head, a bittersweet irony. I had always hated my hair; it was frizzy, curly, hard to manage and a whole hourly process to straighten. Yet, here it was; a remnant of my past ready to be repurposed.

As she masterfully cut and colored my hair turning black into an ashy golden blonde, I felt a surge of hope. It was the color I had always dreamed about but had never been able to attain –not even from the trendiest salon on Newbury Street. I remembered the time when I was making money stripping and I had splurged $350 on a haircut and color, longing for a similar bob style back in 2003. But the expert colorist had turned my hair to ashy, leaving me disheartened. After that, I took to dying my own hair, Feria hair dye always turned my hair a blonde I could live with.

Now, May, with her skill and dedication was finally achieving the unattainable blonde I had envisioned. The whole process lasted over six hours, a lengthy pilgrimage to   transformation. We talked, but rarely; the silence felt sacred. I mainly watched her in the mirros as she cut, dyed and styled, entranced by the artistry unfolding before me. Each snip and stroke felt like a step toward liberation, a rebirth in every sense.

I loved the end result.

"You are amazing and brilliant" I had screeched in excitement. As she put the final styling touches on my hair.

"Well, I don't know if the color is too golden, I can add more highlights but I can't do that now, your hair just went through a lot. We don't want to make it fall out." She said, as she looked through my hair judging her work.

"No, no need, you did it, it's perfect. Thank you." I said with joy.

John had entered the salon, to pick me up.

"You look beautiful babygirl," he said to me as he walked over towards us.

"Oh I love it!" I said with joy in my voice.

What I didn't realize then in my joy, was how hard it would be to maintain the style of the cut. I didn't think about the process and how I would be able to style it on my own, what it required of me.

A realization I would uncover only a few short days after, of how hard it would be attain the style May had created, a realization that would soon temper all my joy and thrill with the weight of new-found responsibility and failure.

I was too swept up in joy in that moment, as though going from black to blonde was somehow going to restore the broken, damaged pieces of me, and me and John.

Chapter 28

Ariel

Christmas came and went and it felt bland. There was no magic, no sparkle, just the mechanical ticking of time. But I was confident. I was protected by my wedding ring—a strange type of confidence, one I never want to feel again. It was like wearing armor made of glass, giving the illusion of security but so fragile you could hear it crack with every careless word, every indifferent glance.

We were in bed as per usual one night, watching Lord of the Rings.

"Look, it's Smeogul," John said to me, kissing my forehead. "My babygirl is Smeogul." It was the scene where Smeogul finally gets the ring, my precious.

"What do you mean, I look like Smeogul?" I replied, my mind immediately turning on me, screaming and laughing inside,

"Yeah, you really do."

I heard John's voice, a soothing balm against the rising tide of insecurity:

"No, my baby girl doesn't look like Smeogul; it's because you love your ring. Like Smeogul, you have your precious."

That relaxed me a bit. I did have my precious, my diamond wedding ring, glinting in the dim light—a testament to promises made. Of course, I longed to feel like Marilyn Monroe in Gentlemen Prefer Blondes, after all, weren't diamonds a girl's best friend? But instead, here I was, settling for Smeogul.

New Year's always had a different feel for me, it was rooted in my upbringing, in my childhood.

In Soviet culture, Christmas didn't hold the same weight. There was no religion, just the rhythm of a state-driven society. The Orthodox Christian Church had its own Christmas, but that was after New Year's, a quiet footnote. So, for us, everything happened on New Year's—the real celebration of letting go of the past, embracing the new, of love and the

warm embrace of joy from family; babushkas, dedushkas, aunts, uncles, cousins. The tree was lit, the food was prepared, lots and lots of food, meat stuffed crepes, salad Olivere, cakes, cookies, candies and Ded Moroz, our version of Santa Claus, came with his bag of gifts, as we the children danced around the Christmas tree singing:

Маленькой ёлочке холодно зимой,

Из лесу взяли ёлочку домой.

Сколько на ёлочке шариков цветных,

Розовых, пряников, шишек золотых.

Встанем под ёлочкой дружный паровоз,

Весело, весело встретим Новый год.

Translated to English the song went something like this;

Little Christmas tree cold in winter,

From the forest took (the) little tree home.

How many on (the) tree balls colorful,

Pink, gingerbread, cones golden.

Let's stand under (the) tree a friendly train,

Joyfully, joyfully we'll meet the New Year.

It was something I would never experience again, it all faded into memories once I stepped onto the US soil.

John didn't care about New Year's. He wasn't big on going out or celebrating. He allowed me a Christmas tree, and I accepted it. It felt like that's what wives did—accept, adjust, make peace with disappointment.

So we spent the night in bed. The same bed where I had watched his indifference grow like a slow cancer, spreading into every part of our lives.

The street we lived on was quiet, almost too quiet for a night like New Year's. There was no celebration outside, no parties spilling into the cold night air. Just the distant hum of silence, the occasional car passing by on its way somewhere better. John never wanted to go into the city, not for New Year's or for any other reason. He liked the quiet. He liked staying in. And every year, we spent it the same way—together in bed, with nothing but

the faint glow of the bedside lamp to mark the passage of time.

This married year was no different. There were no fireworks, no countdown, I drank a bottle of champagne in bed, John didn't like alcohol. So it was me getting drunk by myself, lying next to sleeping John. I lay next to him, staring at the ceiling, not paying attention to the New York, New Year's countdown, feeling that familiar emptiness creep in. It was odd, the way marriage created a new kind of loneliness. Before, when I was alone, I could own it, wear it like a coat. But this was different. Being next to someone and still feeling cold—there was something cruel in that.

I thought about the New Years of my childhood, how my parents had always tried to make it special. How the magic of that one night seemed to hang in the air like frost. It was a time of hope, of new beginnings. But here, with John, it felt like just another night.

I secretly craved the celebration, the party, the excitement of New Year's—the lights, the noise, the laughter of strangers in the city. But instead, I was here, in the silence, bound by a ring that felt heavier with each passing day. No promises of new beginnings. No warmth. Just a ring on my finger and a silent room.

It was January when I met Ariel. Completely out of the blue, at a photoshoot. I had been invited to model for a boudoir BDSM-style shoot, something I had never done before, but the idea intrigued me. The photographer was an artist in his own right, with an eye for capturing the raw and the intimate. He wanted two models to create a striking contrast for the session, and that's how I ended up standing in a dimly lit studio, unsure of what to expect. I didn't expect to discover a new friend that day. But I did.

The moment I saw Ariel, I was drawn to her. There was something about her—a magnetic confidence, a presence that demanded attention without even trying. She had this effortless beauty, the kind you can't manufacture, and a way of carrying herself that said she didn't care what anyone thought. I admired that. Maybe I even envied it.

We hit it off almost immediately, our conversation flowing as naturally as if we had known each other for years. Between shots, she told me about her life, how she had lived in Germany for most of her twenties but she had moved back to the States recently, needing to escape the suffocating grip of her mother. There was something in the way she said it that made me feel like there was more to the story, but I didn't push. We all had our reasons for running from something.

By the end of the shoot, I realized I wasn't just leaving with a series of provocative photos. I was leaving with something I hadn't expected—a connection, a new friend who had somehow slipped into my life like she had always been meant to. Ariel was a force, and I

felt like I was being pulled into her orbit.

John had been surprisingly supportive of my blossoming friendship with Ariel. He loved how our energy seemed to pulse with laughter and spontaneity. I hadn't been out to a city bar in ages and as we settled into our seats at a lively bar in Boston, the noise of the crowd enveloped me like a warm embrace. The music thumped against my chest, and the air was thick with the scent of beer and excitement. Yet, through it all, I was more enthralled in my conversation with Ariel than the surroundings.

"I was too wild in Germany," she confessed, her eyes sparkling with mischief. "My mom couldn't handle me, so she sent me here to live with my grandmother and brother. The clubs in Germany are different from here. It's a whole different scene. Have you been to Germany?"

I shook my head, feeling a twinge of envy. "No, I've never been. I haven't traveled outside the U.S. since I came here at the age of nine, but I would love to go one day."

"It's a crazy place. You've heard of the clubs, right?"

"Yeah, it's crazy" I lied, agreeing with her. I had no idea what she meant by crazy, wild clubs. I wouldn't realize she was talking about the sex clubs until ten years later. I didn't even know such clubs existed.

But at the bar, that night with Ariel I didn't want to sound uninformed, so I played along. The truth was, I knew little about German culture aside from the Holocaust, a shadow that loomed large in my understanding. I couldn't fathom how an entire nation could succumb to such hatred and disregard for human life. As a child, I had devoured books about it; I read and reread—Anne Frank at eleven, again at twelve, at thirteen, and at fifteen. I did a whole term project on the Holocaust, meeting an Author and Survivor of the Holocaust back at Dana Hall. Each time, the stories haunted me; I had watched Schindler's List and cried every time. In my heart, I held onto a resentment I couldn't shake. I had never cared to explore how the culture evolved past Hitler, nor did I have much desire to visit, though I would have admitted back then that it would be interesting to see where the Berlin Wall had once stood.

Ariel's words snapped me back to reality. "Yeah, so now my brother is my pimp," she said with a nonchalant shrug. "It works out. We make do."

"Wait, what?" My heart raced. The words hung in the air, unsettling in their casualness.

"Yeah, it's been tough. I'm going to try to live with this guy I'm seeing. He has a shit ton of money, but I don't like him. I love Joe, but he doesn't want to live with me. It's all going to shit,"

she said, her voice a mix of frustration and resignation.

An urge surged within me—a fierce, protective instinct. I was in a better position than her, and I wanted to shield her from the chaos. I glanced at my ring, feeling the armor of confidence it provided, and then said, "Well, while it's all sorting out, you can come live with John and me. Our couch pulls out, we have room, and I would love your company."

"Thanks, yeah, I'll think about it," Ariel replied, her expression softening. For a moment, the noise of the bar faded, and I felt a strange sense of purpose. Here was someone I could help, someone who could bring color into my monochrome existence. As theconversation shifted to lighter topics, I felt a spark of hope, igniting within me the possibility of new beginnings.

Chapter 29

Ariel Continued

A week later, Ariel called me.

"Thanks so much for the offer to come live with you guys. But I'm gonna try and give it a go with Bill. He got this job offer to travel through Texas and California closing businesses," she said on the other line, her voice steady, almost euphoric.

"Travel might be good for you, and it'll get you off the streets and away from your brother," I responded, though a tightness gripped my throat.

After I hung up, a wave of loneliness swept over me, drowning out any semblance of happiness I should have felt for her. The envy burned quietly, hot and familiar. Ariel was about to step into a new chapter—glossy, nomadic, and free—while I remained here, in this stillness. The tears welled up, unbidden, not just for her leaving, but for the small fantasy that slipped through my fingers: the thought of her being the third. John had seemed happier with her around. Or maybe it was me, happier, more vibrant, less weighed down by the mundanity that had crept into our lives.

Her laugh, her energy—it had filled the spaces between John and me, balancing the unspoken tensions, the creeping distance. I wanted to tell myself that I was enough, that I

didn't need her or anyone else to make this work. But the truth was, Ariel had become a bridge, a connection that I didn't know I was missing until it was gone.

How she embodied a wildness I could never possess, no matter how much I craved it, it was something untouchable, something that made her seem larger than life, while I felt myself shrinking in her absence. She was everything I wasn't—free, untethered, moving forward with such grace, while I stayed behind, held down by invisible chains.

Plath's Ariel echoed in my mind, and the words felt sharp against my thoughts:

> ***God's lioness,***
> ***How one we grow,***
> ***Pivot of heels and knees!—The furrow***
>
> ***Splits and passes, sister to***
> ***The brown arc***
> ***Of the neck I cannot catch,***
>
> ***Nigger-eye***
> ***Berries cast dark***
> ***Hooks—***

There was something in that fierce acceleration, that unstoppable force, that reminded me of Ariel. How she moved forward with or without me. She was a force I could only observe from a distance, spinning out of my reach.

The room felt emptier, John's silence heavier. I knew, deep down, that her departure had taken something vital with it. The void she left wasn't just hers, it was a part of me, too. A part that longed to break free.

In the next coming weeks, the room felt heavier. The silence between John and me became almost suffocating, as if Ariel had taken all the lightness with her. The void she left was noticeable and with each passing day, it seemed to grow, stretching across our once vibrant space. John stayed the same—detached, distant—moving through our shared life like a ghost. But without Ariel, there was nothing to distract me from the slow unraveling of what we had. I thought I could manage it, that I'd adjust to her absence, but instead, it gnawed at me. Every corner of the house felt emptier, colder, as though even the walls were grieving her loss. I tried to fill the space with tasks, meaningless motions—cleaning, cooking, anything to occupy my hands and mind. But nothing could erase the emptiness. I missed her laughter, the wild stories of her travels, the way her presence had made everything seem a little more alive.

John barely noticed the change, or if he did, he never spoke of it. He continued on, locked in his own world, while I found myself staring at my phone, waiting for a call or a text that never came.

Even when I wasn't thinking of her, Ariel lingered in the back of my mind—a wild, untouchable thing I had lost.

When she did call, she sounded worse. Lost, crying—sometimes I couldn't even understand what she was saying. I knew she was high on coke. Bill was a liquidator with a large cash flow, and it seemed like that easy money fueled their chaos.

Every time I hung up, the heaviness in my chest worsened. I couldn't shake the worry.

"I'm so worried about her," I would say to John, lying next to him in the darkness, his chest rising and falling under my head. "Maybe she really should have come and lived with us."

"Maybe," he murmured, half awake, half asleep, kissing my forehead softly. His hand rested on my hair, but his gaze was always fixed ahead, at the tattoo of the bare-chested woman etched onto his arm. I hated how much it pulled his attention, even now.

"I'm so alone," I whispered, feeling the isolation creep in deeper. "I have no friends."

"You don't need any," he said, his voice low and indifferent. "You have me, babygirl. And my sisters."

"I don't think they like me," I said, though it was more of a confession than a complaint.

"They love you," he replied, kissing my forehead again, as if that would quiet all my doubts. But I wasn't convinced. Something about it all felt too hollow, too distant. The ache of loneliness never quite left, not even in his arms.

I busied myself with popping pills—methadone mostly, but alcohol if the pills ran out. I took fertility herbal pills, hoping they would help me have a baby. I imagined that having a child would heal the loneliness, solidify our family life, and be the solution to all our problems. I'd clean, fold laundry, write for hours, anything to fill the silence while waiting for John to come home with food. Between it all, I chain-smoked Newports, one after another, the smoke curling around me like a shield. I worried constantly about running out, I never had any money to buy more. Sometimes I'd force myself outside for a walk, but the cold wrapped around me like icy fingers, pressing into my skin, making each step feel heavier than the last. I couldn't do any photo shoots, and that went on from January into March. Most days, I stayed wrapped in blankets, the TV flickering in the background as I drifted in and out of sleep, the world outsideblurring into something distant, almost unreal.

March brought change: John's birthday and his ongoing obsession with the dream of a threesome as his birthday present. It lingered in our conversations, like a shadow that

wouldn't fade, and I often wondered if it was a way for him to escape the reality of our strained relationship. The promise of adventure, of wild experiences, seemed to tempt him more than anything else.

Then early April rolled in with a phone call—Ariel was back. She left Bill, leaving behind the chaos of their whirlwind romance, and now she wanted to get back with Joe. I could hear the urgency in her voice when she asked if she could come live with us while she sorted everything out. A part of me wanted to welcome her back, to rekindle that spark of excitement she always brought into my life, but another part hesitated, wary of the complications her presence might stir.

During this tumultuous time, I had finally given up the idea of having a baby. It felt like a weight had been lifted, yet a void still lingered in its place. I could no longer chase after a dream that felt increasingly unattainable. In an attempt to fill that void, I bought John a pitbull puppy for his birthday, with my mom giving me the money and driving me to pick up the puppy in Rhode Island. She seemed to think the puppy would be a welcome distraction for both of us.

Taking care of her like a baby, bringing her out for walks, made the loneliness less palpable. PlayPlay, our aging dog, could barely move by then. She spent her days laying in her bed next to my computer desk, a fragile shadow of her former self. I didn't want to live with a pet that would soon be gone, but I hoped the new puppy would bring a sense of life back into the house—a distraction from the heaviness that had settled over us.

As the days unfolded, the thought of Ariel moving in again loomed in the back of my mind. It felt like a collision course, the excitement of a new puppy mixed with the return of an old friend, and I couldn't help but wonder how it would all play out. Would Ariel's presence breathe new life into our stagnant routine, or would it amplify the tensions that already existed? Would the puppy be a symbol of hope or just another reminder of the unpredictability of our lives?

Chapter 30

Crack Whore

Ariel moved in quickly, as if she had been waiting for the moment. She arrived with little more than an army bag filled with clothes, her presence both light and intense, hovering somewhere between transience and permanence. She took the pull-out couch, though most nights she ended up at Joe's, their on-again, off-again love affair adding a layer of complication I refused to acknowledge when John pressed. He kept asking me, "Is she the one to be our third?" I knew what he wanted, what the suggestion meant, but I always deflected. "She's in love with Joe," I would say.

Ariel was my friend, and I couldn't let those lines blur, couldn't afford the mess that would come from that kind of intimacy. Instead, we spent our days together, wrapped in laughter and an unspoken bond, our lives tethered by more than friendship. She pulled me out of the house, filled the silence of the suburban streets with her energy. She was receiving food stamps back then, and our kitchen overflowed with groceries she brought in, filling the empty spaces John and I left unattended.

Meeting her family only added to the strange alchemy of our relationship. Her grandmother was a relic of another time, and her brother—flamboyant, walking the tightrope between sweetness and danger—was nothing like she had described. There was no anger in him, none of the violence she hinted at. But I wasn't fooled. People wear their masks well, and who knew what unfolded behind the thick curtains of their crack smoke filled home? I had learned, too, that everyone carried secrets too heavy to share in the light of day.

And then something shifted.

Joe stopped calling her back, the tenuous connection they'd forged dissolving into radio silence. That's when Ariel started taking the pervie shoots, and I went with her. It wasn't the photography I was used to—the sterile artifice of boudoir poses or the glittery, erotic glamour Ariel had dabbled in before. No, these shoots were different. They didn't barter in cash, but in crack, and the photographers weren't artists; they were predators. I remember the dim light in that room, the way they had us go down on each other, clicking away like it was sport, something far from beauty or sensuality. It wasn't about art. It was about control, about making us disappear beneath their gaze.

The crack helped.

I craved the way it filled my lungs, that bitter, nauseating tingle of baking soda mixing with the familiar sting of cocaine. It was a different kind of high, smoother than I'd

expected, and safer in some strange way. I could smoke crack without seizing.

Cocaine?

No.

I'd learned my lesson the hard way, after that seizure at Blockbuster. John and I had done a line each in the car, and I felt it hit me like a freight train, collapsing under the weight of my own body, but I steadied myself with a pill I put between my tongue before exiting the car. I clearly remember walking the aisles of blockbuster in search for a movie. I wanted a Romantic Comedy, John wanted Horror. The lights felt extremely bright.

I felt the flickering of the fluorescent lights in my mind every time I blinked.

I told myself,

Ok, maybe a bit too much coke.

Was the line even that big? I asked myself as a continuation of my thought.

It wasn't, I told myself, It was a bump, and you took a benzodiazepine.

You're fine. You did it right.

With those soothing thoughts,

I blinked again.

And once more,

And then,

I came to on the floor, paramedics surrounding me, their faces hard, uncaring. They were mean, cold, detached, uncaring, to say rough around the edges is putting it mildly, as if I was wasting their time, another cocaine overdose, I tried to tell them it wasn't a cocaine overdose, they didn't believe me. They wanted to strap me into the gurney.

I told them to let me be.

I told them I had a seizure disorder, which was true, but I omitted the fact that I had just done a bump of coke in the car.

They made me sign I a paper stating I refused their services.

I'd had seizures before, on methadone and Klonopins, back when everything was spiraling. It was the story I told myself to cling to a sliver of reality in the madness. That it wasn't the drugs.

That I wasn't out of control. That I still had some grasp on sanity, even when I could feel it slipping through my fingers like smoke.

But for some reason when I smoked crack, I didn't not seize, my mind relaxed even more so than on benzos, methadone, or heroin.

It was a strange sensation. It was a sensation that I enjoyed.

"Whitney Houston smokes crack," we were laying in bed watching a special on Whitney Houston, high on crack, John, Ariel and me one night, all us sprawled innocently across our new bed. John's parents felt that our water bed, was not a suitable bed for a married couple and replaced it with a king size pillow top, John had bought special made blackened sheets to block any window light that could seep in from the window that was once blocked by the huge canopy, I had replaced all the dark purple, black red sheets, and really I shouldn't write I here, my mother purchased us chocolate/champagne theme bed set, including comforter, pillow cases, sheets, I felt my bed turn into a princess bed. I loved and hated it at the same time, apart of me missed the lull of the waterbed.

"Does she?" I can hear myself asking snuggling closer to John, Ariel on the other side of me sitting up, lighting her lighter with the small clear crack pipe pressed between her lips,

Whitney Houston was singing on the TV, "Yeah, I want to dance. Clock strikes upon the hour and the sun begins to fade, still enough time to figure out how to chase the blues away.......

"I don't believe it", I said as Ariel passed the pipe to me, holding in the crack filled smoke she just inhaled in her lungs before exhaling.

"When the night falls, the loneliness strikes.....

I wanna feel the heat, with somebody, with somebody who loves me. I have been in love and lost my senses...." Whitney Houston sang on.

I wondered to myself, *Maybe she does smoke crack, it makes sense, maybe her brain works like my brain.*

"Yeah everyone knows it, it's the truth, just like R.Kelly is the Pied Piper, and Michael Jackson is Peter Pan."

I enhaled the smoke. I felt it in my lungs.

I exhaled with, "why is R. Kelly a Pied Piper? What does that even mean?"

"He likes little girls, he is pedo. Everyone knows it." John responded,

"But he wrote I Believe I Can Fly, and I am Your Angel"

I said defensively almost offended.

"Yeah and you just proved my point, he sings and little girls run to him and he believe he

can fly." John responded taking a huge hit off the pipe.

"Ariel, its kicked, do we have more rocks."

"Yeah I got a shit ton," She responded, reaching for her bag on the floor.

"Somebody whoo, somebody whoo,

to hold me in his arms....

Ohhh I wanna dance with somebody, I wanna feel the heat with somebody,

.....With somebody who loves me......wHOOOOO......dance,

Don't you wanna dance?" Whitney Houston sang on the tv screen.

Oh I wanted to dance, singing the words I could catch as Whitney

Houston concluded singing her song. I felt nice.

Everything felt nice.

I wanted to dance, I was in the kitchen.

Ariel appeared. Was she in her lingerie? Ariel and I gravitated toward each other, our intertwined dance led us into the living room. Towards the couch, our bodies pulled together by something more than the high. I felt a surge of confidence, I never felt before.

Is this what it felt like to be a man? I wondered to myself, kissing her pushing her towards the wall next to the couch, her back pressing into the wall, her legs spreading, coiling around me, her breathe short, rhythmic, soft, on my lips.

I want this, I told myself. This is for me, Not John, I convinced myself in that passionate moment. I remember my fingers tugging at her sheer black lingerie, the fabric whispering secrets against my skin as it slid beneath my fingertips. One hand danced rhythmically through her long, brown waves, the strands slipping through my fingers like liquid silk, tugging gently as if to draw her closer. The other hand, emboldened by the haze of crack and desire, found its way between her legs, slipping beneath the delicate ace of her underwear. The heat radiated from her, a magnetic pull that was impossible to resist. There was an urgency in the air, an electric thrill that surged through my veins as I felt her soft warmth envelop my fingers.

I hadn't felt this electricity this desire since that one night with Mindy where we got high on coke and made out. I wanted her in bed with me that night. But her ultimatum of choosing her or John just didn't sit right. Of course I would choose John.

Every caress ignited something primal within me, a raw unfiltered need that obliterated the boundaries of our existence. We became two bodies entwined in a moment, lost in the chaotic rhythm of lust, everything else fading into oblivion.

As I explored the contours of her body, I sang to myself, "I wanna be loved by somebody. I want to dance with somebody." The bittersweet essence of those lyrics mixed with the intoxicating blend of pleasure and despair, echoing in my mind. In that suspended reality, we were both liberated and shackled, dancing on the edge of our own desires, where every touch was a declaration and ever gasp was a testament to our shared madness.

Then,

Just like that,

Shattering the moment,

Ariel's phone rang. It was the ringtone she had assigned especially for Joe. Its sharp tone slicing through the haze of our connection. We untangled as swiftly as we had found ourselves tangled in each other.

In that second, I mused to myself that:

I was saved by the ring:

I had lost all control.

I didn't know this me;

she terrified me and excited me.

The urgency in her eyes was enough to pull me away, bring me back to reality. I helped her get ready, smoothed her hair, helped her pick out her clothes, and just like that, she was gone – leaving behind a bitter scent of crack, lust and sweat.

After she left, I went to John who was still sitting in the kitchen chair. I sat on his lap, I kissed him on the lips, and said. "See? She loves Joe."

John kissing my forehead and fondling my breast between his fingers, said; "She is a crack whore," he was kissing my neck now, that spot that made me tingle all over.

"She can still do us, she wants you, baby girl. Works out perfectly."

He was leading me into the bedroom.

I wanted it.

I wanted him to fuck me, rough.

I wanted it to hurt. And through it all, his words still clung to me.

If she was a crack whore, what did that make me?

The though dug deep, lodged itself in my chest, twisting; hurting me more, than John as he pounded away at me from the back; with one hand pushing me further and further into the pillow.

Chapter 31

Easter Sunday - 2008

Easter Morning

I woke as if being dragged out of hell, my body heavy and aching, my head throbbing in steady waves of pain. The sharp, relentless ache radiated from the left side of my forehead, just above my eyebrow, like someone hammering from the inside. *Was this a migraine coming on?* I wondered, pressing my palm against my temple in a useless attempt to soothe it.

Questions swirled, colliding in my mind, but there were no answers, just an overwhelming fog. What happened last night? I pushed myself to remember, to piece together fragments of the evening. John was right next to me, soundly asleep. He wouldn't be sleeping so deeply if something bad had happened to me.

A sudden thought struck me—Maybe I had a seizure? My heart raced as I lifted the sheets, checking the bed for any dampness, I tended to wet myself during a grand-mal. Relief washed over me when I found the bed dry. No seizure. I didn't die. I'm fine.

I told myself, I just needed more rest, convincing myself this was just another anxiety attack; my mind, as always, too quick to spiral into worst-case scenarios.

I reached for the bottle tucked behind a stack of books on the bedside table, my fingers brushing against the cool surface of the pills. Popping a Klonopin, I let it dissolve on my tongue, its bitter edge familiar, soothing. Soon, the fog would fade, the tension would release. I'd sleep again, sinking back into the only thing that felt like an escape.

Easter Afternoon

"Diana! Diana! What the fuck is going on?! It's Easter! What's wrong with John?! Who is that naked old black man on the couch?!"

Mrs. B's voice ripped through the air, shaking me from whatever haze I was in. Her hands were on me, shaking me harder. "Diana! Can you hear me? What happened?" Her words came fast, sharp, like she was trying to pull me back to reality. But I didn't feel her hands on me. I didn't feel anything.

Why am I outside? I wondered. *Am I smoking a cigarette? Is Play-Play here?* My thoughts felt like they were moving through water, slow and sluggish. Is this a dream? It has to be. A weird dream. Mrs. B kept calling my name, her voice louder now, more frantic. I could hear her, but it was like I was stuck somewhere far away, not able to respond.

This had to be some sort of nightmare. My head pounded—I woke up with a migraine earlier.

This must be a migraine-induced delusion, a nightmare, I told myself, trying to make sense of the chaos swirling around me. Mrs. B was gone now, the shouting had faded, and I was left sitting in the backyard. I looked down—I had clothes on. At least I wasn't naked.

"John! Wake up! It's Easter Sunday! Family brunch! What the fuck is all this shit? John, I am going to call the fucking COPS!! JOHN!!!"

I couldn't hear if John responded. Everything went quiet again, the stillness heavy and oppressive. Time stretched out, like forever. Then suddenly, I was back in bed. John mumbled something about missing Easter brunch with the family. Oh shit, I thought, a sudden jolt of panic pushing through the fog in my brain.

I heard the front door fling open, the crash of it hitting the wall. Then came Mr. B's voice, furious, booming, "Get the fuck out of here!" His voice shook the house, and I froze. Who was he kicking out? Was it Ariel?

Then Mr. B stormed into the bedroom, yanking John out of bed by his arm. "Get the fuck up, John! Get the fuck up. Diana, stay there," he barked. John stumbled up, groggy, and the shouting continued—voices echoing from the kitchen or maybe the living room. I couldn't tell anymore. I pulled the blankets over my head, wanting to disappear.

I slipped two more pills from the bottle, let them dissolve slowly under my tongue. The familiar numbness crept in, dulling the edges of everything. My head still throbbed, but I

told myself, *I am safe. I am okay. Everything is fine.*

I rocked myself to sleep, whispering the lie until I believed it.

Easter Evening

I woke to the dim, fading light of evening, that sickly kind of dusk that makes everything look like it's drowning in shadows. John was awake, in bed watching TV on low volume. My head was throbbing, a relentless pounding that felt like the world was cracking open behind my eyes.

Cold seeped into my bones, and my heart wouldn't stop racing, hammering against my ribs like it was desperate to escape. Nausea hit me hard, and I stumbled to the bathroom, but nothing came. Just dry heaving, my body wrung out, hugging the toilet as if it were the only thing keeping me grounded.

Everything was spinning in silence, the kind of silence that's louder than noise. I tried to piece it together—what the hell had triggered all this? My thoughts were scattered like broken glass.

John's parents… we missed Easter brunch.

Fuck.

What had we done?

I dragged myself off the floor, legs trembling, and made my way back to the bedroom. The bed felt distant, like it wasn't meant for me. But I crawled in beside John anyway, curling into the crook of his arm, my head finding that familiar space above his armpit. It was the only place that made any sense.

"What happened?" I whispered, my voice barely there, like it was afraid of the answer.

"You don't remember?" John's voice was thick with sleep, like the night hadn't weighed him down the way it had crushed me.

"I know we missed Easter dinner. I remember your parents... did they kick Ariel out?" The question tumbled out, and with it, the tight grip of panic started to wrap around my chest again.

"No, not her. The dude she was with."

The pieces were there, scattered in front of me, but I was too scared to pick them up. "Joe came over?" I asked, the fog in my mind starting to lift just enough for the edges of the night to come into focus. And then, the memories rushed in, too fast, too clear.

"I remember... the ecstasy... the threesome." The words left my mouth before I could s

stop them, and with them came the flood of images, the night unraveling itself in my mind, vivid and sharp.

Ariel had brought the drugs—small pink pills, smooth, seductive, like promises you can't resist. We swallowed them down without a second thought, chasing the high, the thrill of something forbidden. The ecstasy hit, and the night became a blur of heat, of skin against skin, bodies intertwined in ways that felt endless. Ariel's lips on mine, her body between John and me—each moment electric, charged with a craving I hadn't known I had.

I wanted her. I wanted her more than I could admit, and in that moment, it felt like nothing else mattered. There was no guilt, no shame, just raw, aching desire. The three of us tangled together, lost in the haze of the drugs and the night, everything blending into one. I wanted to feel everything, to lose myself in the pleasure, to have more of her, more of everything.

But now, in the cold aftermath, all that remained was this hollow ache. The pleasure had evaporated, leaving behind the bitter taste of what we'd done. This is what happens, I thought, when you swallow the night whole and wake up choking on it.

"Fuck," I muttered, more to myself than to John. What had we done? What had I done? My body felt like a shell, emptied out by the hunger of the night, left fragile, trembling.

"No, it wasn't Joe. You don't remember?"

"No, I don't remember anything past the threesome. I thought everyone went to sleep."

"You put on your pajamas after and knocked out in bed. Ariel and I wanted crack, so she called her 70-year-old crack dealer. We didn't have money for it, so she slept with him. I came to bed and let them have their fun. My parents freaked out just because we missed Easter dinner."

"So… nothing else happened?"

"No, babygirl," he said, kissing my forehead, "nothing else happened. I would never let

anything bad happen to my baby girl."

Oh, how I wanted to believe him. I wanted to feel the warmth of each word, to let them sink into me and bring me back to life. But the more I tried to wrap myself in his reassurance, the more the nausea crawled up my throat. My body refused to buy into the comfort. It rejected it like poison.

Bad things had happened that night, my body screamed so.

Just as bad as that time when I was twelve, a part of me whispered, a voice that rose from the dark, hidden place inside. I tried to silence it. I had to silence it. I reached for another

pill, letting it dissolve under my tongue, as if it could make that voice disappear.

"Pinky promise," I said, my voice small, trembling, as I stared up at John. "Nothing bad

happened to me."

He linked his pinky with mine, his grip warm and solid. "I promise, babygirl. Nothing bad happened. Nothing bad will ever happen. I'm right here to protect my baby girl."

He pulled me closer, wrapping his arms around me, like I was something precious he had to shelter from the world. He kissed my forehead again, like he was sealing the promise, locking it in.

"It's true," I told myself. "Just believe him."

But my body stayed tense, my heart thudding in a way that felt all too familiar. I wanted to trust him. I wanted his words to be enough. But somewhere, buried deep in the marrow of my bones, I knew. Even as I clung to him, letting him hold me like I was safe, the truth gnawed at me from the inside. It was the specter of my own choices and the shadows of my desires. I lay there, a vessel adrift, filled with questions I couldn't articulate, drowning in the depths of my own memory.

"...So where did Ariel go?"

John shrugged his shoulders slightly, a dismissive gesture that made me feel even smaller.

"I don't know. Her grandma's, maybe. She left with the crackhead. Told you she's a crack

whore."

The words hung in the air, heavy and laden with the weight of truth. Just like that, Ariel slipped away from us, a specter of the night, a reminder of everything I craved and feared. The edges of my memory flickered, and I felt the chill of her absence wrapping around me, a cloak of despair.

As the darkness settled in again, I closed my eyes, wishing for a moment that I could forget it all.

But deep down, I knew that the night was far from over, and I was left alone with the echoes of the choices we'd made.

Chapter 32

Falling Down The Rabbit Hole

Ariel returned the next morning, and she officially moved into our bedroom. That night had unlocked any and all reservations or inhibitions that were faced. I told myself I could make it work. I was John's wife; he wouldn't leave me for her. But each day she stayed, my quiet lifestyle in the house changed. I found excitement in it. People were coming over. I met the liquidator Bill, who was a sweet man with a habit and love for cocaine. He brought a dozen long-stemmed white roses the first night he came over, along with a ton of coke, which was more welcomed than the roses as John had begun shooting up speedballs by then.

"Just shoot me up too! Why not? I want to feel the high you feel. Ariel gets to!"

"No, babygirl, you don't do needles."

"But… it's not fair. Plus, I am saying I want to."

"No, babygirl, and that's it. You want to shoot up, go fucking live on the street."

"Okay, I don't want to; I am fine." I pouted.

By now, John had loaded the needle with the substance of heroin and cocaine, the rubber band tied tightly around just above his elbow. He put the needle in with a practiced ease, slipping into a world I wasn't welcome to with Ariel.

I didn't get it; I wanted to feel what they were feeling. I felt left out in this twisted threesome. I tried so hard to fit back in, but I felt John pull away. It was as though he craved her and had no need for me. Days blurred into weeks, but I clung on, even when every morning I woke up drenched in sweat, dry heaving. It was a continuous cycle of morning anxiety and hangovers until I had my morning drug fix of methadone and Klonopin.

This particular morning, I remember clearly, like it just happened, like it is still happening. That morning, I woke up to a shaking body. It wasn't the drugs, not the familiar claw of withdrawal digging into my bones. No, it was something deeper, something that had taken root and twisted itself around my insides. A level of anxiety I couldn't manage. It festered under my skin, alive and writhing, along with a loneliness so thick it hung in the air like humidity, clinging to me with every breath.

John was asleep, as usual, right in the middle of the bed—the space that once belonged to us.

Ariel lay on one side, curled like a cat, peaceful and still. And me, exiled to the edge,

barely clinging on. I watched the rise and fall of John's chest, steady and undisturbed, while my own heart raced in a frenzy I couldn't control. The gap between us felt like a chasm, a silent reminder that I no longer belonged in the space we used to share.

I pressed my palm flat against the sheets, feeling the cool emptiness of the bed under my hand, and the ache of it hit me all at once. This wasn't my place anymore—no matter how hard I tried to pretend otherwise. My shaking intensified, and it wasn't just physical; it was as though my whole body, my whole sense of self, was fracturing.

I thought about waking John, about asking him, pleading even, to hold me the way he used to. But the thought of his half-lidded eyes, the flat, indifferent way he'd say, "Go back to sleep, babygirl," stopped me cold.

What was the point?

There was no comfort here anymore, no warmth.

I was a ghost in my own bed, haunting a space that had already forgotten me.

Ariel stirred beside him, her hand brushing against his arm, and I watched how he didn't flinch, didn't shift away the way he did when I touched him now. I was envious of how easily she fit into this new version of our life, how effortlessly she had slipped into a place I once filled. How she was welcomed in while I stood on the outskirts, desperate and invisible.

The weight of it, of everything, bore down on me, and I knew I couldn't stay like this. Not on the edge of the bed, not on the edge of my own life. But I didn't know how to climb back, how to reclaim what had been taken from me—or if it was even possible anymore. I stared at the ceiling, tracing the patterns in the darkness, my breath shallow, heart pounding like a distant drum, and for a moment, I thought maybe, just maybe, if I stayed very still, the shaking would stop.

But it never did.

I kept trying to get back in.

I woke John up.

"I don't feel good."

"Just take your medicine."

"No, it's not working. It's bad, and I can't take an extra pill. I don't have enough."

"Fine. I'll get you the methadone," he said in a tone that dripped with anger, like I had dared to disturb his peace.

But he didn't move. He just lay there, heavy, indifferent. I stared at the back of his head, willing him to care. Five minutes passed, each one a reminder of how alone I really was. Then I started bugging him again, my anxiety rising like bile in my throat.

"Fuck!" John snapped, throwing the covers off and getting out of bed. His footsteps were heavy, almost stomping as he went to the safe, muttering under his breath. The metallic click of the lock sounded loud in the quiet apartment. He came back with the droplet, his face twisted in anger, and gave me my methadone in that same rough way, like it was an inconvenience to even offer me relief.

He drank a dose and dropped the bottle back on the nightstand; sliding back into bed without a word, snuggling closer to her. Ariel.

My chest tightened as I watched them, the way he sank into her warmth, his back turned to me. It wasn't the methadone I needed; it was him. But he was gone in every way that mattered.

I lay there, waiting for the drug to take the edge off my mind, hoping for that numbing calm to settle in, to quiet the storm inside me. But it didn't. Something else was rising, something darker, something I couldn't control anymore.

"I want her out of my apartment," I blurted, the words tearing out of me before I could stop them. My voice cracked, raw, as if it had been trapped inside for too long.

"What the fuck? Seriously, what the fuck is wrong with you?" John shot up, anger flaring in his eyes, his voice slicing through the stillness of the room.

Ariel stirred, rubbing her eyes and looking between us with a lazy smirk. She stretched like a cat, completely unfazed by the tension.

"Oh, she just needs a good fuck," she purred, her voice low and mocking, cutting through me with its smugness.

I felt my body shake again, not from withdrawal this time, but from a rage I could barely contain. Something inside me was breaking, shattering under the weight of everything I'd tried to hold together. And I didn't know if there was anything left to save.

In that moment, I felt like a pawn on a chessboard, the rules of the game shifting beneath my feet. Ariel's control loomed large, casting shadows over my existence. I wanted to scream, to fight against the absurdity of it all, but instead, I found myself sinking deeper into a place I had never wanted to be.

The game had changed, and I was losing in ways I never thought possible.

Ariel moved towards me, kissing me, her lips soft and knowing, weaving a strange tapestry of affection that felt both foreign and intimately familiar. I felt myself let go, like a boat unmoored, drifting in uncharted waters. Maybe the drugs were kicking in; maybe this was my mind's way of blurring the edges of reality into a hazy dreamscape.

"I'm just being paranoid," I whispered to myself, a mantra against the rising tide of dread. But even after the fleeting pleasure of an orgasm delivered by Ariel, my body refused to warm, refused to cease its relentless trembling, like a leaf caught in a winter storm.

"I really don't feel good. I need my prescription of Klonopin filled, but it's not due for another few days," I murmured, concern lacing my voice as I curled between John and Ariel, their warmth juxtaposed against the icy grip that clung to my skin.

"John and I will go get you some weed. I know a guy. It will help. I'll text him right now," she declared, her voice steady and authoritative, claiming dominion over the space, as if we were mere players in her theatrical production. "John, go fuck your wife in the shower. It will be good for her." And we, her obedient puppets, followed her command, moving as if enchanted by her spell.

The shower became a cocoon, steam curling around us, the warmth of the water enveloping us, washing away the tension that clung to me like a shroud. John's touch felt good, a temporary escape from the shaking that vibrated through my core. I turned to face him, the heat swirling around us, distorting the lines between our bodies.

He took me from behind, his hand gripping my neck, a tether to both pleasure and pain, grounding me in a reality I longed to escape. I craved more—a raw, primal connection that had once anchored us, but now felt tainted, like a cherished photograph faded by careless hands.

In that moment, the contrast became unbearable—his body pressed against mine, the water cascading over us, warm and thick, and yet, deep within me, an icy knot of anxiety tightened its hold. The steam thickened the air, wrapping around my throat, as if trying to smother my doubts.

Each thrust pushed me closer to the edge, each gasp a reminder of my fragile state.

I wanted to surrender completely, to drown in this ephemeral warmth, but I felt the weight of Ariel's gaze, an omnipresent force, suffocating and omnipotent. Her laughter reverberated in the corners of my mind, a haunting echo that mingled with the rhythm of our bodies, a reminder that I was not alone in this dance of ecstasy and despair. I was losing my grip on the moment, and yet, with each surge of sensation, the lines between pleasure and pain blurred, creating a tapestry of conflicting emotions that left me breathless. The water pooled around my feet, each drop a fleeting memory I couldn't escape—a reminder of what was and what would never be again. I clung to the feeling of the water, hoping it would cleanse the darkness lingering just beneath the surface, but the more I grasped, the deeper I sank into the shadows. The storm raged inside me, howling, unrelenting, a tempest that mirrored chaos outside our steam filled sanctuary. In that cocoon of warmth and wetness, I was lost, adrift in a sea of longing, despair, and fleeting

moments of ecstasy that tasted like ash in my mouth.

Chapter 33

Dorsal Vagal

The next morning I awoke to a heaviness, not just in my body but in the air itself. A thickness like a fog, clinging to my skin, as if I had been buried under the weight of my own thoughts all night. The stew pot still sat cold on the stove. The smell of it had seeped into the apartment, curling into every corner, clinging to me like an accusation — the perfect meal for a perfect family that had never come to pass. The dogs lay curled beside me, their small breaths the only real warmth I felt.

I lay there, in that bed, motionless, stuck somewhere between waking and dreaming, as though my limbs had forgotten how to move. My body felt distant, unresponsive — heavy, but not in the comforting way that sleep can be. No, this was something deeper. It was as if my body was slowly disconnecting from the world around it, slipping further away from any sense of control I had left. Everything felt muted, a layer of cotton shoved between me and the rest of the world.

My chest was tight, my breath shallow, but not from panic, no. This was something else — a kind of shutting down.

I didn't know what to call it back then, but I knew this state well. A slow, numbing surrender, like the world was dimming around me and I was sinking further into a place I couldn't crawl out of. It wasn't fear or anxiety—it was something beyond that, something where even my own fight had gone quiet. My mind told my body to move, to get up, but nothing happened.

There was a ringing — my phone. I heard it somewhere in the distance. I reached for it with a kind of lethargic obedience, my fingers barely gripping the device. It was my mother, no doubt checking on me, but I couldn't answer. Not now. What would I even say? I could hear her voice already, full of concern, laced with the same unspoken disappointment she always carried for me.

I didn't want to hear it. Not now. Not ever.

I let the phone fall back onto the bed and stared at the ceiling. The stillness of the apartment swallowed me. The moments between breaths felt like vast chasms, stretching endlessly.

I was disconnected from everything, even from the thoughts that used to plague me relentlessly. Now, there was just numbness, a space too vast and too deep to crawl out of.

The dogs nudged closer to me, sensing my stillness. I could feel their bodies pressed against mine, but even that seemed far away, like I was watching someone else in my place. How long had I been here? Hours? Days? It all felt the same now.

There was no urge to eat, no urge to speak. Just the weight of the room, the suffocating silence, and the smell of forgotten stew.

I could hear John's voice in my head: "Snap out of it." His tone would be irritated, impatient. But even he couldn't reach me here.

This place inside me wasn't built for him, or Ariel, or anyone. It was deeper than their betrayals. This was a place built out of survival, carved out of the years I had spent burying parts of myself just to keep moving forward.

But now, there was nowhere left to move.

The silence continued to stretch on, like the empty space between heartbeats, and for the first time in a long time, I wasn't sure I wanted to fill it.

John would come and go, sometimes giving me methadone, sometimes not. He would enter the room, eyes heavy and unfocused, only to shower or get dressed, his presence fleeting and absent all at once. "She doesn't want to live with you," he'd say, as if that simple declaration could erase the tangled web of our lives.

"Why not? Can we at least try it?" I'd plead, desperation seeping into my words. "Otherwise, it's the ultimatum: me or her. I am not giving you a divorce. We just got married. This is not happening."

It was a conversation on an endless loop, each iteration falling flat against the backdrop of my despair. Each time I spoke, my teeth would chatter, the cold creeping deeper into my bones. I couldn't get warm. I couldn't breathe. I couldn't feel. I wondered if I was dead — trapped in this half-life where time lost its meaning and everything blurred into an indistinct haze.

The TV, always on, flickered in the dim light, its ceaseless chatter occasionally sucking me in, a siren's call in a world gone silent. The characters moved and spoke, but their voices felt distant, echoing in a void that no longer felt like home. I barely mustered the strength to rise from the bed to feed the dogs or let them out, their small bodies padding around me, sensing my stillness, their energy a stark contrast to my own.

I was dead but alive, suspended in this state of limbo, where the weight of my own

existence pressed down on me like a heavy shroud. I floated through days that melded into one another, a ghost in my own life, haunting the corners of an apartment that had become a cage.

Chapter 34

Beef Stew

"Ma, you don't need to go inside. I got this."

"Я тебе помогу занести сумки и всё," my mom responded in Russian, parking the car in front of the two-family peach-colored house on Clinton Ave.

"Ok, but you don't need to," I said, reaching for the door handle. I appreciated my mom's

reluctance to leave, under the guise of helping me bring in the grocery bags from the car into the apartment.

My mom expressed her love through food. She could never utter the words "I love you" or "я тебя люблю," but she didn't need to. It was felt through food. So, prior to driving me back to John, she packed all the contents of her fridge and pantry into bags for me to take home.

We went around to the trunk of the Hyundai SUV and, without speaking, lifted the trunk lid and took out the bags. We walked quietly into the first-floor apartment. Ariel was standing by my computer desk with an envelope for National Grid. John was sitting in the kitchen, facing the living room and the front door. A green army bag was packed up by the foot of the black couch.

PlayPlay came wagging her tail, and my puppy almost jumped into my arms. My mom placed the bags she was holding on the living room floor, and in a soft voice said:

"Диана, не выглядит что она уезжает отсюда. Может, ты поедешь назад со мной?"

My mom spoke in Russian so only I could understand her. I had told her that John had kicked Ariel out and was waiting for me at home alone.

"Ма все нормально, езжай домой. Я разберусь," I said in a whiny, commanding voice.

"Ok. Bye," was all my mom said, shutting the door behind her as she left. In that moment, I wished she had stayed.

"Well, I am going to go and mail this payment to National Grid,"

Ariel said, waving the

envelope in her hand. She left, walking around me. My feet were glued to the living room's ivory carpet. I couldn't move. It wasn't until Ariel was gone that I felt able to walk toward John. His head was in his hands, and as I moved closer, he reached out for me. I climbed onto his lap, and he laid his head on my chest. I held him, running my fingers through his thinning hair.

"Why is she here?" I whispered childishly, sheepishly into his ear.

"I couldn't send her away."

"What do you mean? She has been living here with you while I was at my parents'?"

"Yes."

With that single word, something in me cracked. I felt it, the way glass fractures under pressure, suddenly fragile.

"Do you love her?" I asked, terrified of his response but already knowing the answer.

"Yes." He said it softly, but it hit hard.

"I thought she was a crack whore you would never leave me for. That's what you said," my voice now a defensive, tearful whisper.

"I know. I don't know what happened."

"Do you love me?" I asked, needing to see his eyes as he answered. I searched them, and there were tears. He was crying.

"I don't know," he said.

But I told myself he loved me.

There were tears.

He loved me.

I could fix this.

"Ok," I said, kissing his forehead like he had done to mine so many times before. "We are going to make this work. You always wanted a threesome, so let's live together. I won't freak out anymore. Why don't you go talk to Ariel, go for a ride, pick up something, and I'll cook us dinner. I'll make beef stew."

In that instant, I envisioned myself as a 1950s housewife. I could do it. I could play the part.

Ariel walked in, and John and I separated. I almost jumped off him, like I was caught doing something wrong. But I felt in control. I had crafted a new mask in the midst of my

psychosis, ready to handle this.

"Ariel, you don't need to leave. We are all going to live together," I said with an eerie calmness.

"John, go talk to Ariel, go for a ride, pick up some dope. It will be good for you guys. When you come back, I'll have beef stew ready."

Turning to John, I softened my tone, like a wife trying to make peace. "I have everything to make beef stew. Just how you like it. Your mom's recipe."

They had listened to me; they left. I was alone. The apartment felt hollow, like a stage after the curtain falls. I stared at Ariel's army bag, sitting there, a symbol of her permanence, her invasion into the space that used to be mine. My fingers itched to rip it open, to shred everything inside, but I didn't. I told myself I was in control. I had a plan. Instead of giving in to that destructive impulse, I picked up the phone and called Mrs. B.

"Hi, Mrs. B. It's Diana. I'm home, and I wanted to know what your exact recipe for beef stew is."

There was a pause on the other end of the line. I could hear her breathing, processing. "Diana, why are you making beef stew?"

"I'm making dinner for Ariel and John. We're all going to live together. We decided." My voice sounded almost robotic, too calm, as if repeating a script I wasn't entirely convinced by.

Another pause, longer this time. "Diana, I don't…"

"I just need your recipe for the beef stew. I have all the ingredients, I think."

Her voice was wary, unsure how to respond. "Diana…okay, if you're sure. Um, you need beef chunks. Roll them in flour first, then heat up oil in the pot and brown them. Add Lipton cubes or Lipton onion mix to the mixture. Brown it all, salt, pepper, cubed potatoes, onions, carrots. Add water, bring it to a boil, and let it simmer for a few hours."

"Oh wow, I didn't realize how easy it was. Thank you." I hung up the phone before she could say anything more.

In the silence, I turned to the kitchen, the instructions playing in my head like an incantation. I moved methodically, calmly, as if on autopilot, rolling the beef in flour, browning it just right.

The smell of onions and sizzling meat filled the apartment, giving it a warmth it hadn't had in days. I stirred, salted, added potatoes, carrots. The stew bubbled, simmered. I kept cooking, kept waiting.

Hours passed. The beef stew simmered, filling the air with the heavy, comforting scent of a meal that would never be eaten. I waited for them to return, for the door to open, for some sign that this fantasy I had constructed might hold. But even after the stew cooled, after the night thickened and the apartment grew colder, they didn't come back.

I snuggled with the dogs that night, their warmth the only comfort I had. I buried my face in their fur, breathing in their familiar scent, feeling their steady, forgiving presence beside me. They were all I had.

Chapter 35

Rock Bottom

It all ended with the slamming of the door. They both dressed quickly, a whirlwind of movement on a mission to make me feel better, promising to return swiftly. But as the minutes ticked away, a new panic set in, creeping into my chest like a cold, dark mist. The anxiety returned with a vengeance, and no amount of cigarettes smoked in bed could ease the tightening grip around my throat. Methadone wasn't working; it felt like a cruel joke.

The flickering of the TV cast ghostly shadows across the room, but even that couldn't distract me from the dread mounting inside. They're taking too long. Way too long, my mind repeated like a broken record, amplifying the thunderous beats of my heart. My body shook, a tremor I couldn't control. I picked up my cell phone, fingers trembling, and called. No answer.

I called again. No answer.

Again. Nothing.

After an hour of waiting, I called again, desperation tinging my voice.

Another hour passed, and I called once more.

Still no answer.

But I didn't give up. I kept calling, each ring echoing like a scream into the void.

Evening settled in when they finally returned. My body was still shaking, an uncontrollable response to the mounting dread.

"What the fuck are you blowing up my phone like a psycho?" John yelled as he stormed into the bedroom, his anger slicing through the remnants of my composure.

"I can't deal with your shit anymore. Here's your fucking weed. I'm going to stay at my parents'," he spat out, tossing the bag at me like it was a grenade.

"Please don't leave me. I don't understand. You were gone for so long.

I don't feel good. I'm having a seizure," I pleaded, the words spilling from my lips, desperate and jagged.

"No, you're fucking not. You're coherent," he shot back, eyes narrowing in contempt.

By now, my body shook uncontrollably, as if I were an earthquake waiting to erupt. I felt it deep within—an impending sense of doom that clawed at my insides.

"Maybe she is really sick," Ariel said, stepping into the room, her tone softening slightly.

"No, she isn't. She's fucking faking it," John sneered, his voice laced with venom.

"Please don't leave, please don't leave me alone," I cried out, reaching for him, my hands trembling in the air between us.

"Fuck off! You controlling psycho. I need time away from you," he barked, each word a lash that made me dry heave in bed, twisting my insides.

"See? She's fucking faking it. She can't even throw up. Fucking fake-ass bitch." His anger surged, a dark wave crashing over me, and I wondered what I had done to provoke this fury. A voice inside me screamed into the void, I don't feel good, desperate for someone to listen.

"Ariel, let's go. I'm dropping you off at your grandma's. I'm going to my parents. She is insane; I can't take it anymore." He had packed a bag of clothes, the weight of it heavy with finality.

"But what about the methadone? I can't go through withdrawals right now," I sobbed, crying and dry heaving, reaching my hands out toward him, pleading for mercy.

He pushed my hands away.

"Don't fucking touch me," he yelled back, the words piercing through the haze of my panic.

"Ariel, let's fucking go!" he barked, picking up the bag with a sense of determination that left me cold.

And with the slamming of the door, the world outside faded, leaving me in a suffocating silence.

I have no memory of how I coped that night; the moments blurred into a haze of despair.

I didn't know if I had, in fact, experienced a seizure, or if my brain had reached its breaking point.

Even then, I still believed I could fix it all, like a jigsaw puzzle with missing pieces. In the morning, John came in, his presence heavy with unspoken words. He handed me a dose of methadone, and without a glance, he left again. His silence hurt more than any harsh word he could have thrown at me, a wound deeper than the chaos that had unfolded.

This went on for days as I remained frozen in bed. I was freezing, dry heaving, barely able to care for the new puppy, but I cared for her better than I could for myself. If my mind had a breaking point, I had reached it. I was lost in a cold, trembling fog, like some ghost of myself, barely tethered to the world.

"Are you seeing her?" I asked him one morning when he brought me my methadone, my voice tearful, fearful and barely above whisper.

"No, this is about you and me. You always being on my case. I need time away from you."

"I don't know what I did. Please. I'm sorry I called your phone so many times. I just didn't feel good."

"You never feel good. We need a break. I'm dropping you off at your parents' house tomorrow. I need time to think."

"But…" there was no arguing. His tone left no room for it. I was a child being punished, stripped of power, trying to figure out what I had done wrong. I shouldn't have called his phone so many times. I could be better, I told myself, as the coldness of his words cut through me.

I hatched a plan in my mind. I could fix this, fix me.

The next day he drove me to pick up my prescription and brought me to my parents' house in Belmont. We didn't speak. The silence between us was thick and suffocating, too heavy for me to break. I was too scared to voice my fears. I had to show him I could be better. This separation was just a test, I convinced myself. I wouldn't even call him.

But I did.

No amount of Klonopins could ease the panic, the fear that gnawed at me from the inside out. It became my second skin, become my only truth.

I no longer existed outside of it. The need to hear his voice consumed me. It was the only thing keeping me tethered to reality.

But he never answered when I called. Each ring fed the panic, a reminder of how far I had fallen.

I called his mother.

"Mrs. B, I don't know what to do. He won't talk to me."

"Diana, I don't know what to tell you. He isn't saying anything to us. I told him he shouldn't be treating his wife like this. But you know how he is, he won't listen to anyone."

He called me after that. His voice wasn't the relief I had been seeking, though. It was a fresh wound.

"I told you, I needed time away from you. Stop fucking calling me."

"But I just want to come home."

"Well, you better learn your lesson then!"

He hung up.

My stomach twisted, and my chest tightened. I stared at the phone in my trembling hands. The message was clear: I was a burden. A weight he couldn't carry. I had to stop. I had to do better. I wouldn't call him or any of his family again. I would prove I had learned my lesson. I didn't call.

Five days later, he did.

"Baby girl, come home," he said, and I felt the knot in my chest begin to loosen, just enough to breathe again.

I ran to my mom, desperate to leave. "Ma, I need to go home. Please, please drive me home."

"Why can't he come pick you up? I don't understand," my mom responded, her confusion evident. But despite the questions hanging in the air, she picked up the car keys anyway; she must have felt my desperation these past weeks.

"If you're ready, I'll drive you now."

Yes. Yes, I was ready.

He wanted me home.

I was going to do better.

I had learned my lesson.

I didn't call.

I thought to myself on the silent ride home.

Chapter 36

Black Fuzzy Socks

Somehow, I had started to get out of bed, my limbs heavy like lead, and began going for walks with Nikki, the baby pit bull puppy who was, at that moment, my only lifeline. I moved for her, not for myself, shuffling along the cracked sidewalks of our neighborhood, where the trees loomed like sentinels, their branches gnarled and bare, mirroring the turmoil inside me. Each step felt like wading through molasses, but Nikki's unbridled enthusiasm made the world feel just a little less suffocating. Her playful leaps, a stark contrast to my stagnant spirit, reminded me that life still pulsed somewhere beneath the surface.

After one such walk, I returned home to find black fuzzy socks folded neatly on my bed, waiting like an ominous gift, untouched by the dust of neglect but stained with the essence of betrayal. I didn't put them there. A wave of unease washed over me, a chill that clung to my bones like the relentless winter I couldn't escape. Was someone in the apartment? My heart thudded in my chest as I grabbed my phone and called John. His voice answered surprisingly fast, but it felt like an echo from a distant reality.

"Whose socks are on my bed?" I demanded, my voice a brittle whisper of authority, cracking under the weight of dread.

"Ariel went over to the apartment. She wanted to leave you a present."

"What the fuck? She comes when I'm not here and leaves me socks? She doesn't want to talk to me. She stole my husband, and she fucking leaves me socks!" My words erupted, sharp and jagged, slicing through the silence of my empty home, each syllable steeped in the despair of betrayal. I felt like a ghost wandering through my own life, searching for traces of warmth amidst the frost.

Silence hung like a noose between us, heavy and oppressive, before he spoke again, his tone an unsettling mixture of calm and irritation.

"I locked the front door. How did she even come in?"

"I gave her the key."

"You gave her the key? The fucking key I don't even have?" My voice escalated, each word a nail driven into the coffin of my composure. "I have to sneak into the house every time I need to enter, and she has a fucking key? I don't have a key to my own apartment.

It's my apartment! My name is on the lease. I should call the cops! What did she steal?" Now I was yelling and threatening, and I couldn't control the words spewing out of my

mouth like venom. My throat tightened as I raged against the absurdity, my words spiraling into a crescendo of confusion and despair.

"She didn't steal anything; she was trying to do something nice for you."

"Fuck your 'nice'! She was trying to do something nice for me?!? She doesn't give a fuck about me. She stole you! And I get SOCKS?? FUCK YOU BOTH!! Go FUCK EACH OTHER!!!

LEAVE ME THE FUCK ALONE" I yelled back, the words burning like acid on my tongue. I hung up, the click reverberating like a death knell in the suffocating stillness of my apartment.

My body felt freezing cold, shivering as if the very air around me conspired to freeze my heart in place. A continuous chill had developed throughout my body, seeping into my bones, leaving me trembling. I rummaged through the apartment, a frantic search for something—anything—that felt out of place. The shadows clung to me, whispering their secrets, reminding me of how quickly warmth could be replaced by ice. But nothing was missing. The cash I had hidden in the far depths of my closet inside an empty prescription bottle was still there, a reminder of survival, safe and untouched.

Maybe she was just being nice, I told myself, soothing myself, slipping my feet into the fuzzy black socks. They were cozy and warm—the warmth I craved but couldn't feel. Yet they felt like an anchor, dragging me deeper into a sea of despair. I was the walking dead, an empty shell navigating the remnants of my life.

The socks wrapped around my feet like a suffocating embrace, but they couldn't fill the gaping void inside me. Each fiber felt like a betrayal, a reminder of her presence that had intruded upon my sanctuary. I paced the room, the softness of the socks contrasting sharply with the jagged edges of my emotions. I felt lost, spiraling into the depths of a mind that could no longer distinguish reality from nightmare.

I sank onto the bed, feeling the weight of the world pressing down on my chest. Was this how it would be? Haunted by reminders of someone who had intruded into my life without warning?

The socks were just a gesture, but they felt like a mockery of my suffering, an emblem of the life I had lost, like the shards of a mirror reflecting my fractured self.

Nikki nudged me with her wet nose, pulling me back into the present, a flicker of warmth amid the encroaching darkness. I could feel her breath, a lifeline tethering me to the moment, to a sliver of hope in the desolate expanse of my heart. I needed to focus on her, on the walks we would take tomorrow, on the small joys that still lingered, even in the face of such overwhelming despair. I took a deep breath, trying to shake off the chill that wrapped around me like a shroud.

Maybe, just maybe, the black fuzzy socks could be a symbol of something different—a reminder that warmth still existed in the world, even when it felt like everything was falling apart. But for now, I just sat there, lost in a sea of thoughts and emotions, staring into the TV, the black fuzzy socks making an attempt to keep me warm, but nothing could warm me. *I am the Ice Queen* I thougt to my myself, my heart frozen, my blood turned to ice. I was desperate to escape, but there was no escaping me, my frost: my ice.

Chapter 37

Computer

I was starting to get used to just me and the dogs. I wondered if I could live like this through July. More and more, I found myself wanting to be outside. The sun seemed to reach for me, but I barely felt the warmth of May. I didn't see the flowers bloom or the trees stretch into leaves. All I saw was gray.

After a week, I finally managed to pull myself into the shower. The water, so hot, felt like it was melting me. I turned it up higher, higher, but still, I couldn't feel it, not really. The heat slid off my skin like I wasn't there. Somewhere beneath the steady drum of water, I heard someone in the house. I wasn't expecting anyone.

I had a photoshoot scheduled for that early evening, hoping an extra two hundred might cover rent. "I could live like this," I kept telling myself, like a mantra, repeating it through the steam.

But the noises from the house distracted me. Something was off. I turned off the water, my hand trembling as I reached for the towel I had draped on the covered toilet seat.

Wrapping the towel around me, my heart began to pound, heavy and wild in my chest.

There should be no one in the apartment.

I stumbled into the kitchen, and there they were—John and Ariel—rifling through my things by the computer desk.

"What the fuck are you doing?!" I screeched, my voice cracking through the silence. They didn't respond, didn't even look at me.

I ran, breathless, to push John away from my computer. He was unplugging it, tearing it from the wall. Ariel stepped in front of him, blocking me, throwing herself between us

like a human shield. I wanted to stop him, I needed to stop him, but all I felt was rage and fear, crashing together like a tidal wave, limiting my movements, freezing me still.

Ariel shoved me hard against the wall, her hand around my throat. The cold gleam of John's gun was in her other hand.

"Ri-Ri, put the fucking gun down! Where the fuck did you find it?"

"In your closet, babe," she said, purring with a cruel, sarcastic calm.

"Why are you doing this?" The words came out as a sob, a pathetic plea. "Take whatever you want, just not the computer. My life is on it!"

I was crying now, hard, my body shaking under her grip. In that moment, I wanted her to pull the trigger. I wanted it to end. She didn't lower the gun; she just kept it on me, like I was nothing.

"Ariel needs a computer," John said, his voice flat, indifferent.

"But it's my computer," I whispered, naked and pressed against the wall, unable to move. I had no fight left in me, no breath, no resistance. I was frozen in that place between terror and defeat.

"I gave it to you, and I can take it from you," John said, his hands pulling the hard drive from my desktop like it was nothing. Like it wasn't my whole life.

"Ariel, grab the screen. Let's fucking go."

She let me go then, the pressure around my throat loosening as she set the gun down on the desk, a casual gesture that made me feel even smaller. She took the screen, and they left. I fell to the ground, sobbing. Everything was gone—my writing, my pictures, a part of me ripped out of the wall because Ariel wanted a computer.

I don't know how long I sat there, on the cold floor. I don't know where I found the phone. All I remember is this one thought: call the police. Just do it. Its ok, to call the police.

Just dial 9-1-1

Easy….

I picked up the phone.

I started to dial.

But my fingers didn't dial 9-1-1.

Instead, they dialed Mrs. B.

I was still sobbing when she answered.

"It's John," I choked out. "He ….took …..the ….computer."

"Diana, I don't understand."

"He stole my computer. My writing. I just want my writing back."

"Diana, slow down. What did John do?"

"He came in with Ariel while I was in the shower and took my computer. Oh I can't breathe!" I cried.

"Ariel held his gun to me!" I was shrieking now, words tumbling out between sobs and sniffling.

"I should call the cops! I should, but I won't. I just want my writing. Mrs. B, please, please, I just want my writing. He can keep the computer."

"Diana, stay put. Don't do anything rash. Let me see what I can do."

I stayed put. I canceled the evening photoshoot and crawled into bed naked, I couldn't dress myself. There was no going back from this. I swallowed a handful of pills that night, hoping to erase the memory of them ripping apart my life, pulling my words and images from their place in the world. I didn't want to admit, even to myself, that I would have to leave.

When I woke the next morning, for a moment, I thought it had all been a nightmare. I ran to the desk, half-expecting to see my computer there. But the desk was empty. All that remained was John's black Beretta, carelessly abandoned on top of it. I picked it up, heavy in my hand, the safety off. I didn't want to know if it was loaded; I didn't even know how to check. I flicked the safety back on, like John had taught me and tucked it into John's closet, hiding it away like a secret I didn't want to understand.

The Odyssey of You and Me

I lived in the shadow of who I could be,
Trapped in the version you sculpted of me.
How we met?
A nightmare I don't repeat,
Her body cold beside me—no heartbeat.
Took years to remember the night she died,
Nineteen and frozen, I couldn't even cry.
Wasn't allowed to call 911,
Just sat there numb while you were gone.

You found me stripping, chasing that fix,
I was hooked before I could even resist.
Seven years deep, ate when you said,
Had to get your permission just to be fed.
You looked fresh—Mavado on your wrist,
Diddy-style sweats, never missed a drip.
And there I was, lacking, insecure,
Hiding layers, shades of fear,
Foundation on my skin,
layers masking the truth that was never seen,
Never Known.

I was your mini me, Aaliyah to your R. Kelly,
Lost in your world, too scared to be free.
Every move I made mirrored your game,

But deep down, I was drowning in shame.
You liked it when I called you Daddy,
Named me Babygirl, said I was happy.
Roles we played, but I was never free,
Just another name in this twisted odyssey.
I remember the day you sent me to hunt,
MySpace accounts, searching for a third to stunt.
A threesome you claimed you deserved,
After all, you wed me, kept your word.
That day I should've known our journey was done,
You met me the same way it had begun.
I was your third, but she died that night,
Foaming at the mouth, no hope in sight.
You told me she survived, said it was all right,
But her name was buried, out of my sight.

Manipulation, you had me under,

High on methadone, caught in your thunder.

Cotton swabs from the clinic you'd bring,

I was lost in your web, where I couldn't feel a thing.

Riddled with shame and guilt,

I searched for the third on ModelMayhem and Craigslist,

You pimped me out, and I didn't even know it.

Convinced it was me who was meant to be sold,

Just to sustain this life you created, a story retold.

I held on to you, couldn't let you go,

Even when you said I was free, it was a show.

You didn't want me anymore, but I stayed in the dark,

Chained to the silence, afraid of the spark.

I believed your lies even when I felt the truth,

I believed you when you said it wasn't you and you never would.

Diana Kouprina ©

Book IV

Revenge

It felt surreal, having my computer just disappear, like a hole opening in the universe, sucking away what little stability I had. I tried to cling to the hope that all the contents would somehow be returned, as if they might crawl back through that black void, as though John or Mrs. B would adhere to my pleas, would suddenly be moved by some sliver of decency. But that hope was fleeting, a fraying thread, even in my state of madness. The emptiness hummed, its silence mocking me, the absence of what was mine more present than the objects that remained.

Kyle, my landlord, was sitting on my bed, smoking a bowl. His presence was fog-like, hazy, drifting in and out of my space, filling the room with a dull sense of being—just enough to keep me tethered to something. We'd become friendlier lately—strange how shared vices can do that.

I think he felt bad for me, though his pity had the hollow ring of indifference. I had asked him for some weed that morning, the moment I finally had to accept the truth: my computer was gone, stolen away in the night like a piece of me. This wasn't a nightmare. It was real. John let Ariel hold a gun to me. The cold metal, slick with fingerprints, pressed against my skin. They robbed me.

"No, no," a voice murmured softly in my head, like a lullaby sung from the depths of some dark place. "It wasn't all that bad." The voice soothed, but its sweetness was poisoned. I wanted to believe it, but I knew better.

"I'm sorry you're going through this," Kyle said, his words thick with smoke as he inhaled deeply. He passed me the bowl, an offering, a temporary reprieve from the gnawing ache in my chest. He liked sneaking downstairs to smoke, away from his wife, his responsibilities. I found his presence comforting, even if just for ten minutes. Ten minutes where the silence between us stretched, heavy and oppressive, like the weight of all the words we didn't say.

"Maybe you should go out with friends. It can't be good for you to be in bed this long," he said, exhaling smoke like a ghost escaping his mouth. The cloud swirled in the room, thickening the air, making it harder to breathe.

I shrugged, took a deep hit, and coughed out, "Yeah, maybe." The weed hit hard, my lungs protesting, the burn sharp enough to remind me that I was still alive. That I hadn't drifted entirely into the void.

"Alright, I gotta head back up. The old ball and chain will get pissed. Maybe I'll sneak down later." His words barely registered. I was already somewhere else.

"Okay," I said, my mind spinning, sinking. What friends could I even go out with? I didn't have any. I was a ghost, drifting through a life that wasn't mine, tethered to people who didn't see me.

But then it hit me—I did have someone. Joe. Ariel's Joe. His name came to me like a whisper from the past, curling around my thoughts. He'd given me his number one night while we were waiting for Ariel to get ready, her perfume filling the air like a promise. We sat on the front porch, smoke curling from our cigarettes, and he'd turned to me, his eyes unreadable in the dim light. "You know, kid, if you ever need anything, I can hook you up. I got you." His voice had been smooth, laced with something unspoken. He'd handed me his number on a piece of paper, and I'd later saved it in my cell phone, just in case. I threw the paper away, never telling John or Ariel. A secret kept in the dark, like all the others.

If there was ever a time to use it, this was it. This was the emergency. This was the moment when the shadows wrapped themselves around me, urging me forward, whispering in my ear that revenge was the only thing that could fill the hollow space left behind.

It was time to call Joe.

The more I stared at my phone, the weight of it in my hand, waiting to press the call button, the more confident I grew. My thumb hovered over the keypad of my old BlackBerry. I liked the idea of hanging out with Joe, of getting closer to Ariel through him, twisting the knife with every detail that would eventually reach her. I worried, briefly, that he wouldn't answer. But I crossed my fingers, holding on to the last shred of reckless hope, and pressed the button.

After three rings, a groggy male voice answered.

"Hello?"

"Hi, it's Diana."

A pause. "Who is that?"

"Diana. You know, Ariel's friend. You've come by the house a few times. You gave me your number, said if I ever needed anything…" My voice trailed off, feeling suddenly small, but I pressed on.

"Hey, kid, what's up!" His voice came alive, as if he'd snapped to attention.

"Could you take me out tonight? I'm having a hard time. I don't know if you heard…"

"Yeah, yeah, I heard." He cut me off with a bitter edge. "Ariel told me how she's been fucking around with your man."

My stomach twisted. "You saw Ariel?"

"I see her all the time. I fuck her all the time. Been telling her she's playing a sick, fucked-up game."

His words settled over me like ash. The betrayal, though expected, still burned, but it wasn't about John anymore. I didn't even flinch.

"Oh shit," I muttered, forcing calm. "Are you around tonight? Can we hang out?"

"Sure, kid. I'll pick you up at 9."

As I hung up, a strange calmness washed over me. I was already moving, mechanical, as if every step I took had been rehearsed. I showered, I shaved. I got ready, not just for a night out but for the revenge I'd been crafting in my head.

It wasn't about John. He was a hollow figure, discarded in the background of my rage. No, this was about Ariel. She could keep him for all I cared. But she hadn't just taken my husband—she'd gone after my writing, after the very essence of me. She'd ripped my words from the walls like they were worthless, stealing my journals, my writings, seven years of school papers, and an award-winning script I had written for a class at Suffolk. It was a two-person play about the craving and struggle of heroin addiction, a work I had poured myself into.

She had it all now, every word, every piece of my soul inked onto those pages.

It felt like a desecration. Stacy had destroyed my journals once, and I'd never recovered from that.

This?

This was worse. I felt shame wrap around me, tightening like a noose. Shame on me for letting them steal my computer. Shame on me for not calling the cops.

Shame on me.

But now I had a plan.

A way to hurt her where she'd truly feel it – through Joe.

I would seduce him, I had concluded in my mind as though it was a simple solution to all my problems.

I knew it wouldn't be hard. His desire for me was obvious in the few times we'd met. That phone exchange had confirmed what I'd already sensed. Going out tonight would lead to more; it would lead to sex.

And I was ready for it.

Joe picked me up at 9 p.m. sharp. The streetlights cast long shadows, the world cloaked in the quiet hum of night. I wore a short, flowy mini dress that clung to me in all the right places, the fabric soft against my skin, leaving little to the imagination. My black Aldo sandals added height, the heels clicking softly on the pavement as I approached his car. The evening air was warm, with just enough of a spring bite to make me feel awake, alive.

I slid into the passenger seat, the door closing with a muted thud. We greeted each other with a kiss on the cheek, a brief exchange of warmth before the night truly began.

"Where do you wanna go, kid? What do you want to do?" His voice had that familiar

edge—casual, careless, like he'd been waiting for this moment.

"I don't know… anything and everything." My answer came out too quickly, the words reckless, daring him to take me somewhere far away from the mess I was drowning in.

"All right, how about a strip club?" he asked, almost too easily, as if it were the most natural place to go.

"Yes, let's do it. Haven't been to one in years. And haven't been to one as a guest—not a

stripper—in like, never." There was a strange excitement in the thought, a return to something I'd long since abandoned, yet tonight, it seemed perfect.

He glanced over at me, eyes gleaming with something unreadable. "Want some ecstasy or oxy, or both?"

"Both, please," I answered without hesitation, the words dripping from my lips like honey. The night was mine, after all. I was taking it back.

"All right, kid. Let's not overdo it." He handed me an oxy, and I took it with a grin, feeling its cool weight on my palm.

"What about the ecstasy?" I pouted, my lips curving into a teasing smile as I flirted with him, letting my eyes dance over his face.

"Well, that could be for later." He smirked, his eyes flickering with amusement. "All right, kid, let's go have some fun."

We drove off into the night, the car humming beneath us, carrying me farther away from the darkness inside my head. I leaned back in the seat letting the oxy dissolve into me, letting the numbness creep over the raw edges of my thoughts. I could breathe again, if only just a little.

The euphoria kicked in, soft and slow, just enough to blur the jagged lines of reality.

The streetlights blurred as we moved and for a moment, I could forget. Forget Ariel, forget John. Forget the loss that gnawed at the back of my mind. I was no longer tethered to the weight of what they'd taken from me. The night was a temporary escape, a way to reclaim the power they'd stripped from me.

I let the feeling wash over me as Joe drove, letting myself drift into the haze, knowing full well that it wouldn't last long, but not caring. Not tonight.

We went to a strip club on Route One, a place drenched in neon, where the air was thick with the scent of stale sweat and cheap perfume, the kind of place where you go to lose yourself, to let the night swallow you whole. Joe was a king there, greeted with knowing smiles and nods, and that only heightened the thrill pulsing through me. It wasn't just his name that carried weight tonight—it was mine too. I wore confidence like a second skin, gliding into this world as if I'd never left it. Champagne fizzed in my veins, sweet and sharp, the bubbles a fleeting distraction.

For once, I wasn't counting tips. The crumpled dollar bills I threw out felt like pieces of another life, one I had shed for this night.

The dancers moved in slow, practiced rhythms, their bodies shimmering under dim lights. Their eyes caught mine, and I smirked, feeling the distance between who I was and who I had become. I watched them, feeling a strange pang beneath the surface, as if a part of me still longed for that simplicity, that structure—the stage, the rules. But tonight, I was the one in control. Confidence spread like wildfire, the kind that burned away doubt, leaving only the hunger for more.

Joe's eyes lingered on me all night, and I could feel his desire, his need to touch me, to take me. But it was mine to give. By the time we left, I knew exactly what I wanted. In the car, he pulled up to my place, and without thinking, I leaned over, pressing my lips to his, pulling him into me. Our kiss was hard, desperate—his hands already on my body, tracing the lines of my waist, sliding over the curve of my hips. I let him touch me, let him taste just enough.

But as always, there was something missing—a hollow ache buried deep, a piece of me still longing for something I couldn't name. Something that felt out of reach, even now.

"Why don't you come in for a few hours?" I whispered, biting his lip, teasing him with the promise of more. "And you've got the ecstasy, right?"

"Yes, ma'am, I do," he said, his voice low and thick with need.

We stumbled into the house, the door slamming shut behind us, lost in the darkness, lost in each other. There was something primal in the way we moved, a shared desperation. But even as we tore at each other's clothes, as our hands explored, there was a strange,

quiet yearning underneath it all. I felt it with every touch – the need to forget, yes, but also the need to be seen, to be held in a way that went deeper than flesh. It hovered between us, unspoken.

Once we were in the bedroom, I took control. I bound his arms with leather straps John had used on me previously and kept in the shoebox under the bed with the porn, and the dildos; the leather straps now bound Joe, his body felt tense beneath mine. He looked at me eyes dark with want, but there was trust there too – an unspoken surrender, I smiled, feeling powerful, biting down on my lip gently, and feeling more and more invincible. I let my hands roam over him, tracing every inch, feeding off his helplessness. But even in the heat of it all, I could feel the distance – the gap between the physical and the emotional. I went into a trance; I envisioned I was Cleopatra, yes, commanding my Caesar, the game, played and well orchestrated, but even Cleopatra, in her power knew loneliness.

I knew, knew loneliness.

I felt that loneliness deep within me, even in the haze of ecstasy and sex. With every thrust, within each rhythmic movement of my body, I felt power, hunger and loneliness.

I took him apart piece by piece, dragging him to the edge and pulling him back, teasing out every ounce of control. And yet, somewhere beneath the surface, I felt a quiet ache. Not for him – not for Joe – but for something more, something lost. A part of me longed to reclaim not just my body, but my heart, my soul. To reclaim, the words, the dreams they had stolen from me. But for now, I settled for this.

For this moment of power. For this fleeting euphoria.

Every touch, every whispered breath was a reclamation of what had been taken. But as I looked down at him, bound and helpless beneath me, I couldn't shake the lingering question:

Was it enough?

Joe was gone in the morning, long before I woke up. The sheets beside me were cool, his scent barely lingering in the air, as though he had never really been there at all. A part of me ached for the warmth of a body next to mine, for the simple comfort of someone's presence, someone to anchor me against the vast, empty silence of the room. But another part of me recoiled, a deep sense of disgust settling in my stomach. The emptiness I felt wasn't from his absence; it was something much older, more familiar, that hollow space between the flesh and the heart.

Still, my only real solace was knowing this would get back to Ariel. I pictured the way she would react when she found out, the way her face might twist with something resembling pain—or jealousy.

Maybe it wouldn't be enough to break her, but it would cut. And that thought offered me a strange, bitter satisfaction.

That was the only relief that mattered.

That's not to say I didn't enjoy Joe and his company. I did—more than I expected to. More than I ever enjoyed John's, and that truth came to me clearly in the soft morning light. Joe was different. He wasn't a means to an end the way John had become. He was something more... something real, even if just for one night. But that was where it ended. I didn't need him to stay.

The damage was done, the revenge already in motion. There was no turning back.

Still, there was a lingering feeling that maybe; just maybe, I wanted him to stay a little longer.

Just enough to fill the silence.

Goodbye

Two days later, late morning, early afternoon, John came into the apartment. I wasn't expecting him, plus I didn't want to face any face-to-face consequences of him finding out about Joe. He came into the bedroom, startling me. The TV was on; I was half-asleep, half-awake, and omewhere else entirely when he walked in.

He looked beaten, distraught, his skin looked gray.

"Can I come lay with you, babygirl?" he said gently. I was worried he knew. But it didn't seem like it. This was something else.

"Ok," I mumbled, unsure of what was to come next, moving over from his side of the bed to mine.

"I just want to snuggle my babygirl," he said, kicking off his Adidas shell tops and climbing into bed. I was under the covers, cold, but it was a warm day out, and he was wearing his grey Adidas sweats, the ones he wore to the reception of our wedding.

We snuggled in silence. I was too scared to ask what it meant. My thoughts were racing—could this mean he picked me? It's over? This was the time limit, the ultimatum, the timeframe. Rent was due next week. I told him to end it and come home, and I would pay the rent; I had money to cover it.

Was this it? Could we pick up as though nothing happened, go back to our routine of just me and him?

My heart raced.

A voice in my head whispered, *no this is not IT.*

No, its not.

Yes, this is it, I yelled at the little voice, the little whisper inside my head.

You're just anxiety, I told that little voice.

And I did, I did feel anxious.

Or maybe I am just excited.

I told myself everything I wanted to hear, silencing any little whisper inside my hand, but feeling my hands shake, feeling the cold set in.

No, no, I'm just excited, I kept convincing myself further.

But I needed to know why he came home. I needed to hear he had chosen me. I lay there, trying to form the words, feeling his body next to mine. I was back in the safety of his arms. I couldn't get the words out, but I had to if I wanted to breathe again.

I just had to.

"Does this mean you're back?"

"Yes, babygirl."

"It's over with Ariel for good?"

"Yes, babygirl, it's all over."

I breathed. This was just what I wanted, but my anxiety didn't let go. My heart thumped louder.

"You don't love her anymore?"

He didn't answer.

Why is he silent? I thought to myself.

What does silence mean?

I couldn't let go.

"So what happened?" I pressed on, unable to stop myself from picking at the scab. I wanted to make it bleed again. "You told her you don't want to be with her?"

"No, she was arrested."

"Wait, what?"

"Yeah, she got busted last night for trying to rob some guy."

"So right now, she's in jail?" I said aloud, thinking to myself, *I don't get it. What is happening?*

He isn't choosing me; he's coming, defeated, because Ariel is locked up.

Fuck, my mind screamed.

"Why didn't you bail her out?" I tried to sound concerned.

But my mind was screaming: *this is so fucking wrong. Get out, get him out of here.*

"I couldn't make her bail. I went to my parents, but they wouldn't give me the money."

"So you came here…"

"I came home," he corrected me, kissing my forehead gently, as though that single gesture could soothe all the chaos swirling inside me.

"But… what if you could pay her bail and she got out—would you go back to her?" I pressed, the question feeling like a weight I needed to unburden myself of, even though I knew the answer might crush me.

"I don't know, babygirl. I'm home now. It doesn't matter." His voice was soft, tired, defeated.

But "I don't know" wasn't good enough. I needed the scab torn off, needed to see the blood spill from this festering wound. I couldn't handle the half-truths or ambiguous promises.

"But if she wasn't arrested… would you have come home?"

He hesitated. "No, probably not. But she was, and I'm here now."

"Mhm," I muttered, the sound catching in my throat. My mind raced, crashing into walls of doubt. I hated this feeling. This gnawing, wrong feeling that hollowed me out, piece by piece. I had to purge it.

I pulled away from him, my body moving before my mind could catch up. I climbed out of bed, the sheets, a heavy reminder of how close I'd let him back in. My feet carried me to the closet.

Without hesitation, I dug into the corner, behind the little wooden dresser, where the prescription bottle sat hidden. I tipped it over, shaking loose the cash I'd stashed there—$800 in total.

"How much is her bail?" I asked, the words cold and steady, a sharp contrast to the storm inside me.

"Eight hundred," he replied, his voice tinged with something—relief, maybe hope. I handed him the money.

"Now you can pay her bail. But you need to pay me back," I said flatly. "This was supposed to go toward rent for us."

His eyes lit up, a glint of excitement flickering through the exhaustion on his face. He smiled—a real smile, the kind I hadn't seen in what felt like a lifetime. "Yes, I'll pay you back. I'll be back."

I forced a nod. "No one should be left alone in jail," I muttered, hollowly, watching as he pocketed the money with the kind of energy I hadn't seen from him in weeks. He left as quickly as he had appeared, the door clicking shut with a finality that echoed in the silence of the room.

In that moment, something shifted inside me. The room felt colder, heavier. I knew—I knew I had to leave. The weight of realization pressed down on me, suffocating in its clarity. I had to call my mom, tell her it was over. Tell her to come get me, or at the very least, let her know I would need to come back home.

Defeated.

Broken.

A loser.

The black sheep of the family.

I know it was the next day, where we were going and why, I can't remember. No matter how hard I try, that memory is blank. Even as I write this now, all I hear is a little voice in my head saying: *You had to go pay the bail, it turned out John couldn't do it. Mrs. B gave you a ride. That's what happened.*

But I have no visual memory. Just that voice. My visual memory starts with me sitting in the front of Mrs. B's Dodge Durango, a car I had come to know all too well. The same car where Mrs. B tried to teach me how to drive. But I could never grasp it, clinging onto the wheel as if it was supposed to rescue me.

Was it the drugs?

Or the anxiety?

Both?

I still don't know. But today, I can say I've finally learned to ride a bike without the fear of crashing and breaking bones. And for me, that is something.

I felt anxious in the car. Something deep inside of me knew this would probably be the last time I'd sit in that seat.

We were driving. Mrs. B, looking at the road ahead, finally broke the silence.

"Diana, why? Why did you agree to pay her bail? She belongs in jail."

"I don't know. I felt bad."

"Do you think she feels bad for you?"

"I don't know…it doesn't matter" I shrugged, my voice trembling, unsure. That strange pitch it had developed was back, the voice of someone cornered.

"I just don't understand, Diana. He came home to you. He was going to stay. You could've worked this out. Ariel is a criminal who deserves to be behind bars. Why are you paying her bail?"

"Mrs. B, I don't know. It wasn't supposed to be like this."

"Diana, like what?"

"I don't know." I shrugged again, and she drove in silence.

There was nothing else to say.

What happened next is blank.

Another gap, another blank space in my mind.

A week, or a few days? I do not know, filled with blanks, until I finally got the courage to pick up the phone and call my mother.

"Mama," I cried when she answered, "I need to come home. It's over."

My mom didn't come right away, but that phone call began the process. The landlords let me stay way into end of June. Somehow, I packed—no, I didn't pack, I threw everything into trash bags. It was easier to transport that way, since we didn't rent a U-Haul. My clothes, my shoes—all stuffed away without care. It was hard to even imagine going back to my parents' house. The thought sent a cold shiver down my spine every time it crossed my mind.

John would still come by sometimes, bringing me methadone. I know he did. I remember drinking it. But I don't remember him. He would bring me methadone even after I moved back to my parents' house in Belmont. I remember the methadone, but not our exchanges. Not the conversations. Just the bottle, the ritual of swallowing, and the fog it brought with it.

I was still executing my revenge with Joe. By sleeping with him, I knew I was hurting them both, but mainly Ariel. We continued sleeping together even after I moved back to my parents' house.

Each time we met, I could feel the sting of betrayal I was inflicting—not on John, who had already faded into the background because I didn't believe he loved me enough to care—but on Ariel, the woman who had taken everything from me.

Joe would tell me what Ariel and John were up to. It was through him that I found out Ariel and John had moved in together, into my apartment. She had stepped into my life completely. I was replaced.

That knowledge gutted me. The space that had once been ours—where John and I had lived, loved, and fought—was now theirs. My bed, my furniture, my memories. She had taken it all. I could feel her shadow consuming every corner of my life, as though she was swallowing me whole, and I had no power left to resist.

Later, it was through Joe that I learned Ariel was pregnant. That pill was hard to swallow. I tried to keep my composure when he told me, but inside, I felt like I was unraveling, coming a part at the seams. The rage that had once kept me going was replaced by something darker, something heavier—an ache that wouldn't go away.

The only relief, the only sliver of joy I felt, was when Joe would say, I bet that kid is mine. I just know it. She even told me.

But then he'd laugh, a bitter sound that echoed between us. But she needs that asshole John to be the baby daddy. So that's how it's gonna be.

I wondered if he was just saying that to make me feel better, throwing me some twisted lifeline to hold onto in the mess of it all. I clung to those words like they meant something, like they gave me some sense of power over the situation, even though deep down, I knew they didn't.

And today, as I sit here with everything I do know, I still wonder if it was true. If that

child—their child—wasn't even John's. If, in the end, Ariel's perfect little world was built on a lie.

In the month leading up to my return home, I faced the heart-wrenching task of finding a new

home for my puppy, Nikki. She was growing rapidly, and my mother had firmly stated, "We already have a cat and a dog. No more." Despite Nikki and Riley, our rat terrier, getting along well, my mother's decision was final and non-negotiable. Leaving Nikki with John wasn't an option; he admitted he couldn't care for a puppy. Ironically, by the end of August, Ariel was pregnant. I wondered if she had been expecting earlier, and I had only learned of it later.

The process of rehoming Nikki was agonizing. Each potential adopter felt like a betrayal, a severing of the bond we shared. I was tormented by the thought of her feeling abandoned, her trusting eyes searching for me in vain. The despair was suffocating, a relentless ache that gnawed at my soul. I felt as though I was drowning in a sea of sorrow, each wave pulling me deeper into the abyss.

Eventually, I found a family willing to take Nikki in. Handing her over was like tearing out a piece of my heart. I watched as she was led away, her tail wagging, oblivious to the permanence of our separation. I stood there, tears streaming down my face, feeling utterly desolate. The world around me seemed to blur, the colors fading into a monochrome of despair. I was left with an overwhelming emptiness, a void that echoed with the loss of my beloved companion.

This chapter of my life was marked by a series of losses—my home, my relationship, and now, Nikki. Each loss compounded the other, creating a labyrinth of grief from which there seemed no escape. I was engulfed in a darkness so profound that it felt as though I would never find the light again. The weight of my sorrow was unbearable, pressing down on me with an unrelenting force. I was adrift in a sea of despair, with no shore in sight.

I don't have many visual memories of those days leading up to leaving with my mom. The details blur like a photograph left too long in the sun, fading into nothingness. The only clear memory I have is of her coming to pick me up, her presence a cold reminder of everything I had lost. I can't recall the words we exchanged, only the emptiness of it all. Packing up, the final moments when everything was reduced to trash bags—my life stuffed away in plastic and forgotten corners. She insisted on using trash bags to minimize space in the car. It was all so mechanical. The things that once held meaning now felt like burdens, just things to haul around, as though that would make them matter again.

Here's the list of what I took, and why:

I took two of John's BB guns and everything that went along with it.

Why? Because he loved his weapons, and by taking them, I would take a part of him with

me—something to hold on to, something that once made him who he was. The guns, the bullets, the throwing knife stars. And the grenade. I don't know why I wanted it so badly. It was heavy, iron, real in a way that made me shiver when I held it. I remember him telling me, with an almost manic calmness, that grenades don't just explode, you have to pull the pin. He was right. I could feel the weight of it, and yet I held it, wondering if it would slip from my hand and destroy everything I still pretended to care about. I asked him where it came from, and he said his cousin had snuck it out of the army for him. That fact, that betrayal, made me sick. But even sicker was the idea of leaving it behind, leaving something that had once tied me to him.

I showed it to my brother and sister, but they didn't react the way I thought they would. They weren't fascinated by it, weren't impressed by John's so-called treasures. They were terrified.

And in their fear, I saw the truth: these things weren't mine. I wasn't supposed to hold on to them. So, I left the weapons behind, leaving them where they belonged—tied to him, but not to me.

I took the two black marble ashtrays.

Why? Because John loved them, and I hated him for it. But also because, in some strange way, they were mine now. They were part of the ritual of his life, part of the little universe he created that I had somehow become a part of.

His little gargoyle statues. I took them. Why? Because my mom loved them, and she had always wanted them. But also because he loved them, and somehow, I wanted to take them from him, strip him of everything that he thought made him important.

I took the season-changing Japanese art wall décor, made of marble.

Why? Because it wasn't just John's—it was Nana and Papa's. And they had given it to him. And in that moment, I couldn't let him have it. It wasn't his. It had never been his, and I couldn't let him keep it. It wasn't just about the art. It was about taking back what was mine. What they had tried to give him.

I took the two black tables.

The 2 little dressers. One tall dresser.

Anything I could fit, anything that held value to him. It was the last thing I could do to feel like I was taking back control. These things were his, but now, they were mine to claim.

I took his wedding band,

Why? Simply because I felt that he didn't deserve it.

I wore mine, I deserved my rings, those weren't leaving my finger.

We realized we would have to make a few trips. And so, I stayed a bit longer, spinning my days with Joe, drowning out the questions, the discomfort. I told myself it wasn't the end yet, that I could still change things, that I could hold on a little longer. We made a few trips, and it wasn't until the end of June that I actually moved out. And in those final days, I was numb—nothing more than an empty shell, packed away and crammed into a car that felt too small for the weight of everything I was trying to escape.

Breaking Through

I have been blinded by you,
I couldn't see the truth—
didn't even know,
hidden behind black curtains,
no light shining through.
You cast me into a darkness,
a tunnel made of glass,
turning me into a marvel,
the hollow husk of a lifeless tree.
You blinded me,
stole my light,
and called it love.
You let me wither in that darkness,
starving me of life.

Every time I reached for light—
an overgrown branch here, a desperate reach there—
you cut me down,
severing my branches,
blocking out all light.
It took years, but I grew out of your darkness,
found the light,
shattered the glass,
and planted myself in soil.
At last, I have life,
the warmth of soil to cradle me,
to keep me from freezing
between the glass.
No longer hollow,
no longer the brittle thing
you left behind.
I have found my roots,
and the light that will not leave.

Diana Kouprina ©

Home Sweet Home

That summer, I was hopeful—hopeful that my stay at home would be brief. John had found my replacement, and I would find mine. It was simple, wasn't it? All I needed was another man, another tether to keep me grounded, to keep me from falling. Anyone but myself.

I came back like a feral animal, suddenly captured in a cage I didn't realize I had walked into.

And now, it was suffocating me. The walls, the routines, the roles—everything a trap. I wanted out so badly, but there was nowhere to go but deeper into the claustrophobia.

Yet, that summer, I convinced myself that once immigration was resolved, I'd be free. That all hinged on John showing up for the interview. No lies. Just the truth—we were still legally husband and wife. All he had to do was stand by my side, if only on paper.

I started a gratitude journal, desperately clinging to it as if it were a rope pulling me out of quicksand. I was trying to manifest salvation. I'd read The Secret religiously, as if it were my bible, a lifeline John had given me a year earlier. He had handed it to me, saying it would snap me out of depression. And in my desperation, I held onto it with white-knuckled faith, writing each morning with the hope that my life would somehow magically transform.

But here's the thing about manifestation: I didn't know then that it would take me years to realize, to truly manifest, you have to feel. It's not just about the words, the hopes, the lists of things to be grateful for. You have to feel them deep inside, let them take root. And back then, I wasn't feeling anything. I was scribbling words, burying the truth beneath layers of forced optimism, refusing to face the reality I was living.

Hope without truth is just another form of denial. But I was still learning that. Still holding out for a miracle, blind to the fact that I was nowhere near salvation.

I was filled with so much hope, teetering on a fine edge between reality and delusion, bordering a level of psychosis I had never touched before. It wasn't just hope—it was mania. And in that manic hope, I drank daily, washed it down with Klonopin daily. The prescriptions still came, though the clock was ticking—soon I'd outgrow my father's health insurance, and then there would be nothing left but the void.

Even now, I marvel at what I accomplished in those months, fueled by adrenaline, hope, and

benzos, spiraling through a psychotic break. Somehow, I started my own business—a PR firm, connecting models and photographers in Boston, planning events, and partnering with top nightclubs to host fashion shows. No one was doing fashion shows in clubs back then, not in Boston, not in 2009. I was ahead of the curve, creating something new, something mine. The money came in—though never as much as I had imagined—but enough to keep me floating.

And then I flew to California, the trip wrapped in dual purposes. On the surface, it was to heal, to find clarity. But underneath, it was revenge. Revenge on John. Revenge on Ariel. I wanted to twist the knife a little deeper, feel the satisfaction of their wounds. Bill, the liquidator, was waiting for me in Santa Barbara, also broken over Ariel. We were a perfect pair of shattered souls, bonding over our shared bitterness. He had offered me an escape—come live with him, rent-free, all expenses paid. All I had to do was buy my ticket. So I did.

Before I flew out to California, I called John from a penthouse suite in New York City. It was an opulent cage—a bourgeois room a man I was dating had brought me to, only to leave me there.

He ended things with me on the drive into the city. Who does that? He didn't even have the decency to break up before the trip. It was one of those what-the-fuck-just-happened moments, but the room was paid for, the card was on file, and I wasn't going to let it all go to waste. He had told me I could stay, but he hadn't said not to charge everything else to his card. So, I did.

For three days, I drained his credit—ordering room service, lounging in bed with champagne, imagining myself someone important, walking through Times Square as if it were my kingdom.

High on delusion, I picked up the hotel phone, the receiver cold in my hand, and called John. He answered, his voice cutting through my drunken haze like a knife.

"Hello," he said, his tone sharp, sober, a brutal contrast to the cloud of mimosas and benzos I was floating in.

"I'm in NYC," I slurred, the confidence false but thick, anger bubbling in my veins, "and when I get back to Boston, you're going to pay me back!"

Silence on the other end, but I didn't care. I had spent the morning at brunch, eggs Florentine and bottomless mimosas, and I was riding the wave of alcohol and entitlement.

"I'm flying to California next month," I continued, my voice rising, "and I need my money.

I paid that bitch's bail! You owe me! Do you hear me? You owe me!"

But John was gone. He had hung up, leaving me screaming into the void, yelling into the hollow space where his voice had been.

Here, dear reader, I wish I could paint for you the beauty of Santa Barbara—the freedom, the sun-soaked days, the effortless flow of money and pleasure. But that would be a lie. Yes, the money flowed, and so did the cocaine. Bill and I did plenty of it. I quickly learned that if I balanced the coke with more Klonopin, I could ride the high without tipping over the edge.

Cocaine, benzos, and weed—that's all that sticks in my mind from those days. I didn't feel anything, not really. Even now, I only have flickers of memory: flashes of parties, the first night I arrived, Bill wrapping me in a hug, whispering, "breathe, you're free".

But I didn't feel free. I felt trapped in my own numbness. That first night, we cut lines of coke on the coffee table in his new three-bedroom house. A house that should have felt like an oasis, a place where I could start over. But I wasn't present for any of it. Bill tried to show me all of Santa Barbara—the beaches, the sprawling vineyards, the pristine streets—but my mind stayed locked on a loop, replaying Ariel and John over and over like a broken record.

I wanted John back. More than anything, I wanted my old life back. I was consumed by the craving for it—the familiarity, the security of marriage, the illusion of stability. But I had convinced myself otherwise. Told myself I didn't really want him, that it was just my mind clinging to the past. Denial was a drug of its own, mingling with the false hopes and real substances I was taking in daily. I kept writing in my journal, filling pages with empty affirmations of self-love, pretending I was grateful, pretending I was falling in love with myself, or with the men who filled my days, but none of it was true.

I had flown to Santa Barbara with the vague idea that maybe I could fall for Bill. That maybe he could be my second husband. After all, he was kind, he was broken in the same way I was, and on paper, he could have been perfect. But I couldn't use Bill like that. I knew that deep down, there was something else I was looking for—something far more elusive, buried deep beneath layers of denial, a desire I didn't even fully understand yet. Something I hadn't admitted to

myself.

I couldn't admit to myself.

Point A to Point B

How I got from point A to point B, I don't remember. My mind was clouded, swirled with the haze of benzodiazepines and alcohol, men and clubs, parties that never stopped.

But through it all, I managed to make money and never sold my body.

Not in the way I feared, not in the way I had done in the past.

Yes, I posed for nudes. But that's all they were—nude photographs. The kind that could have been beautiful, something I might have appreciated later, if only I could.

I couldn't.

I can't.

Because when I look at them, I see the truth in my glazed-over eyes.

I was barely hanging on, floating above my body.

Not living.

Just existing in an empty vessel.

John had stopped answering my calls after I returned from Santa Barbara. It was around the same time we were called for the interview with immigration, the only thing that could have freed me.

But, I don't remember calling Mrs. B. I know I did. In that moment, I had no choice. I called everyone. I called him over and over again, but he wouldn't answer.

Still, I told myself he would be there. He would come through. He had to.

I climbed the stairs to the government building like it was a mountain. My stomach churned, but I told myself he would meet me in the JFK lobby. He would be there. I repeated it like a mantra, like it was the only thing keeping me tethered to reality.

I passed security, hands shaking, and told myself it would be okay. He will be here.

I waited in the lobby, staring at the sterile walls, willing time to stop, willing him to walk

through the door.

When the immigration officer approached, his clipped tone broke through the fog of my

thoughts.

"Hi, Diana Bonia, are you ready?"

He will be here.

He will.

He has to be.

"My husband…he's running late, but he will be here momentarily."

The officer nodded, but I saw the flicker of impatience in his eyes. "Okay, I'll check back in with you in a few minutes."

Minutes stretched to eternity.

"He will be here. Don't panic," I told myself, over and over, like a prayer I couldn't quite

believe.

He will be here.

Ten minutes passed.

Then another.

"Diana Bonia?" the officer called again, the finality in his tone.

"Yes," I said, blinking hard, trying to focus.

"Is your husband here?"

"No, not yet. I'm so sorry for the delay. He's just…detained at work."

The officer's face was unreadable, but the words that followed broke something deep inside me.

"We can't wait any longer. I'm afraid we'll need to reschedule."

I felt the ground shift beneath me.

Reschedule?

How could I? How could I explain that this was the last chance?

That this wasn't just paperwork—this was my life?

What if John didn't show to the rescheduled interview?

Voices in my head yelled at me from various directions, ricocheting against my skull.

"It's okay to reschedule. Oh, thank you. I didn't know that. I'm so sorry. He just…got held up."

I choked on the words, but I forced them out, hoping they could somehow make sense of the mess I had made.

The officer barely acknowledged my frantic apologies. "You'll receive a notice in the mail in two weeks."

"Okay, okay, thank you," I whispered, numb.

I don't know how I made it out of the building.

My body was shaking, my legs unsteady beneath me. How I didn't collapse right there, a grand mal seizure overtaking me in front of everyone, I'll never understand.

I don't know how I called my mother after that, sobbing, barely able to form the words. He didn't come. He didn't come.

I don't remember calling Mrs. B, but I know I did. In that moment, I had no choice.

I called everyone.

I called Mr. B.

I called the business,

I called him again,

and again,

and again,

but he wouldn't answer.

I was alone.

Completely alone.

Yet through it all, I clung to hope.

I floated in the sea of denial, clinging to the belief that somehow, it would all work out.

That he would show up for the rescheduled interview.

That I would somehow get my chance at freedom.

Almost two months later;

I got the letter.

A letter of deportation.

My final sentencing, written in cold, bureaucratic ink.

Deportation

Even now, dear reader, as I write these final chapters, when I have already untangled my immigration mess, and am currently a documented immigrant with a right to work in the U.S., even now my hands are shaking, my heart is racing, my legs feel weak, and nausea rises in my throat. I am sitting on the 73 bus from Belmont to Harvard Square, because I can't write while sitting still—I need the motion of the bus, the comfort of a known destination. Only then does the writing become soothing. I type it all out in my notes and email it to myself to edit and format later, because even now, it's hard to step back into that time.

It's one thing to lose a husband and a home, to be replaced. But to face deportation, the loss of a country, sent to a destination unknown—it felt like something else entirely. The deportation letter said I missed a hearing, that a letter was sent to Clinton Ave. It said I had a hearing scheduled for January and that I was being considered for deportation to Armenia or Georgia.

Nowhere in that paperwork did it acknowledge that I had come to the U.S. legally under my father's student visa, that I had lived legally under his H1B work visa. Nowhere did it mention that I was born in the USSR, as my birth certificate pamphlet book clearly stated. Some days I wonder if that little booklet belongs in a museum.

That letter set in motion a frenzy of chaos in an already chaotic relationship—that of my mother and father. It wasn't just about a failed marriage or not having a bachelor's degree; this felt like a different kind of failure, one that my father refused to help with. He didn't want to give me money for immigration attorneys. Instead, he wielded the loans and my incomplete college education like a noose, tightening it around me, suffocating me in guilt and shame.

I had always hungered for my father's approval, chasing it in the ways a little girl does—pleasing, achieving, even disappearing. But that hunger had turned into a desperate ache, a kind of invisible scream that rang in my ears. It was a scream for acknowledgment, for him to see me, to fix me, to fix this. But instead, I was suffocated beneath the weight of his disappointment, crushed by the failures he collected like broken promises. His words, cold and distant, stung like wind against raw skin, each one making it harder to breathe.

A scandal erupted in the house—my parents' voices rose to a fever pitch, my mother's sobs echoing through the rooms, punctuated by the crash of thrown objects. My brother retreated to his room, shutting himself away from the storm, while my sister and I huddled upstairs in our shared attic bedroom, waiting for it all to end. But in those moments, it felt like it never would, like this was just the beginning of another spiral.

Eventually, my mother won the fight. But the victory was hollow. My father agreed to

give me money for an immigration attorney, but at a cost. The funds would come from my brother's and sister's college savings. It was another failure etched into my skin, a debt I couldn't escape. I was made to write a legally binding document promising repayment. My diamond ring and Movado watch—once symbols of achievement, of status—became collateral, a physical embodiment of my shame.

We all signed—me, my brother, my sister—and with that, the search for an attorney began. It was as if we had entered a different kind of hell, one where every step forward was a reminder of what I had lost, of how deep this wound had cut into my family. The guilt weighed heavy, but there was something even heavier pressing down on me: the knowledge that no matter what I did, no matter how hard I fought, I would always be marked by my father's disappointment. And that, perhaps, was the greatest exile of all.

In hindsight, I wonder if my father was right. Maybe it would have been better if I had untangled my immigration situation on my own, if I had learned, understood the labyrinth of it all. But I couldn't then—I couldn't think. I was barely clinging on, grasping for anything that could ground me. The only thing I had was my soon-to-be-ending Klonopin prescription, and I knew what would come after that: withdrawals, the cold, gnawing edge of it. It was like seeing a cliff approach and being powerless to stop it.

I had to find an immigration attorney—someone who could unravel something I couldn't even begin to untangle. It was a mess beyond my comprehension, and I felt like I had no more fight left. I had returned home like the Corpse Bride, setting out in exile, with pieces of myself falling away as I moved through the days. Bits of me broke off in silence, unnoticed by the world but all too visible to me. And secretly, in the dark, I had to sew those pieces back on alone, stitching them together with the frayed threads of my mind.

My sister was there for me, listening to my cries in the dead of night, the kind of cries that sounded like they came from a wounded beast. She held me together when I felt like I was falling apart. I would stumble to the bathroom, vomiting into the toilet, and she would be right there, silently covering my tracks so my parents wouldn't know the truth. She became my shield, hiding the darkest parts of me from them—the parts that couldn't face the fact that I was an addict. The withdrawals were just beginning, creeping in slowly like an unrelenting shadow, and I was terrified of what would come next. My body was breaking down, but I couldn't let them see. My sister made sure they didn't. In the attic, she became my quiet guardian, the one who kept the secret I couldn't bear to admit.

I eventually found an immigration attorney. It wasn't the one I wanted; it was the only one I could afford, and my mother and I were desperate. The search itself was brutal—each rejection felt like another door slamming shut, another reminder of how deep I was sinking. Most attorneys offered the same solution, their voices clinical and detached: Just get divorced as soon as possible, and marry again.

As if it were that simple.

They said it like it was the most practical thing in the world, as if I could just step outside, find a husband, and be done with it: as though I hadn't already been grasping for someone, anyone, to fill that void. They tossed it out as a solution, like recommending a new coat of paint for a chipped wall. No mention of the cracks beneath, the pieces that were already falling apart.

"Just get married again and you'll be a green card holder in no time", they'd say, their voices confident, one attorney after another, as if this was a minor inconvenience, easily fixed. But it wasn't.

The immigration attorney I found didn't tell me I had to get divorced right away. Instead, he recommended filing for the I-360, a petition for adjustment of status under the Violence Against Women Act (VAWA). He admitted he had never handled such a case before, but he said I had a compelling story. All I needed, according to him, was to get an interview with a judge or immigration officer. He was confident he could lift the deportation and secure that interview, all for a flat rate of five thousand dollars.

For what it's worth, he did get the deportation lifted, but in the end, he failed—failed to untangle the simple truth that should have been the core of my case: that I had come to the U.S. legally, lived here legally, and that nothing had changed until I married a U.S. citizen. That piece of me, the one that screamed for justice, for recognition of what was right, was never sewn back into place. He hadn't fixed it, and I was still left carrying the weight of it all.

But that January, I trusted him. I trusted my attorney like a drowning person trusts a raft, clinging to anything that seemed to offer relief. I did everything I could to keep immigration off my mind, to not let it devour me whole. And then, the withdrawals came, like an unstoppable force. I had no health insurance, no therapies. My last prescription had run out, and I had no choice but to surrender to the physical and mind numbing withdrawals. Some days I felt my mind racing, like I was about to have a cocaine overdose, other days all I could do was stare at the TV screen. I had forgotten how to be, who to be. I was wearing different masks, different personalities I had crafted for my parents, for strangers, for family, friends, and each mask, each personality was crafted solely to please the person I was interacting with. It wasn't me; it was just a reflection of their thoughts, of what they wanted to see in me. The true me, was floating somewhere above,

Unable to get inside my own body or take control of it, I was stuck on the outer banks unable to get in.

And so, in the midst of legal chaos, I was alone with my body's rebellion—alone in the attic, where my sister whispered comfort in the dark, trying to soothe my madness. She was there, a child, going through her own battles, and watching her older sister experience a psychotic break in the secret of the attic walls. She watched me have a grand mal seizure, and I know that traumatized her. I can't handle watching someone else have a

grand mal, I know what to do and I react quickly but when I step back and began to process what I am witnessing I freeze. There was a time John had a grand mal, he had overdosed on cocaine, we were secretly getting high in our bedroom, while his parents where watching American Idol in the living room. John had gotten up and was going to the kitchen for water, my brain was buzzing, he opened the bedroom door and went down in the halfway floor. He made a creepy sound going down, and his mom ran from the couch she was sitting on, he began to shake on the floor and she tried to lift him to

move him. I told her, "Don't. He is having a grand mal seizure, you can't move him, just make sure he doesn't bite his tongue". I sounded composed or so I thought I did but whatever I was saying fell on deaf ears. Paramedics were called and by the time they arrived he was done seizing, and he refused to go to the emergency room. As I write, this I wonder what happened after. Did we get in trouble for getting high, or did John make up some weird lie and his parents believed him.

I knew it traumatized me seeing John have a grand mal, I can only imagine the trauma it caused my thirteen year old sister. Even though the battles I fought inside myself were silent, unseen, I unleashed them all in the night and grasped onto my sister as though she was my rescuer, the one who could save me from all this madness.

And, Through it all, I gave my trust to the attorney, he had promised me freedom, he knew the law. In the end the promised freedom was a lie, a waste of ten thousand dollars. There was no freedom from this. There was only surviving and facing myself. Which I couldn't do; I could write false words of how I loved myself in my new journal but those words fell flat, they were a lie I was telling myself, trying to convince myself of something I didn't feel.

Cold Turkey

The day had come when all the little dissolving pills had run out, and there was no way I could get more. All I could do was drink. Being a functioning alcoholic going through benzodiazepine withdrawal is no easy feat. I don't know how I survived those first two or three years. My body and mind, splintered by the absence of Klonopin, found a new rhythm of suffering.

When my PCP stopped prescribing me Klonopin, I knew it was time to go into therapy. I spent ten years in therapy, and although it helped, something was still missing. Therapy got my mind to a place of average functioning without drugs or medication, but I didn't tell my therapist about my drinking. I made sure I was always sober for our sessions, though sometimes I skipped them to sit at a bar across the street, sipping margaritas. I was honest about my eating disorder, but only after I felt confident I had beaten it. I talked about addiction only when I was sure it no longer had a hold on me. It took years. And yet, even after all that time, my mind still felt broken.

After I found the attorney, I placed all my trust in him. I didn't read the paperwork I signed, submitting whatever he asked for without question. The day of my deportation hearing, I still had a few Klonopins left—I popped a couple before walking into the courthouse. I felt like a walking dead Barbie in high heels, disoriented yet somehow holding it together. I wasn't even called into the courtroom, and at the time, I felt relieved. But now, I wonder if I should've been there, standing before the judge, pleading my case. Would my voice have made a difference? At the time, I trusted my attorney to handle everything, and he did. My deportation was removed based on my I-360 petition under the Violence Against Women Act. I clung to the idea that everything would resolve quickly.

For a while, it seemed like it would. My petition was accepted, and six months later, Prima Facie was established. I was able to apply for health insurance which felt like a small victory. I found a doctor, a new PCP, who prescribed me Klonopin. I didn't tell him about my addiction, only about the stress of my immigration situation. But the dose he gave me was so much lower than what I had been used to. The seizures started again—sharp, random, a reminder that withdrawal was still lurking in my bloodstream. I drank as much as I could stomach to drown the shaking, but I hated being drunk. I drank not for pleasure but to move, to socialize, to numb the endless noise in my mind. My thoughts scattered like broken glass.

Every time I thought of John, I had a physical reaction—a searing pain that radiated through my chest. And then, when I craved an extra pill, I'd start this internal war: one part of me begged for it, called me names, tore at my willpower. The other part fought back, scolding, trying to hold the line. But eventually, the begging would win. The impulsive side of me always won.

I met him one night, drunk outside a club. I had just concluded a fashion show and celebrated with the usual cocktail of pills and alcohol. I'd come to the club with the owner, but the security didn't care—they took one look at me and said I was too fucked up to go inside. So, I stood outside, swaying in my stilettos, gripping a lamppost, wondering what the hell to do next. That's when I heard a male Russian voice nearby; he wasn't speaking to me, or was he?

And then I heard him clearly, he was speaking to me, he asked if I spoke Russian in Russian, his voice in that instant felt like a calling home. but without thinking, "Ты говоришь по-русски?"

he asked.

I responded, "Yes," meeting his eyes with mine. His eyes were dancing and in that instant I saw his soul, a glimpse into it. And it was in that instant I felt a true calling home; the home that no longer existed, in a country that is no longer.

It was August 8, 2009. I remember the date because I wrote it down in my journal, the one I started after John.

What I didn't realize then was that this man, who I thought would be a rebound, would change my life in ways I couldn't have imagined. He wasn't my Prince Charming; he was Dionysus.

Bluntly honest, with good intentions, but deeply connected to my soul in a way that unsettled me. He made it clear from the start: he didn't want to get married, and he was still married, uncertain of what his future held. And I said, me too.

But in my mind, I was already planning a wedding. He became my new obsession, my coping mechanism. Whenever stress or anxiety overwhelmed me, I thought of him. I tried to make myself dependent on him, but he wouldn't let that happen. What happened instead was that he became my best friend. A mirror of myself. He had the same darkness inside him, but he was better at controlling it. He had a stronger moral compass, one that I lacked.

In him, and in the whirlwind of our relationship, I played roles. Part of me loved being the mistress. I wanted to play the role of Ariel, but he saw through all that. Despite everything, he stayed with me through the years that followed. I often wonder why he stuck around, not because I thought he was too good for me, but because I broke the one promise we made to each other—to never lie. But I lied. I needed to. I had to have a Plan A and a Plan B. I wanted him, craved him, but he was my forbidden fruit—the one I ate, knowing I could never marry him.

When things went wrong with immigration, that's when Plan B would kick in—a plan I had learned quite skillfully from Stacy: if you can't marry the one you want, marry the

one who wants you more. I dated secretly, hating it every time. Each encounter felt like I was betraying myself. In the end, I told myself that if I were ever meant to be married, it would need to be to John.

During my cold turkey rehab phase in 2016, I wrote to John's mother seeking forgiveness. To my surprise, she responded, telling me I should come over, that everyone would love to see me, including John. I took that as a sign from the universe—this was it, my path. I had to go back to him. The last time I saw him, we didn't speak. It was the divorce meeting—quick, clinical, and yet filled with an unbearable, unspoken pain. Resentment hummed between us like static, but beneath it all, there was something else—a strange electricity. If he had asked me right then and there to say, Fuck it, let's forget the divorce and get back together, I would have said yes.

I wanted him to ask. I needed him to ask. I played out the scene in my head a hundred times—the words I'd say, the look on his face. But he never said anything. His silence was a closed door, and as much as I wanted to turn the handle, I sat frozen in the chair next to him, signing where the magistrate told me to. There was nothing I could contest—the prenup was ironclad.

In 2016, I ran over. I fought with my mom, who said I shouldn't go, that I needed to let it all go, but I couldn't. I couldn't just let it go. And so, I went.

John talked to me that first and only time. Not much was said, but enough that it echoed in my mind long after.

I had enough balls to ask him the question I still had no answer to.

"Why didn't you come to the immigration interview?"

"I don't know," he said, not meeting my eyes. I remember that interaction as though it just happened. The air had a chill, and he and I stood around the fire pit he built in the patio of his parents' estate. There was something in the air that night, something thick and unspoken.

I was too scared to press. So, instead, I asked, "What's up with you and Ariel?"

"Well, she was in prison for a few years."

"Yeah, yeah, I heard, your mom told me earlier" I said softly, shifting my weight between my feet, moving and not moving.

"And now what?"

I needed to know where I stood in this, the ex wife, was he envisioning a future with us, together

with our kids by other people, riding off into the sunset, as I was. I held my breath as I waited for the answer.

"Now she's trying to reconnect with her dad in Florida."

"Well what does that mean?" I pressed on. I couldn't let it go.

In those moments all I cared about was knowing whether or not he was still with her.

"Are you still together?"

I held my breath.

"No, we ended it when she went to prison."

I breathed a sigh of relief, but it left a strange taste in my mouth, like I wasn't breathing, but I was, I had to have been, I was alive. I was standing.

I was having this conversation. But in the reality of it all, in retrospect I can tell you I wasn't breathing.

I was gulping air and suffocating at the same time. I began to feel the pinch of my knee high, square toe, square heel boots. I was cold, yet my purple cashmere sweater dress was suffocating me, I wanted it to tear it off, the soft cashmere against my skin felt like iron wool.

"You broke up with her while she was in prison?"

"Yeah, it was too crazy. I still brought our son to visit her. She is his mother after all."

I had so many questions, but I was too scared to ask them. We stood there in silence. One

question kept playing in my mind, looping like a mocking refrain:

Are you sure you're the father? I was amazed I didn't blurt it out.

But I didn't.

And his silence told me everything I needed to know.

We were done talking.

That didn't mean his mom didn't set up other times for me to come over. Each time I did, John barely spoke to me—until he didn't speak at all. It was an eerie silence, like I was no longer even a ghost in his world.

But even in 2019, I would try to run to him again. After realizing that I was officially

undocumented and stuck in immigration limbo, hanging on by the thread of appeals—based solely on the fact that my attorney had failed to submit my paperwork on time and hadn't disclosed vital information in the initial petition that proved, without a doubt, that I had married my now ex-husband—I called John.

I just wanted him. I had put him on a pedestal inside my head; where he had no fault, the flaw, the failure was mine to bare, there was no abuse, I was the willing participant, John loved me; I tried to convince myself of this naïve lie, and convinced, or rather tried to convince anyone and everyone who would listen, except for the man with whom I shared a bed; that John and I would be getting back together. I envisioned John as Great Gatsby coming to the rescue. He was my Mr. B. rescuing me from Baryshnikov, the scene where Mr. Big in Sex and The City flies to Paris, after Miranda squeezes his hand earnestly and says, "GO Get Our Girl." I pictured John doing the same, his mom squeezing his hand, his family around saying, "Go Get Our Girl" in a rhythmic chant.

I replayed the scene over and over in my mind.

Instead of Miranda and Big, it was John and Mrs. B in my head, planning out how he would come rescue me.

John was Gatsby,

John was Mr. Big,

John loved me,

John was coming to rescue me and set everything right.

I told myself over and over, until I began to believe it.

I was manifesting it into reality,

I had convinced myself.

I told none of this to the man I had been with for nearly ten years, the man with whom I had a child, who had divorced his wife and worked his own life around me. But marrying him for paperwork just didn't sit right with me.

It felt wrong, shallow.

It wasn't what I wanted.

What sat right with me was running back to John.

But he refused to see me.

His mom stopped talking to me.

In that I knew;

That was the end.

And yet, in my heart, I still believed in some small part of me that maybe, just maybe, if I tried hard enough, if I could convince myself or even him, that this was the only path left to me, he would return.

But it was done. I had no one to run to anymore, except myself.

The Ending...
Is just the Beginning

Restoration begins with letting go,
Knees quiver, fragile like glass,
Legs melt, wobbling like jello,
Hands tremble, as if caught in a breeze,
The body hums, alive with memory,
This is the reclamation of what was stolen,
Once stripped bare, hollowed out,
Now, it returns—slowly, surely.

Who could have known,
That such joy could bloom again,
After so much darkness?
Who would have thought,
That the soul's return
Could be so tender—so raw?

It seeps in, quietly at first,
After drifting away for so long.
It starts in trembling hands,
Legs soft, like jello,
Knees buckling,

The heart pounding in its cage,
Excitement wells up,
Slow and steady,
Coursing through my veins,
Thicker than blood.

I am almost whole…
Hope flickers—distant, but real—
That one day, I will be complete,
Restored to what I once was,
Before the world tore at me,
Ripped me down to nothing.
This is what restoration feels like— The soul finding its way back,
Piece by piece,
To the body,
That waits,
Silent, trembling,
ready to heal.

I have come far, I know this now. I must admit, that…

In sooth, I have wandered 'twixt two realms of life, and tasted deeply of each— of fear and of desire.

The first, a shadowy grip upon my soul,

didst lead me to confinement, to the suffocation of self, guiding me into mine own demise.

The other,

the path I now traverse,

hath broken me free, shattered the chains of breathlessness,

Ushering me into restoration.

'Tis a clearer road at that, devoid of dark disguise.

©Diana **Kouprina**

I was able to restore my mind intuitively through prayer, through herbs, through anything I could grasp that I could afford, I became my own healing psychological guinea pig, as usually I could afford the most minimum, as being an undocumented, stateless individual in the US, my rights were minimal. There was only so far I could go with therapy, because at the end of it all, therapy can only take you so far when you are still hiding in the shadows like a feral animal, scared to come out, to be judged, to be shamed, to be deported, as I was. My healing only truly started when I began to write again.

When I was able to tap into the spirit voice that from an early age guided me through life, my soul, I had tried so hard to diminish and to deny it, its existence, the weary soul I punished so hard for its existence.

My Weary Soul

You walked in sorrow all this way,

The odyssey of torment is almost near,

This is your time to breathe,

To reflect upon the length you've come.

Sit upon this ancient tree stump,

Where once a mighty tree stood tall, now become a place of quiet rebirth.

Amidst this open meadow, you have uncovered.

Let the pain roll off your shoulders,

Allow for stress to drift away into thin air.

Hold on to the truth that lays before you,

As it awakens body, soul and mind, making you whole once more.

Follow the path that once consumed you,

Allow it to Illuminate the way.

For in the end, it is your truth,

The sole purpose of your soul.

I went back to basics, to the first time I was raped, I opened up those wounds. I slowly untangled

the blame and the shame.

Yes, it happened to me.

I don't say it often,

For it was my fault,

I know that, as sure as day.

I should have known better

Than to trust a stranger, lurking in the 90s, Messenger maze.

Yet, I did.
On that fateful day,
I told no one
Where I went.
"Just to the movies," I said,
"With friends." My voice echoed, hollow,
As the door closed,
Behind me,
The room's shadow
Swallowed silence whole.
Off to the movies, I went.
But he was there.
I cringed at the thought of his hands upon my shoulders.
Still, It was the movie I wanted to see the most.
Titanic was showing,
After all.
Yes, the fault is mine,
And mine alone.
I didn't run— I followed. I followed him,
All the way home.
To this day, I wonder why.
No reason makes sense.
I followed him,
Dreaming of escape,
Back to my own safety.
I should have run.
But I didn't.

Instead, I boarded the train with him,
Rode past where
I needed to be.
I stayed still,
Silent as night.
Yes, The fault is mine to bear.
In that apartment,
In the sky,
By the grand piano— Seduction was the game.
He gave me a drink I shouldn't have had.
But I drank it anyway.
I knew the toxins,
Felt disgust brew

Burning deep inside my throat.
Still, I drank.
The fault is mine.
I drank the poison,
And I alone.
Yet, in this flaw,
My fault,
My demise,
I wonder… What of him?
Where was his shame,
His guilt?
Who was he,
To hurt me so?

To lace my drink,

Steal my voice,

Throw me on the mattress,

Bare, clothe torn off.

To use me,

Abuse me,

Invite his friend,

Upon the matted floor

To pry my mouth open,

To tear me apart.

He knew all along I was a child— A mere 12, Naïve, Scared, Alone,

Abandoned By a life that

Had given way.

Yes, I should have known better

Than to trust a stranger Lurking in the 90s' haze.

But what of him? Where is his guilt,

His shame?

His punishment?

His own demise?

For my demise

Is mine to bear.

For years to come,

Always there.

Diana Kouprina ©

I prayed to God, I prayed to Cleopatra, I prayed to the Universe, I prayed to the Roman Gods, and to the Greek Gods, I studied the bible, and I studied Wicca. Grasping, trying to understand and trying to believe that there really is something more outside the hell I was living in.

O Ye of little faith, have faith in me,

All for my torch of hope to be your guiding beacon, leading you toward the light at the end of

this forsaken path which no one dares to venture.

You have journeyed far through unclear roads wandering through hidden forests of overgrowth.

It is time to take a breath, you traveled far, you made it here, where my voice is loud and clear.

It is time for you to trust in me, for I shall not forsake you, I am the voice you muted long ago,

too afraid to sing aloud for it might come out sounding out of tune.

I am the instrument you have forgotten, left behind, collecting dust in memories of past.

Feel me, release me from the chains that bind, separating body, soul, and mind.

For I am the prayer you left unspoken, the voice you always silenced,

Too fearful to release it into the void.

O! Ye of little faith, have faith in me,

For I am the spirit that forever guides you between the realms of living and of the dead,

For I am the one who is always there, a little glow of

intuition nudging you along the way.

O! Ye of little faith, have faith in me,

For I am you and you are me.

Cleopatra

O, my dear Cleopatra, Daughter of Isis and Osiris, Fathered by the Great Alexander,

You have guided me thus far, through storms and madness of the sea.

You breathed life back into me, when mine was lost, adrift.

You brought me back for this second round— A battle for a life of light

Amidst the darkness of the void.

At last my prayer to you is not beseeching, but one:

Of gratitude,

Of strength,

Of light.

My queen,

My god,

My universe.

I prayed to you for strength,

To guide me out of hell.

O, my dear Cleopatra, how far we have come within this second life of light.

At last this is my prayer to you:

Of gratitude,

For giving me strength,

For a life of light,

For never leaving me forsaken.

For breathing life into me,

When death was ready to claim my soul.

For giving me the purpose of true desire.

Alas, this is my prayer to you,

Of gratitude for all you have given.

My queen,

My god,

My universe.

I begged for forgiveness, at times I bargained, at time gratitude was clear and other times I

couldn't feel it. It is hard to allow the banished soul to take up space within the body, and it is

just as hard to forgive one self, when all your life you walked in shame.

Diana Kouprina ©

I went through years where I didn't know who I was, an empty vessel walking around, grasping at various lifelines and falling flat on my face.

I had to come to terms with the simple fact that I had died, and was brought back to life. That there was a chance I could have not been brought back to life. I grappled with the why, and what it all meant.

I had to understand and accept the simple truth of life that it is not about trying to be good, to be perfect. It's about feeling life. I always aimed to be the good girl,

Who earned the praise, the hugs, the love,

The pats on the head for perfect ways –

The girl who did no wrong,

A girl consumed with notions of perfection, outshining every star in sight.

I tried my best to reach perfection, to follow every rule they set, but within me lived a wild spirit,craving to understand the muted lines of grey, refusing to be tied down in a world where heaven collides into one with hell.

I quieted the spirit's voice, silenced her and paid the price, until she left me – mind and soul, alone on earth to sustain.

I wanted to be the good girl, yearning for the world applause,

But chasing after flawlessness I never paused to grasp,

That good was never good enough. I had to break again on healing hands.

Learning how to plant my soul, let it root, to let go and to let it flourish,

I did without a second thought.

In turn my rooted soul within the soil, enlightened me one day during a floral bloom,

That mind body and the spirit all reside in harmony of one.

That the only love I ever needed, was my own, and mine alone,

Through soaring fire I was never meant to tire, a good girl never meant to be.

For I am the Phoenix rising higher through the flames,

For all to see, reborn and rooted this time from within.

I had to learn that to love or hate, that feeling I felt deep inside toward me, toward the ones that

hurt me, was my feeling, my choice to make.

The choice is yours to love or hate.

But trust me when I say, love –

For I've seen hate,

I've felt the fury,

I saw the ugliness I hid,

Behind a mask, where the seen becomes unseen.

In the mirror distortion staring back at me –
My body too fleshy, thighs rubbing against another,
Fatty meat protruding all around.
O! The disgust I felt
The shame, the guilt,
The blame, the pain,
I hid so well.
No one could hate me
As well as I
No one could break me
As well as I.
The truest taste of all desire,

I felt it from within,
Always cutting through outer skin.
I've felt the torment of the mind,
The dismay,
The disdain – the hate of others and of the self,
Consumed with the dissatisfaction, playing words of hate,
On repeat in my brain.
To break the loop,
I've learned upon this journey of survival, love is life,
I'd rather love, to breathe.
So trust me when I say, love –
I am offering you a shortcut in this life,
An untold secret of the world,
Where hate makes fortunes, and Love –

Is just a cliché thrown around in meaningless way,

Never felt, but always told.

Even then, love is true,

When given to the self.

It's so much easier to hate, I know firsthand,

To turn love into a cliché, than to shower the self with love,

Which in truth is the only antidote to hate, from which darkness stems

To see the illuminated way, love must always trump the hate.

But, to love or hate, the choice is always yours to make.

I had to learn that parts of me were stolen, and others I gave away not caring what happened

next. That I allowed others to control me, that I trusted everyone but me.

You were me and I, was you

But that in turn meant nothing to you at all.

Instead a game was played of Russian Roulette with my life at stake

Although I never knew it,

we all wear masks but no one told me that my life was on the line.

I didn't know you would steal my light, that burned deep within,

the light I hid from others, always feeling shame. I didn't know the mask you wore

was weaved together out of the bits and pieces of my soul.

You knew, you always knew,

But never told me, that behind your mask your pure existence was a sham,

Of exhuming power and control, of keeping me restrained

within these prison walls.

Sometimes I wish I never met you, then again I wouldn't be me.

The unmasked version of the self, for the outside world to see,

The soaring spirit I was always meant to be.

I learned that to be whole, I had to embrace me, my mind and my spirit voice; fusing myself

together.

My spirit voice lives through me,

In poetry and motion,

Between the lines of words, of meaning,

Between the black and white, within the grey,

Resides a spirit voice that shine through me.

I find my soul in solace, within the rhythm of my voice.

In poetry and pictures, of words, of tales untold, poetry for me

Always moves in motion of the imagery within the rhythm of the beat.

One letter after another creating one words at a time, connections made,

A ballet of sentences created, a dance is formed, flowing in the rhythm of the movement between the beat.

I began to garden based on sole intuition, trusting my inner spirit voice to guide me, feeling like I had no idea what I was doing, but finding relief in pulling weeds and digging holes, and with each change of the season, I slowly saw the growth of flowers re-emerging each season.

In my garden, my hands plunge into the earth,

the soil is a living thing, clinging to my fingers, gritty and raw, a reminder of my struggle. I dig, and thorns bite back, each scrape a silent scream of defiance,

the infested baobabs stand their ground,

roots twisted like the thoughts I cannot untangle,

weeds coil around my resolve,

whispering the secrets of a life buried beneath the surface.

Fingers bleed, crimson offerings to the stubborn ground,

each scoop an excavation of hidden truths,

the tangled mess of growth and decay reflecting the chaos within me.

Here, beauty flirts with despair,

where hope intertwines with the sharp edges of reality,

the heart learns to break and mend, finding solace in the rhythm of the seasons, each heartbeat a

testament to resilience.

In this sacred space, the weight of the world dissolves, and I become one with the earth, a

witness to the cycle of life, the delicate dance of creation and destruction.

I nourish the soil, and in turn, it nourishes me,

a silent pact of existence, where pain and growth entwine, and in every seed sown,

I find the echo of my own heart, a flickering light in the vast, unyielding dark.

I learned that I could no longer hold on to the past, nor cling onto the people seeking their forgiveness and never acknowledging their wrong doing. I had to finally let go of Stacy and that was harder to do than letting go of John. But I had to accept that she hurt me, that our friendship was not healthy for me.

We all wear masks, but no one told me –
I didn't know it was a secret.
I just wanted to blend into the lines of black and white,
Upon my meet with you.
I didn't know you would be the thief, stealing my burning light.
Through those deep brown eyes it took years to see the truth—
Who you were beneath the veil,
I didn't know the disguise you wore was masterfully crafted

From bits and pieces of my identity.
Sometimes I wish I never met you;
I wonder how my life would have unfolded.
But there you were one day in class,
The new, popular girl with too much blush.
I was there enamored by your presence, still clinging on,
Having just survived to never be the same again.
You preyed upon me, the wounded animal and piece by piece, made me forget
You became me – the mask you wore, and there was me
Trying to copy you never seeing that you were me and I was you.
We all wear masks, but you didn't tell me –
You wore yours always around me.
I in turn showed you truth, and in awe of you mimicked the way you flipped your hair,

When perfecting my chameleon ways, crafting a mask of perfection for the outside world to see,
All the while knowing I could never be.
But you didn't tell me that behind your mask you had no feelings, floating in façade.
Sometimes I wish I never met you;
I wonder who I would have been.
Sometimes I wish I never met you, but then again, I wouldn't be me.
The unmasked version of myself living in authenticity for the whole world to see.
Sometime I wish I never met you, but then I wouldn't be me –
The one I am today, a transparent soul rooted from within,
Walking the path I was always meant to lead.
If I had never met you, I wouldn't be who I am today.
But sometimes, I wish I never met you;
I wonder who I would have been.

Ultimately, I learned that the truth does set you free, and that the real happy ending isn't loud or triumphant. It is quieter, slipping into your life without fanfare, in the smallest parts of your day—the ones you never thought to look for.

It's in that first sip of coffee, where the bitterness wakes you up slowly, where for a brief moment the world feels still, like it's holding its breath. Or in the smell of bread rising in the oven, something so simple, so ancient, that it makes you pause as if time itself has stopped for you. It in pulling weeds, and playing in dirt, and feeding the soil; it's in riding a bicycle down streets you've pedaled through a hundred times, the air rushing past, stirring your hair, carrying away everything heavy—if only for a moment. It's in those long, languid afternoons, when you pick up a book you'd forgotten, and the words wrap around you like a memory, reminding you of who you were and who you might still become. These moments—fleeting, almost invisible—are the ones that patch up the cracks, the tiny fractures we never knew were there until they started to heal.

And in those small moments, today, I ground myself. I find joy in them. I find peace in those little moments, in the small traditions I've created and built upon with my very modern-looking family. I find peace in knitting my daughter scarves, reflecting on memories of Babushka Polly knitting me wool socks in the winter. I would watch her for hours, learning not by words, but by the rhythm of her hands. When I knit now, I feel her with me. The same feeling washes over me when I make crepes. I am soothed in the love of my ancestors past.

I find joy in the little moments of letting go, when at one point in my life I feared it so deeply. Today, I know what is meant for you will always return. True love loves you through all your crazy, and I've been blessed to experience that love, that rubber band effect.

Rubber Band

If I let you go, Will you come back to me?
As so few seldom do.
If I release you,
Will you love me still?
If I step back in silence,
Watching from afar,
Will you return to me?
If I let you go,
Will you spring back to me— Like a rubber band,
Stretched thin but never broken,
Always bending, never snapping?
Yin and Yang,
Dark and light,
A fluid balance Of trust and knowing,
That our souls are intertwined,
Bound as one.
Will you let me go?
Trust me to return,
When my soul has awakened And blossomed into itself.
If I let you go,
Will you release me too?

Free of control,
Balanced in harmony.
Yin and Yang,
Two halves of one soul,
United beyond time.
Is this real love?
As Such a love, Is so seldom found.

Diana Kouprina ©

I had only dreamt of it before, never truly understanding it, but always wanting it.

Finally, I get it.

But that love story doesn't belong in these final pages. It doesn't belong in this book. This book is about letting go—letting go of my shame, letting go of my fear. I know I'm not innocent; I lived in darkness, and at times, I craved more of it.

EPILOGUE

I was young when I began to play the game of pain.
Abandonment was its name.
He never hurt me with his hands.
I felt no pain
No broken bones, no bruises to show of my affliction,
no spilled blood upon the counter.

Although my voice was lost, drowning slowly in the murky salty water.

My mind always masquerading

Tip toeing around the broken shells,

Of shattered glass upon the floor,

One wrong move,

One wrong step,

One wrong breath,

Would be a mistake made, giving reign to torment I couldn't endure.

Spiraling me into a darkness, upon which death was the only welcome door.

No he never hurt me with his hands,

A slap here or there

But I deserved it, screeching out of tune.

Who was I to yell

To raise my voice,

To think, to speak so out of turn.

After all, it was me who gave up control,

Gave him reign of power over me.

No, this wasn't pain it was just a game, I had to, hold my breath before breathing,

To look not stare, to not disturb,

To speak when spoken to

To Always do as I was told.

A good girl I had to be,

A good wife, I was meant to make,

Hiding wounds, and tears of pain,

Hiding scars

Staying silent

Wearing heels, dyeing my hair,

Wearing layers of foundation, to cover up the scars that never seemed to heal,

Doubling up on mascara, layering up the lipstick, smoothing over imperfections, pulling on the

final mask of joy.

Turning myself completely into someone else,

That was never me.

To appease anyone who would take notice,

Becoming an empty shell and not a person.

All the while my soul was stuck out at sea,

Screaming out for someone to please come rescue me.

NO, he never hurt me…. No sticks were thrown to break my bones,

Just words were always stinging slowly,

Seeping into me, making me believe them to be real.

Turning them into the the only words

My mind could hear or understand.

I felt it all but I felt nothing, I blocked it all, locking up the door.

I threw away the key, keeping my soul out at sea, with parts of me screaming out for someone to

please come rescue me.

But no one ever came, my screams were silent

Never heard by anyone locked away inside my mind's abyss.

No, he never hurt me

But my soul did drown, becoming the mist of sea.

As words don't heal, like broken bones,

Never forgotten nor released.

No he never hurt me, my voice was just no longer there, as I became the foam of sea.

I have failed time and time again, but through that failure, I have finally learned.

This book is of letting go of the darkness, of the anger, and the hate that consumed me entirely for years, something I now know I need to release, to change the pattern. It is about the difficulty of losing and recovering one's mind. And most importantly, it is a story for you, my dear reader. If you happen to be the broken one reading these pages, identifying with my craze, I want you to know

YOU ARE NOT ALONE.

Here is my story, my introduction, which tells you I made it through.

I can't quite say I am thriving, but I can say I have gone from

victim mentality to survival mentality.

I have failed, and repeated the pattern,

I failed again, and repeated the pattern,

And again and again over it went for years,
a broken record on the loop.

I tried to untangle it all in my head to understand why and how and I have finally learned—and now, I let it all go, out into the world, so I can write the real book of survival and love, real love, family love, soul-mate-twin-flame type of love, modern love that binds us all together, in a thriving environment for my daughter, who I know for certain now will not be repeating our ancestral past, she will have her failures and I will guide her through it all because in the end I have learned, I have unburdened my darkness, I have let go of shame and guilt and I found love.

The Bell Tolled for Me

The day I died, I heard the bell.

The warning signs tolled thrice.

I did not heed the warning of the knell.

Instead, accepted my invitation out of this hell,

I rose above into the heavens,

Leaving behind this body upon the earth,

Desires full, I rose up in harmony

With my ancestral souls of past,

What once was lost, regained again.

I wanted to remain upon this flight of up above,

Leaving behind my plight of hell,

Roaming freely upon the earth,

Seized to exist within the heavens realm,

As my soul, began to find its home within the light.

Alas! And, to my own surprise!

I was told by angels, sight,

That my time was not one of right.

I heard, the striking of the clock

The bell tolled thrice,

The tolling knell would not await,

The shining light blinked twice.

'Twas time to make haste, of souls return

Back into the body that could not wait.

Back into the soil I would go,

In darkness to be reborn again.

Hark! Exclaim, the angels of the light:

As, I felt myself drifting down into the night,

"Remember this, Remember always,

At the tolling of the knell,

it is time for you to leave the hell,

You walk through upon the earth of past,

'Tis time for you to taste true heaven,

That doth exist on earth,

Within this palpable rebirth."

To fluorescent lights I did awaken,

Feeling frost upon my skin,

As my first gulp of air was taken,

I no longer heard the tolling of the bell.

Diana Kouprina ©

Marble Floor

Click clack, click clack
One, Two, Three, four
Clickety clack, click clack
On marble floor
I am the echo of myself,
Each footstep a crack in the silence,
A defiant hymn
In an empty cathedral of marble,
made up of air filled with despair,
I had built.
A queen in a kingdom built of glass,
Hiding out from shadows of the past.
The heels strike the ground
As if it matters—
As if I matter—
To anyone but me.
Click clack, click clack,
One, Two, Three, Four,
Clickety clack, click clack,
Imprisoning the echo of my heels,
The pointy nose, the narrow front,
Squeezes the life out of my toes,

Reflections sharp, but fleeting fast.
I wear my confidence like a mask,
Heavy as nightfall,
And yet—
The weightlessness of it stings.
I walk to be seen,
But there is no one left to see,
No one but the walls that curve inward,
Imprisoning the echo of who it was I used to be.
Click clack, click clack
One, Two, Three Four
Clickety clack, click clack
In this dance,
I command, I conquer,
I collapse,
A flash of steel beneath soft flesh,

A crown that glitters, cold, unheld.
There is power in this stride,
A burning flare that could illuminate the sky,
Glimmering in hope for life.
But here, in this marble desperation,
It fades before it touches the ground.
Click clack, click clack—
One, Two, Three, Four,
Clickety Clack,
Click Clack
Each step,
A song to no one.
I wish I could be seen,
A memory of self past.

Diana Kouprina ©

Rain Chant

Rain, rain, wash away this grief I bear,
Fall upon my crown, unbind the weight I wear.
Drench my hair, every thread and strand,
As your hands, with purpose, cleanse the land.
Each drop, a spell, whispered through the air,
Healing wounds unseen with quiet care.

Rain, rain, wash away the strain,
Break the chains that bind my name.
Let torrents pour, and set me free,
To the wild unknown, from sorrow's sea.
Rain, rain, wash away all pain,
Deliver me whole, let me rise again.

Diana Kouprina ©

The Road Unseen

The road unseen will become seen,
When you release, when you lean,
Into the flow of what must be,
Trust the process—trust and feel.
The left or right is not for you to decide,
It becomes clear when trust is there.
Release it all, and let it be,
The journey shapes your destiny.
In shadows deep, the path is clear,
When doubt evaporates into thin air.
The left or right is not for you to decide,
It becomes clear when trust is there,
In the self and in the soul,
Where the unseen becomes felt from within.

What's hidden now will soon unfold,
Trust the whisper, soft yet true,
It's guiding every step you do.
The left or right is not for you to decide,
It becomes clear when trust is there.
The road unseen will be revealed,
When heart and mind are gently healed.
Release it all, and let it be—
In time, your truth will set you free.

Diana Kouprina ©

Acknowledgments

To my dear reader, thank you for reading this story. Some places and most names have been fictionalized to protect the identities of those involved.

We all have villains in our stories, and in some, we are the villains.

This book is based solely on my memories, and memories can be finicky. There is so much more I wish I could remember, and even after writing the final lines of this book, new pieces continue to surface.

This story is for you, the reader. It is the story of my failures, my mistakes, and my survival. It is a story of forgiveness, understanding, and growth.

The lesson I hope you take from these pages is this: through failure, we learn. If you are drowning, if life feels like it's pressing down on you, I understand. My words are here to serve as a lifeline, to reach out and be a helping hand. Healing is not easy, nor does it happen overnight. It unfolds hour by hour, day by day, sometimes over years, or even a lifetime. But the most valuable thing is that you survived—you lived.

There is so much joy to be found in living.

Give yourself time to learn how to do better before you demand better of yourself. Be kind to yourself. Love yourself most of all.

Thank you for reading.
I write to heal.
I write for you, so you know you are not alone.

To my family: thank you. We have come so far, healing and growing together. Over the past 15 years, you have helped me restore myself, piece by piece, bit by bit.

Thank you, Ashton Loren Ryan—my agent, my business partner, my friend. Thank you for believing in me when I didn't yet fully believe in myself or my words. Your faith helped bring this book to life..

I know the future is bright, and the path ahead is finally clear.

About The Author

Diana Kouprina is a
survivor of child abuse, domestic
violence, sexual abuse, and trafficking. Her
journey to healing took 14 years, during which she
embraced behavioral therapy, spirituality, and holistic
approaches to reclaim her voice and power. Today, her mission
is to eradicate domestic violence in all its forms. Diana believes
that abuse is not solely physical—by the time it manifests as
physical violence, it may be too late. She is the co-creator,
co-producer, and co-host of Wildthepodcast.com, which is pre-
sented live by JessTV. As a published author with Wingless
Dreamer Publishing and Wild Press, she is dedicated to
raising awareness and fostering change through her
work.